The Multi-Dimensions of Industrial Relations in the Asian Knowledge-Based Economies

CHANDOS
ASIAN STUDIES SERIES:
CONTEMPORARY ISSUES AND TRENDS

Series Editor: Professor Chris Rowley,
Cass Business School, City University, UK
(email: c.rowley@city.ac.uk)

Chandos Publishing is pleased to publish this major Series of books entitled *Asian Studies: Contemporary Issues and Trends*. The Series Editor is Professor Chris Rowley, Cass Business School, City University, UK.

Asia has clearly undergone some major transformations in recent years and books in the Series examine this transformation from a number of perspectives: economic, management, social, political and cultural. We seek authors from a broad range of areas and disciplinary interests: covering, for example, business/management, political science, social science, history, sociology, gender studies, ethnography, economics and international relations, etc.

Importantly, the Series examines both current developments and possible future trends. The Series is aimed at an international market of academics and professionals working in the area. The books have been specially commissioned from leading authors. The objective is to provide the reader with an authoritative view of current thinking.

New authors: we would be delighted to hear from you if you have an idea for a book. We are interested in both shorter, practically orientated publications (45,000+ words) and longer, theoretical monographs (75,000–100,000 words). Our books can be single, joint or multi-author volumes. If you have an idea for a book, please contact the publishers or Professor Chris Rowley, the Series Editor.

Dr Glyn Jones
Chandos Publishing
Email: gjones@chandospublishing.com
www.chandospublishing.com

Professor Chris Rowley
Cass Business School, City University
Email: c.rowley@city.ac.uk
www.cass.city.ac.uk/faculty/c.rowley

Chandos Publishing: is a privately owned and wholly independent publisher based in Oxford, UK. The aim of Chandos Publishing is to publish books of the highest possible standard: books that are both intellectually stimulating and innovative.

We are delighted and proud to count our authors from such well known international organisations as the Asian Institute of Technology, Tsinghua University, Kookmin University, Kobe University, Kyoto Sangyo University, London School of Economics, University of Oxford, Michigan State University, Getty Research Library, University of Texas at Austin, University of South Australia, University of Newcastle, Australia, University of Melbourne, ILO, Max-Planck Institute, Duke University and the leading law firm Clifford Chance.

A key feature of Chandos Publishing's activities is the service it offers its authors and customers. Chandos Publishing recognises that its authors are at the core of its publishing ethos, and authors are treated in a friendly, efficient and timely manner. Chandos Publishing's books are marketed on an international basis, via its range of overseas agents and representatives.

Professor Chris Rowley: Dr Rowley, BA, MA (Warwick), DPhil (Nuffield College, Oxford) is Subject Group leader and the inaugural Professor of Human Resource Management at Cass Business School, City University, London, UK. He is the founding Director of the new, multi-disciplinary and internationally networked *Centre for Research on Asian Management* and Editor of the leading journal *Asia Pacific Business Review* (www.tandf.co.uk/journals/titles/13602381.asp). He is well known and highly regarded in the area, with visiting appointments at leading Asian universities and top journal Editorial Boards in the US and UK. He has given a range of talks and lectures to universities and companies internationally with research and consultancy experience with unions, business and government and his previous employment includes varied work in both the public and private sectors. Professor Rowley researches in a range of areas, including international and comparative human resource management and Asia Pacific management and business. He has been awarded grants from the British Academy, an ESRC AIM International Study Fellowship and gained a 5-year RCUK Fellowship in Asian Business and Management. He acts as a reviewer for many funding bodies, as well as for numerous journals and publishers. Professor Rowley publishes very widely, including in leading US and UK journals, with over 100 articles, 80 book chapters and other contributions and 20 edited and sole authored books.

Bulk orders: some organisations buy a number of copies of our books. If you are interested in doing this, we would be pleased to discuss a discount. Please contact Hannah Grace-Williams on email info@chandospublishing.com or telephone number +44 (0) 1993 848726.

Textbook adoptions: inspection copies are available to lecturers considering adopting a Chandos Publishing book as a textbook. Please email Hannah Grace-Williams on email info@chandospublishing.com or telephone number +44 (0) 1993 848726.

The Multi-Dimensions of Industrial Relations in the Asian Knowledge-Based Economies

EDITED BY
SUNUNTA SIENGTHAI, JOHN J. LAWLER,
CHRIS ROWLEY AND HIROMASA SUZUKI

Chandos Publishing

Oxford • Cambridge • New Delhi

Chandos Publishing
TBAC Business Centre
Avenue 4
Station Lane
Witney
Oxford OX28 4BN
UK
Tel: +44 (0) 1993 848726
Email: info@chandospublishing.com
www.chandospublishing.com

Chandos Publishing is an imprint of Woodhead Publishing Limited

Woodhead Publishing Limited
Abington Hall
Granta Park
Great Abington
Cambridge CB21 6AH
UK
www.woodheadpublishing.com

First published in 2010

ISBN:
978-0-08-101448-6

British Library Cataloguing-in-Publication Data.
A catalogue record for this book is available from the British Library.

Produced from electronic copy supplied by the editors and the contributors.

CONTENTS

1. Overview of Economic Growth and Industrial Relations in Asian Knowledge-based Economies   1

Sununta Siengthai, John J. Lawler, Chris Rowley and Hiromasa Suzuki

2. Industrial Relations in the Turbulent Times   31

Sununta Siengthai

ACKNOWLEDGMENTS

This project was initiated in 2007 to investigate how industrial relations system in Asian countries coped with the 1997 Asian financial crisis and globalization process. The main question was whether labor unions would still have their social and economic roles in the societies that are experiencing rapid socio-economic, cultural and political changes. As the project evolves, time does add more to our observations in that more statistics are now ready than when we first started. Yet, there are still many aspects that we cannot answer as few empirical studies have been done in the Asian region on industrial relations, as a discipline of study, compared to issues related to human resource management. Lack of grass-root researchers among workers or those who had been workers and turned into researchers seem to be one of the reasons. In the U.S., for example, certain school of labor and industrial relations was in fact founded by the fund from the labor unions. This set certain patterns of labor movement and development as one of the mainstream of social paradigm. In reflection, the slow progress of labor unions to create impact at the societal level such as the amendment of labor laws, etc. could perhaps be due also to the fact the there is still a low level of social mobility in the society. Implicitly, this could suggest a certain level of rigid social stratification. However, this is still some question to be further investigated.

As editors of the book, we are grateful to many colleagues for their commitment and contribution. Without their spirit as teachers and students of industrial relations, we would never be able to have this book completed. We are also grateful to many union leaders, rank-and-file members and workers who have given us information and insights on issues of their concerns during various interactions throughout this project. Our appreciation goes to many colleagues in the circle whose interaction has benefited greatly the development of this book project. Sununta Siengthai wishes to express in particular her gratitude to Koji Taira, Linda Y.C. Lim, John D. Kasarda, Sumalee Pitayanon for their role modeling as genuine academicians with theoretical practicality in perspective. Her thanks and appreciation are extended to Malee Siengthai, her sister, who had provided her constant library search support throughout this project and in other related research conducted in relation to this book project in the past several years. Finally, we thank Parada Buranathan for her excellent research assistance in updating the country statistical data, Sunisa Srisakul for her assistance in typing the manuscripts, Sue Gruzelier for her assistance with the proofreading. Any errors remaining are solely our responsibilities.

John J. Lawler
Chris Rowley
Hiromasa Suzuki
Sununta Siengthai

LIST OF FIGURES

LIST OF TABLES

LIST OF ABBREVIATIONS

AIWA	Philippine Metalworkers Alliance
Alpa-S	Air Line Pilots Association- Singapore
CFL	Chinese Federation of Labour
CGFWU	Chinese General Federation of Workers' Unions
CGLL	Chinese General Labour League
CLA	Council of Labour Affairs
CPF	Central Provident Fund
CPWU	China Petroleum Workers Union
CTTWU	China Telephone and Telegraph Workers Union
CPI	Consumer Price Index
CSR	Corporate Social Responsibility
DOLE	Department of Labour and Employment
DTI	Department of Trade and Industry
ECOP	Employers' Confederation of the Philippines
EDB	Economic Development Board
EK-LMC	Enchanted Kingdom - Labour Management Council (EK-LMC)
EEO	Equal Employment Opportunity
FCWU	Republic of China Federation of Craft Workers Unions
FLSL	Fair Labour Standards Law
FKTTWU	Federation of Korean Taxi Transport Workers' Unions
FKTU	Federation of Korean Trade Unions
FPWU	Federation of Postal Workers Unions
GDP	Gross Domestic Product
HRD	Human Resource Development
HMC	Hyundai Motor Company
HMWU	Hyundai Motor Workers Union
HRM	Human Resource Management
IAC	Industrial Arbitration Court
ILO	International Labour Organization
IMF	International Monetary Fund

IMF	International Metalworkers Federation
KCTU	Korea Confederation of Trade Unions
KBE	Knowledge-based economy
KFCTU	Korean Federation of Communications Trade Unions
KMT	Kuomintang
KFMWU	Korea Federation of Metal Workers' Unions
NTUC`	National Trade Union Confederation (In Taiwan)
NTUC	National Trades Union Congress
NWC	National Wages Council
PAP	People's Action Party
PMA	Philippine Metalworkers Alliance
SARS	Severe Acute Respiratory Syndrome
SBF	Singapore Business Federation
SMEs	Small and medium enterprises
SIA	Singapore International Airlines
SICC	Singapore International Chamber of Commerce
SMF	Singapore Manufacturers' Federation
SNEF	Singapore National Employers Federation
TCTU	Taiwan Confederation of Trade Unions
TFRWU	Taiwan Federation of Railroad Workers Unions
THWU	Taiwan Highway Workers Union
TPWU	Taiwan Power Workers Union
TPWU	Taiwan Petroleum Workers Union
TRWU	Taiwan Railroad Workers Union
TTTWU	Taiwan Telephone and Telegraph Workers Union
TTWMWU	Taiwan Tobacco and Wine Manufacturing Workers Union
TMPCLO	Toyota Motor Philippines Corporation Labour Organization
UE Rate	Unemployment Rate
UP SOLAIR	University of the Philippines School of Labour and Industrial Relations

ABOUT THE AUTHORS

Dr. Maragtas S.V. AMANTE is currently a full professor of the College of Economics and Business Administration, Hanyang University in Ansan, Korea. Before joining Hanyang University, Prof. Amante had been a Visiting Research Fellow, Institute of Developing Economies (IDE) – JETRO, in Tokyo early in 2007 and was a full professor at the School of Labor and Industrial Relations, University of Philippines in Diliman, Quezon City, the Philippines. He has more than 20 years of experience in teaching, research and consultancy work in the areas of industrial relations, economics of human resources, and compensation. His research, publications and advocacy emphasize the interdisciplinary approach, using the tools of the social sciences, law and management, to promote decent work, and innovative resolution of issues in employment relations. He had performed consultancy work for various stakeholders in industrial relations, including trade unions, employers, and government. From 2002 to 2006, Dr Amante was a consultant and facilitator with the ASEAN Secretariat and the Japan Ministry of Health, Labor and Welfare, on a series of meetings and dialogues in various ASEAN capitals, with government, employers and workers representatives to develop a common regional framework of industrial relations, to sustain economic integration in East Asia.

Dr. Katsuyuki KUBO is an Associate Professor of Economics at the School of Commerce, Waseda University. Previously, he spent three years as a lecturer of economics at the Institute of Economic Research at Hitotsubashi University. Dr. Kubo received his B.A., M.A. in economics from Keio University and Ph.D. in Industrial Relations from the London School of Economics. Dr. Kubo teaches and researches in the area of compensation and incentive strategy, corporate governance, labor economics and organizational economics. Dr. Kubo's research is in the area of corporate governance, executive compensation and performance related pay in the workplace. In particular, he is interested in whether top managers have financial incentive to work for various stakeholders of the firm, i.e., employees. He also analyzes the impact of merger activities on employment conditions, such as employment and wages. His main works include "The Relationship between Financial Incentives for Company Presidents and Firm Performance in Japan", Japanese Economic Review (2008) with Takuji Saito, "The Determinants of Executive Compensation in Japan and U.K: Agency Hypothesis or Joint Determination Hypothesis?" (2003), in Fan, J.; Teranishi, J.; and Hanazaki, J. (eds.) Designing Financial Systems in East Asia & Japan, Routledge.

Dr. John J. LAWLER is currently a Full Professor of the Institute of Labor and Industrial Relations, University of Illinois at Urbana-Champaign, U.S.A. Professor Lawler has been teaching and researching for over 30 years in the areas of HRM and industrial relations. He has been teaching and researching on Asian economies such as Thailand and Taiwan for many years.

Dr. Joseph S. LEE is a full professor at the National Central University, Taiwan. Prof. Lee currently is Wen Say-ling Chair professor of management at National Central University and director of Institute of Knowledge Economy and Management. He received his Ph. D. degree in economics from University of Massachusetts-Amherst. Earlier, he was a professor of economics at Minnesota State University for 22 years before he returned to Taiwan and became vice president of Chung Hua Institution for Economic Research, and Dean of School of Management at National Central University.

Professor Lee's major research interest is in Labor relations, Knowledge-based Economy, Human Resource Management, and Economic Eevelopment. He has published many books and articles in professional journals, including, "The Role of SMEs in Taiwan's Development Process," "US Direct Investment in China" (with Lawrence Lau and K.C. Fung), "The New Knowledge Economy of Taiwan" "Labor Market and Economic Development in Taiwan".

Professor Lee is also an active member in community service. Currently he is the President of Association of Industrial Relations, Taiwan. He is also a member of editorial board of several international scholarly journals,

Dr. Young-bum PARK is a Professor of Economics at Hansung University in Seoul, Republic of Korea, and teaches labor economics and industrial relations. He hold a PhD in Economics from Cornell University. From 1988 until February 1997 he was a senior research fellow at the Korea Labor Institute- a government-sponsored research institute examining labor issues. Professor Park has published extensively on industrial relations, economics and related fields in Korea and Asia. He has also participated in many government committees related to labor issues. From May 1999 to December 2007 Professor Park was a member of the Presidential Tripartite Commission of the Republic of Korea. Since January 2008 he has been the chairperson of the Evaluation Committee of Policies of the Labor Ministry.

Dr. Chris ROWLEY (BA, MA-Warwick, D.Phil-Oxford) is Professor of Human Resource Management, Editor of the leading journal *Asia Pacific Business Review* and book Series Editor for 'Studies in Asia Pacific Business' and 'Asian Studies: Contemporary Issues and Trends'. He has taught at Cardiff Business School and the University of London. His previous employment experience includes a variety of work in the public and private sectors. He has given range of talks and lectures to universities and companies internationally. He has had consultancy experience with unions, business enterprises and government departments.

Professor Rowley researches in a range of areas, including international and comparative human resource management and Asia Pacific management and business, especially in Korea, Malaysia and Thailand. Recently he has been awarded a research grant from the British Academy to examine employment practices in Korean multinational companies in Malaysia (2003), an ESRC AIM International Study Fellowship for UK-Korean comparisons in management research and practice (2004) and a British Academy grant for analysis of Korean companies in Thailand (2005).

Professor Rowley has published very widely, with over 100 articles, over 70 book chapters and other contributions and 16 edited and sole authored books. He has recently co-edited *Globalization and Labor in the Asia Pacific Region* (2001), *Managing Korean Business* (2002), *The Management of Human Resources in the Asia Pacific Region* (2003) and

Globalization and Competition: Big Business in Asia (2005). He has also written *The Management of People: HRM in Context* (2003) and regularly contributed to *Mastering Management Online* from the *Financial Times*.

Dr. Sununta SIENGTHAI (B.A., Chulalongkorn University, 1975; M.A.,1979 and Ph.D., 1984, University of Illinois at Urbana-Champaign) has been a full-time associate professor of the School of Management, Asian Institute of Technology (A.I.T.) since 1999. She has been teaching, training and extensively and intensively researching for over 20 years in the areas of Human Resource Management, Industrial Relations and Organizational Behavior in the public and private sector organizations. Her research exposures include being a tenure faculty at the National Institute of Development Administration (NIDA) and at Thammasat University in Thailand, a research fellow of the Institute of Southeast Asian Studies (ISEAS), the JSPS Fellow at the Kyoto Institute of Economic Research, Citibank Fellow at the Kenan Institute of Private Enterprise, University of North Carolina at Chapel Hill, and the University of Michigan at Ann-Arbor (under the Fulbright Senior Visiting Program). She has publications include articles in the international referee journals such as International Studies of Management and Organization, Administrative Science Quarterly (ASQ), Research and Practice in Human Resource Management, and Journal of Workplace Learning as well as book chapters, conference proceedings. She has served in various administrative roles in the universities and is an editorial board member of the Research and Practice in Human Resource Management Journal. She has served in an advisory role to the Thai Government and an external collaborator for the United Nations Agencies such as ILO, UNDP, JICA, etc. over the past years. She has written about industrial relations in Thailand and believes in the constructive role of labor unions.

Dr. Hiromasa SUZUKI received his doctorate from University of Rouen (France). He is Professor of Labor Economics at the Waseda University, Faculty of Commerce, Tokyo (Japan). From 1970 to 1986, he served the I.L.O., Geneva (Switzerland) as research officer in the field of wages and industrial relations.

Prof. Suzuki was an exchange professor at the Colorado College, Co. (U.S.A.) (1995-1996), invited researcher at the C.N.R.S. (National Center for Scientific Research), 1998 and taught in Lima, Peru, at ESAN Business School (July-August 2003). Currently he is teaching Labor Economics at the Faculty and Employment Relations at the Graduate School of Waseda University. He holds also a special researcher's position at the Japan Institute for Labor Policy and Training.

His current research centers on employment issues, such as diversification of forms of employment, work-sharing, foreign workers. He is specialized in international comparison of these issues. He has extensively published on those issues in Japanese professional journals, as well as English and French journals. Recent publications include "Hirakareta Asia no Shakaiteki Taiwa" (Social Dialogue in opening Asia, Editor Nihon Hyoronsha, 2002), "Gaikokujin Rodosha Mondai no Tenbou – Kokusai Hikaku no Shiten Kara (Overview of the issue of Foreign Workers from a comparative viewpoint), Kikan Rodou Ho, No. 208, 2005, "L'individu, le collectif et l'Etat dans les pays d'Asie du Nord-Est" in "Mondialisation, Travail et droits fondamentaux" (Edited by I. Daugareilh), Bruyant, Bruxelles, 2005.

Dr. David WAN is Head of Programme, Human Resource Management, School of Human Development & Social Services, SIM University, Singapore. He was previously with the School of Business, National University of Singapore, heading the HRM Unit from 2004 to 2008. His research interests include employee relations, strategic HRM, unionization process, corporate governance as well as hospitality & tourism management.

David has been a Council member of the Singapore Human Resources Institute (SHRI) since 2005, Co-chair of its Academic Advisory Board and co-chair, Education & Training Committee; a Panel judge of the Singapore HR Awards (2005-2009); Panel member of the HR Accreditation (given out by the SHRI); and Advisor for the 2008-2010 Singapore HR Challenge.

Chapter 1

OVERVIEW OF ECONOMIC GROWTH AND INDUSTRIAL RELATIONS IN ASIAN KNOWLEDGE-BASED ECONOMIES

Sununta Siengthai, John J. Lawler, Chris Rowley and Hiromasa Suzuki

1. INTRODUCTION

The book traces the development of the post-financial crisis industrial relations systems in selected Asian countries, namely Japan, Korea, Taiwan, Singapore, Thailand and the Philippines, which are regarded as knowledge-based economies. To a large extent, these countries had all been affected by the 1997 Asian financial crisis. In 1997, the crisis originated in the Asian financial sector, which led to other sectors' declining performance and drove substantial numbers of firms out of business. However, since many countries could still depend on their export growth, and the U.S and Europe were their main export markets, these countries could gain some resilience at the time. Yet, in the 2000s, all of the countries are still undergoing deep change in the economic restructuring in order to cope with globalization process and impact of the advanced technologies, especially the new information and communication technologies (ICTs), which drastically change the business landscape.

We are experiencing a transition from an 'information society' to a 'knowledge economy' where knowledge technologies such as knowledge engineering and knowledge management are used to produce economic benefits (http://en.wikipedia.org/ wiki/Knowledge economy). The term "*knowledge-based economy*" results from a fuller recognition of the role of knowledge and technology in economic growth (OECD, 1996). Knowledge, as embodied in human beings (as *"human capital"*) and in technology, has always been central to economic development. But only in the last decade has its relative importance been recognized as its importance is growing.

Knowledge is increasingly being codified and transmitted through computer and communications networks in the *"information society"*. Also required is tacit knowledge, including the skills to use and adapt codified knowledge, which underlines the importance of continuous learning by individuals and firms. Innovation, which enhances competitive advantage of the business firms and the nation, is driven by the interaction of producers and users in the exchange of both codified and tacit knowledge in the knowledge-based economy. In the knowledge-based economy, firms search for linkages to promote inter-firm interactive learning and for outside partners and networks to provide complementary assets. These relationships help firms in various ways such as to spread the costs and risk associated with innovation among a greater number of organisations, to gain access to new research results, to acquire key technological components of a new product or process, and to share assets in manufacturing, marketing and distribution. As they develop new products and processes, firms determine which activities they will undertake individually, in collaboration with other firms, universities or research institutions, and with the support of government.

Employment in the knowledge-based economy is characterised by increasing demand for more highly-skilled workers (OECD, 1996). Changes in technology, and particularly the advent of information technologies, are making educated and skilled labor more valuable, and unskilled labor less so. Studies in some countries (OECD, 1996) show that the more rapid the introduction of knowledge-intensive means of production, such as those based on information technologies, the greater the demand for highly skilled workers. Other studies show that workers who use advanced technologies, or are employed in firms that have advanced technologies, are paid higher wages. This labor market preference for workers with general competencies in handling codified knowledge is having negative effects on the demand for less-skilled workers.

Government policies will need more stress on upgrading human capital through promoting access to a range of skills, and especially the capacity to learn; enhancing the knowledge distribution power of the economy through collaborative networks and the diffusion of technology; and providing the enabling conditions for organisational change at the firm level to maximise the benefits of technology for productivity. This economic transition requires new rules and practices that determined success in the industrial economy operating in an interconnected, globalized economy where knowledge resources such as know-how and expertise are as critical as other economic resources (http://en.wikipedia.org/wiki/Knowledge economy). These changes require new ideas and approaches from policy makers, managers and workers alike. How can a country enhance and maintain its competitiveness in the global market will depend on how well it can develop its own knowledge sources for value added products and services.

The government policies would be needed to continuously develop the country's human resources so that they become knowledge workers who will be able to learn and adapt fast to the need of their firms to survive and grow in the fierce global market competition. All countries represented in this book are establishing themselves as a knowledge-based economy (KBE) wherein the share of employment has been steadily shifting from industrial-based to more service based on knowledge and from production jobs to professional, technical, clerical and service jobs within the information and communication technologies (ICTs) environment.

In this chapter we will describe the economic and employment growth of each selected country, as well as the industrial relations situations, which provides the readers with some relevant background information for the country case studies in the chapters to follow.

2.   JAPAN

After the Asian financial crisis in 1997, Japan, which is the largest investor in Asian region, experienced two years of negative economic growth rates in 1998 and 1999 (Table 1.1). In the following years, its economic growth rates fluctuated, with the highest growth rate being about 3% in 2006. The real GDP has increased from US$ bil. 4640.98 in 1997 to US$ bil. 5201.02 in 2007, which is about 12.07% or about 1.34% annually. In term of inflation, it is observed that the country has been able to maintain the cost of living effectively from a high 1.77% in 1997 to about 0.33% in 2007. The unemployment rate also has been less than 6.0% throughout the period under review.

For example, the unemployment rate was highest, at 5.4% in 2002 and lowest, at 3.4% in 1997. Japan increased its labor force participation rate from 82.2% in 1997 to 86.1% in 2007.

Table 1.1 Japan's Economy at a Glance

Years	Real GDP [1] (bil.US$)	GDP growth rate (%) [1]	CPI [2] (2005 = 100)	UE [3] (10,000s)	UE Rate* % [3]	Employment (10,000s) [3]	Employment Rate (%) ** [3]
1997	3994.14	1.57	102.60	230	3.40	6557	82.20
1998	3908.33	-2.15	103.29	279	4.10	6514	82.40
1999	3097.57	-0.02	102.95	317	4.70	6462	82.50
2000	4018.27	2.83	102.22	320	4.70	6446	83.10
2001	4024.69	0.16	101.44	340	5.00	6412	83.70
2002	4035.15	0.26	100.53	359	5.40	6330	84.20
2003	4094.16	1.46	100.28	350	5.30	6316	84.50
2004	4205.41	2.72	100.27	313	4.70	6329	84.60
2005	4284.16	1.87	100.00	294	4.40	6356	84.80
2006	4378.84	2.21	100.25	275	4.10	6382	85.70
2007	4467.88	2.03	100.31	257	3.90	6412	86.10

Sources:
1. http://www.ers.usda.gov/Data/Macroeconomics/Data/HistoricalRealGDPValues.xls
2. http://www.ers.usda.gov/Data/Macroeconomics/Data/HistoricalCPIsValues.xls
3. http://www.stat.go.jp/english/data/roudou/report/2007/ft/pdf/summary.pdf

Where: UE = Unemployed
       UE rate = Unemployment rate

      * Based on age-group
      ** Based on employment status

When looking at employment by sector, the statistics available (Table 1.2) suggest that the manufacturing sector, wholesale and retail (including restaurants and hotels) sectors, and community-based and personal services are the three largest sectors that absorb most of the workforce. The agricultural sector still provides some employment, but a very small proportion when compared to the employment that each of the three largest sectors generate, i.e., about one fourth to one fifth of each.

Table 1.2 Employed Persons by Sector in Japan, 1997-2007 ('000s)

Sector	1997	1998	1999	2000	2001	2002	2003	2004	2005	2006	2007
Agriculture, Forestry, Hunting and Fishing	3,500	3,430	3,350	3,260	3,130	2,960	2,930	2,860	2,820	2,720	2,720
Mining and Quarrying	70	60	60	50	50	50	50	40	30	30	40
Manufacturing repair and installation service	14,420	13,820	13,450	13,210	12,840	12,220	12,070	11,770	11,690	11,910	11,980
Electricity, Gas, Water and Sanitary service	360	370	380	340	340	340	320	310	350	360	330
Construction	6,850	6,620	6,570	6,530	6,320	6,180	6,040	5,840	5,680	5,590	5,520
Wholesales, Retails, Restaurants and Hotels	14,750	14,830	14,830	14,740	14,730	14,380	15,480	15,370	15,290	15,170	15,200
Transport, Storage and Communication	4,120	4,050	4,060	4,140	4,070	4,010	3,980	3,950	3,850	3,960	3,970
Financial Intermediation	NA	NA	NA	NA	NA	NA	1,610	1,590	1,570	1,550	1,550
Finance, Insurance and Real Estate	5,750	5,930	5,990	6,160	6,290	6,400	6,460	6,840	7,290	7,410	7,610
Community, Social and Personal Service	15,420	15,660	15,520	15,640	15,910	16,220	13,610	14,010	14,230	14,400	14,430
Activities Not Adequately Described	340	360	410	390	440	560	590	670	740	710	770
Total	65,570	65,140	64,620	64,460	64,120	63,300	63,160	63,290	63,560	63,820	64,120

Sources:
1. http://www.laborsta.ilo.org/STP/do
2. http://www.stat.go.jp/english/data/handbook/pdf/c12cont.pdf

The statistics on industrial relations in Japan indicate that the numbers of strikes, lockouts and disputes in the country have declined significantly during the decade of 1997 – 2007, i.e., from 178 in 1997 to 46 in 2006 (Table 1.3). The number of workdays lost decreased even more significantly, from 110,171 in 1997 to only 1,831 in 2006. In addition, the numbers of workers involved have also decreased from 47,185 in 1997 to 1,820 in 2006. Meanwhile, union membership decreased gradually, i.e., from 12,285,000 to 10,080,000 with an average rate of change of 1.95% per annum. This seems to imply that there has been either more cooperation among labor and management over the decade under review or the union role has been declining over the years after the financial crisis took place. However, the figures seems to suggest that the company policies and their HRM might have significantly increased job satisfaction of employees and hence less conflict in the organizations. As indicated by available statistics, the economic growth rate of Japan have never been higher than 5% over the last decade. Meanwhile, the growth rate of legal minimum wages only minimally increased to a limited effect over the decade (Table 1.4).

Table 1.3 Workers and Employers' Industrial Action, Workdays Lost and Union Organisation in Japan, 1997-2007

Year	Strikes, Lockouts and Disputes	Days not worked	Workers Involved	Union Organization	Union Membership ('000s)
1997	178	110,171	47,185	1,229	12,285
1998	145	101,508	26,291	1,209	12,093
1999	154	87,069	25,673	1,183	11,830
2000	118	35,050	15,322	1,154	11,539
2001	90	29,101	12,172	1,121	11,210
2002	74	12,262	7,015	1,080	10,801
2003	47	6,727	4,447	1,053	10521
2004	51	4,485	6,998	1,031	10,309
2005	50	1,417	4,119	1,014	10,138
2006	46	1,831	1,820	1,004	10,041
2007	NA	NA	NA	1,008	10,080

Sources:
n.a.= not available from ILO and Japan yearbook (http://www.stat.go.jp/data/nenkan/zuhyou/)
1.http://laborsta.ilo.org/STP/do
2.http://www.jil.go.jp/english/laborinfo/library/documents/workinglifeprofile06_07.pdf
3.http://www.eurofound.europa.eu/eiro/studies/tn0706028s/tn0706028s_1.htm
4.http://www.jil.go.jp/english/laborinfo/library/2_03.htm
5.http://www.jil.go.jp/jil/bulletin/year/1999/vol38-03/03.htm
6.http://www.stat.go.jp/data/nenkan/zuhyou/y1640000.xls

Table 1.4 Average Monthly Wage in Japan, 1997 – 2007

Year	Average Wage (monthly, Yen)	Change (%)
1997	287200	n.a.
1998	289600	0.0084
1999	291100	0.0052
2000	293100	0.0069
2001	297500	0.0150
2002	296400	-0.0037
2003	296500	0.0003
2004	293100	-0.0115
2005	292100	-0.0034
2006	296800	0.0161

Sources:
1. http://www.mhlw.go.jp/english/database/db-1/20/2010pe/xls/2010t5pe.xls
2. http://www.jil.go.jp/kokunai/statistics/databook/07/7-3.xls
3. http://www.jil.go.jp/kokunai/statistics/databook/07/7-1.xls
4. http://www.jil.go.jp/kokunai/statistics/databook/05/5-1.xls
5. http://laborsta.ilo.org/STP/do

3. KOREA

During 1997 – 2007, Korea experienced economic growth in the range of -6.85 to 9.49%, which is quite extreme (Table 1.5). The economic growth dropped sharply but then bounced up to 9.49 in 1999 and then again decreased sharply to 3.84 in 2001 and fluctuated in the following two years and then fluctuated in the range of 3 – 4.5% per year until 2007. The inflation rate was highest at 7.51% in 1998, when the economic growth rate plunged. However, that situation of stagflation did not persist as in the following year, inflation rate fell to 0.81. The available statistics seem to suggest that after 1998 Korea could control the inflation rate very well as it stays in the range of 0.81 – 4.10 per cent.

In terms of employment growth, the employment rate in the country is highest at 63.7% in 1997 and 2005 (Table 1.6). However, when we look at the unemployment rate, the statistics available indicate that the highest level of unemployment rate is 6.8%, which was in 1998. This seems to suggest that in Korea the underemployment or disguised unemployment rate may still be high and a very significant phenomenon. It may well suggest that there is still a much lower degree of urbanization in Korea. When we look at employment by activity, since 1997 employment in each sector in Korea seem to be fluctuating but in decreasing trends towards 2007. The sectors that are significant in terms of employment generation are respectively manufacturing, agriculture, and wholesale and retail trade and some skilled-related services, but they all show some declining trends towards 2007. Other sectors that are not major sectors of employment generation but show signs of increase in volume of employment generation are hotel and restaurants; real estate, renting and business activities; education; and other communities, social and personal services. Thus, we can expect that the economy is going through some transformation in term of economic activities. This will certainly have some impact on the industrial relations system.

Table 1.5 Korea's Economy at a Glance

Years	Real GDP ($ Billion)	GDP (%)	Inflation	UE ('000s)	UE Rate	Emp. ('000s)	Emp. Rate*
1997	462.52	4.65	4.43	556	2.2	21,106.0	63.70
1998	430.82	-6.85	7.51	1461	6.8	19,994.0	59.20
1999	471.69	9.49	0.81	1353	6.3	20,281.0	59.60
2000	511.71	8.49	2.26	979	4.4	21,156.0	61.50
2001	531.35	3.84	4.10	899	4.0	21,572.0	62.10
2002	568.38	6.97	2.69	752	3.3	22,169.0	63.30
2003	585.99	3.10	3.55	818	3.6	22,139.0	63.00
2004	613.70	4.73	3.61	860	3.7	22,557.0	63.60
2005	639.46	3.96	2.73	887	3.7	22,856.0	63.70
2006	671.39	4.99	2.68	827	3.5	23,151.0	63.10
2007	121.65	4.50	3.72	783	3.2	23,433.0	63.40

Sources:
1. http://www.ers.usda.gov/Data/Macroeconomics/Data/HistoricalRealGDPValues.xls
2. http://www.ers.usda.gov/Data/Macroeconomics/Data/HistoricalCPIsValues.xls
3. http://laboursta.ilo.org/STP/do

Note: *Based on employment status

Table 1.6 Total Employment by Activity in Korea, 1997-2007 ('000s)

Industry	1997	1998	1999	2000	2001	2002	2003	2004	2005	2006	2007
Agriculture, Hunting and Forestry	2,276.00	2,399.00	2,264.00	2,162.00	2,065.00	1,999.00	1,877.00	1,749.00	1,747.00	1,721.00	1,670.00
Fishing	109.00	82.00	85.00	81.00	83.00	70.00	73.00	76.00	68.00	64.00	56.00
Mining and Quarrying	26.00	21.00	20.00	17.00	18.00	18.00	17.00	16.00	17.00	18.00	18.00
Manufacturing	4,482.00	3,898.00	4,006.00	4,293.00	4,267.00	4,241.00	4,205.00	4,290.00	4,234.00	4,167.00	4,119.00
Electricity, Gas and Water Supply	77.00	61.00	61.00	64.00	58.00	52.00	76.00	72.00	71.00	76.00	86.00
Construction	2,004.00	1,578.00	1,476.00	1,580.00	1,585.00	1,746.00	1,816.00	1,820.00	1,814.00	1,835.00	1,850.00
Wholesales & Retail Trade, etc.*	3,915.00	3,818.00	3,904.00	3,833.00	3,931.00	3,991.00	3,871.00	3,805.00	3,748.00	3,713.00	3,677.00
Hotels and Restaurant	1,890.00	1,753.00	1,820.00	1,919.00	1,943.00	2,007.00	1,981.00	2,057.00	2,058.00	2,049.00	2,049.00
Transport, Storage and Communication	1,162.00	1,169.00	1,202.00	1,260.00	1,322.00	1,371.00	1,333.00	1,376.00	1,429.00	1,470.00	1,498.00
Financial Intermediation	761.00	762.00	723.00	752.00	760.00	734.00	751.00	738.00	746.00	786.00	809.00

Table 1.6 Total Employment by Activity in Korea, 1997-2007 ('000s) (contd.)

Activity											
Real Estate, etc. *	1,139.00	1,094.00	1,202.00	1,361.00	1,530.00	1,664.00	1,726.00	1,914.00	2,037.00	2,168.00	2,350.00
Public Administration and Defense	648.00	745.00	870.00	758.00	701.00	702.00	757.00	768.00	791.00	801.00	797.00
Education	1,103.00	1,144.00	1,122.00	1,191.00	1,236.00	1,335.00	1,484.00	1,506.00	1,568.00	1,658.00	1,687.00
Health & Social Work	328.00	360.00	380.00	428.00	484.00	551.00	539.00	594.00	646.00	686.00	745.00
Other Communities, Social & etc. *	944.00	888.00	926.00	1,251.00	1,368.00	1,456.00	1,419.00	1,627.00	1,727.00	1,781.00	1,845.00
Households with Employed Person	229.00	202.00	201.00	186.00	206.00	215.00	192.00	125.00	130.00	138.00	161.00
Extra-Territorial Organization and Bodies	13.00	20.00	18.00	19.00	16.00	18.00	22.00	24.00	24.00	20.00	15.00
Total	21,106.00	19,994.00	20,281.00	21,156.00	21,572.00	22,169.00	22,139.00	22,557.00	22,856.00	23,151.00	23,433.00

*Wholesale & Retail Trade, Repairs of Motor Vehicles, Motorcycles, Personal & Household; Real Estate, Renting and Business Activities; Other Communities, Social & Personal Services.

When we look at the statistics of *industrial action* taken by workers and employers during 1997-2007 (Table 1.7), it is found that the numbers of strikes, lockouts and disputes have increased from 78 cases in 1997 up to the highest of 462 cases in 2004 and then started to decline sharply to 115 cases in 2007. However, in terms of workers involved, the number seems to be quite significant and does not sharply reduce, as reflected in the number of incidents occurred. *This fact* seems to suggest *that industrial action* taken in recent years involved large companies or enterprises. On the other hand, while the number of unions is increasing, the total number of union members is declining after the *increasing trend of* 2000 – 2005.

Table 1.7 Workers and Employers' Industrial Action, Workdays Lost and Union Organizations in Korea, 1997-2007

Year	Strikes, Lockouts and Disputes	Workers Involved ('000s)	Days not Worked	Union Organization	Union Members ('000s)
1997	78	44	445	1,484	5,692
1998	129	146.1	1,452	1,402	5,517
1999	198	92	1,366	1,481	5,592
2000	250	178	1,893	1,527	5,652
2001	235	88.5	1,083	1,526	6,150
2002	322	93.9	1,580	1,568	6,506
2003	320	137.2	1,298	1,606	6,257
2004	462	185	1,199	1,550	6,017
2005	287	117	848	1,506	5,971
2006	138	131.4	1,201	1,559	5,889
2007	115	n.a.	479	1,688	4,713

Sources:
1. http://laborsta.ilo.org/STP/do
2. http://english.molab.go.kr/english/Industrial/Industrial_Dispute.jsp
3. http://www.koilaf.org/KFeng/engLabornews/bbs_read_dis.php?board_no=5499&page=2& keyField=&keyWord=&keyBranch=
4. http://www.koilaf.org/KFeng/engStatistics/bbs_read_dis.php?board_no=33&page=1& keyField =&keyWord=
5. http://www.jil.go.jp/kokunai/statistics/databook/07/7-3.xls
6. https://www.kli.re.kr/_FILE/ENGSTATBOARD/0131b2f91e681fef1a6f77a45bf4683d.pdf
7. https://www.kli.re.kr/kli/html_eng/05_labor/engstatboard/down.asp?parent=65

The average monthly wage rate growth in Korea, which reflects the quality of life and well-being of workers, has fluctuated growing at negative rates in most of the years during 1997-2007 (Table 1.8). The highest increase was 8.9% in 2003. This suggests that Korean economic growth has been maintained at the price of workers' quality of life to a certain extent. It will be interesting to see how workers' organisations can help maintain the quality of life and well-being of members in the future.

Table 1.8 Average Monthly Wage in Korea, 1997-2007

Year	Average Wage per month/won	Wage Growth rate (%)
1997	1,326.20	-0.7
1998	1,284.50	3.2
1999	1,475.50	-0.4
2000	1,601.50	-2.1
2001	1,702.40	1.3
2002	1,907.00	-1.2
2003	2,074.00	8.9
2004	2,279.70	-1.4
2005	2,458.00	-0.3
2006	2,594.80	-0.1
2007	2,772.00	1.5

4. TAIWAN

In economic terms, Lee (1995) noted that Taiwan's economic history can be divided into five phases, namely post-war reconstruction (1946-1952), the first import substitution phase (1953-1960), the export expansion phase (1961-1972), the second import substitution and export enhancement phase (1973-1980) and the final phase of the development of skill-intensive industries from 1981 onwards. Even though Taiwan did not seem to be much affected by the 1997 Asian financial crisis, the country has however undergone significant transformation into a knowledge-based economy (KBE). The GDP growth rates have been fluctuating in the range of 4.02% to 6.59 %, with an exception of -2.17% in 2001, when the employment rate also dropped from 97% to 95% (Table 1.9). It is interesting to note from the available statistics that the current GDP growth rates do not seem to be sufficient for employment generation as unemployment rates increased after 2001. In addition, inflation rates also increased.

Table 1.9 Taiwan's Economy at a Glance

Year	Real GDP ($U.S. bil.)	GDP Growth rate	CPI	UE (000s)	UE Rate %	Empl. (000s)	Empl. Rate %
1997	274.75	6.59	0.9	256	2.7	9,176	97.29
1998	287.25	4.55	1.72	257	2.7	9,289	97.31
1999	303.76	5.75	0.14	283	2.9	9,385	97.07
2000	321.28	5.77	1.28	293	3	9,491	97.01
2001	314.3	-2.17	0.02	450	4.6	9,383	95.43
2002	328.88	4.64	-0.2	515	5.2	9,454	94.83
2003	340.39	3.5	0.28	503	5	9,573	95.01
2004	361.33	5.26	1.61	454	4.4	9,786	95.57
2005	376.03	5.26	2.31	428	4.1	9,942	95.86
2006	393.61	4.68	2.68	411	5.1	10,111	96.09
2007	409.44	4.02	3.72	419	5.1	10,294	96.09

Sources:
1. http://www.ers.usda.gov/Data/Macroeconomics/Data/HistoricalRealGDPValues.xls
2. http://www.ers.usda.gov/Data/Macroeconomics/Data/HistoricalCPIsValues.xls
3. http://laborsta.ilo.org/STP/do
4. http://eng.stat.gov.tw/public/data/dgbas03/bs2/yearbook_eng/y021.pdf
5. http://eng.dgbas.gov.tw/public/data/dgbas03/bs2/yearbook_eng/y022.pdf

Note: (Empl. Rate = employment rate)

When we look at the available statistics on employment by sector (Table 1.10), it is observed that sectors that have significantly generated employment opportunities in 1997 are respectively manufacturing; wholesale & retail trade, restaurants; social and personal services; construction; and agriculture. However, among these sectors, it is only manufacturing sector that still experienced growth in 2007. The rest are in fact experiencing some declining trend in term of employment growth. In 2007, other sectors, although still show increasing trends in employment growth. These are, for example, transport, storage, and communication; financial intermediation; real estate; public administration and defense; education; health & social work; and professional & technical services. The latter group in particular, suggests the growth of KBE.

Table 1.10 Total Employment by Activity in Taiwan, 1997-2007 ('000s)

Industry	1997	1998	1999	2000	2001	2002	2003	2004	2005	2006	2007
Agriculture, Hunting, Forestry and Fishing	878	822	776	740	706	709	696	642	590	554	543
Mining and Quarrying	13	12	11	11	10	9	9	7	7	7	6
Manufacturing	2,570	2,611	2,603	2,655	2,594	2,572	2,600	2,681	2,732	2,777	2,842
Electricity, Gas and Water Supply	35	35	35	35	36	28	29	29	28	28	28
Construction	885	865	843	832	745	724	701	732	791	829	846
Wholesales &Retail Trade, Restaurants	1,995	2,047	2,130	2,163	1,679	1,693	1,698	1,726	1,726	1,759	1,782
Transport, Storage and Communication	465	477	476	481	532	579	590	605	634	665	681
Financial Intermediation	351	385	406	412	373	380	378	390	406	407	404
Real Estate	n.a.	n.a.	n.a.	n.a.	40	41	44	55	61	66	74
Public Administration and Defense	323	315	318	315	315	316	352	357	336	334	332
Education	n.a.	n.a.	n.a.	n.a.	484	488	514	538	556	563	588
Health & Social Work	n.a.	n.a.	n.a.	n.a.	268	281	292	303	323	334	340
Other Communities, Social& Personal Services	n.a.	n.a.	n.a.	n.a.	496	496	497	510	513	524	523
Business Services	240	260	284	313	n.a.	n.a.	n.a.	n.a.	n.a.	n.a.	n.a.

Table 1.10 Total Employment by Activity in Taiwan, 1997-2007 ('000s) (contd.)

Social & Personal Services	1,421	1,461	1,502	1,534	n.a.	n.a.	n.a.	n.a.	n.a.	n.a.	n.a.
Support Services	n.a.	n.a.	n.a.	n.a.	153	158	180	183	194	205	215
Professional & Technical Service	n.a.	n.a.	n.a.	n.a.	202	220	224	234	258	264	301
Information & Communication	n.a.	n.a.	n.a.	n.a.	190	191	187	195	199	209	206
Arts, Entertainment & Recreation	n.a.	n.a.	n.a.	n.a.	93	107	110	114	116	111	101
Total	9,176	9,289	9,385	9,491	9,383	9,454	9,573	9,786	9,942	10,111	10,294

Sources:
1. http://eng.stat.gov.tw/public/data/dgbas03/bs2/yearbook_eng/y025I.pdf
2. http://laborsta.ilo.org/STP/do

Table 1.11 indicates that minimum monthly wages have been fluctuating, but seem to be increasing in 2007. Table 1.12 shows that unit labor costs have been declining after 2001, but seem to be increasing again in 2007. In addition, the number of strikes, lockouts and disputes have been increasing as well as that of the union organizations, particularly in 2007. This seems to suggest that unions are taking action to negotiate with employers to protect the benefits of their members.

Table 1.11 Minimum Monthly Wage in Taiwan

Year	Minimum Wage per Month/ Taiwanese New Dollars
1997	41,792.88
1998	43,763.60
1999	45,264.80
2000	45,270.80
2001	47,174.10
2002	46,101.80
2003	52,379.50
2004	45,366.30
2005	47,511.80
2006	49,023.30
2007	49587.10

Sources:
http://eng.stat.gov.tw/public/data/dgbas03/bs2/yearbook_eng/y030I.pdf
Note: * New dollar = Taiwan new dollar

Table 1.12 Workers and Employers'

Industrial Action and Number of Unions in Taiwan, 1997-2007

Year	Strikes, Lockouts and Disputes (cases)	Union Organization
1997	2600	64
1998	4138	94
1999	5860	156
2000	8026	273
2001	10955	464
2002	14017	1277
2003	12204	4158
2004	10838	4290
2005	14256	4310
2006	15464	4476
2007	19729	4574

Sources:
1. http://eng.stat.gov.tw/public/data/dgbas03/bs2/yearbook_eng/y033.pdf
2. http://eng.stat.gov.tw/public/data/dgbas03/bs2/yearbook_eng/y035I.pdf
3. http://laborsta.ilo.org/STP/do
4. http://www.cepd.gov.tw/encontent/

5. SINGAPORE

Singapore experienced ups and downs in economic growth after 1997 and seems to have picked up growth momentum after 2004, when it achieved a 8.41% growth rate (Table 1.13). Then, the growth rate declined to around 5.22% in 2007, which is still considerably high. The rate of inflation has been low, in the range of -0.40% to about 2.10%. The unemployment rate during the period under review was highest in 2003, when it was 4.0% but declined to 2.1% in 2007. The employment rate by age group of 25-49 was over 80% by 2006.

Table 1.13 Singapore's Economy at a Glance

Year	Real GDP ($ bil.)	GDP Growth rate	CPI [a]	UE ('000s)	UE Rate (Annual Ave.)	Empl. ('000s)	Empl. rate by age, 25-49
1997	79.25	8.51	2.00	30.9	1.4	2,046.1	**78.7**
1998	78.57	-0.86	-0.27	55.1	2.5	2,022.7	**78.6**
1999	83.61	6.42	0.02	61.9	2.8	2,062.6	**77.8**
2000	91.48	9.41	1.36	60.5	2.7	2,171.1	76.7
2001	89.55	-2.10	1.00	62.4	2.7	2,148.1	79.4
2002	92.24	3.00	-0.40	82.9	3.6	2,135.2	77.8
2003	92.51	2.46	0.51	93.2	4.0	2,206.6	77.9
2004	102.46	8.41	1.66	80.1	3.4	2,319.9	78.5
2005	108.97	6.35	0.47	76.8	3.1	2,495.9	79.1
2006	115.62	6.10	1.00	69.7	2.7	2,495.9	81.2
2007	121.65	5.22	2.10	60.2	2.1	2,732.5	82.0

Sources:
1. http://www.ers.usda.gov/Data/Macroeconomics/Data/HistoricalRealGDPValues.xls
2. http://www.ers.usda.gov/Data/Macroeconomics/Data/HistoricalCPIsValues.xls
3. http://laborsta.ilo.org/STP/do
4. http://www.mom.gov.sg/publish/momportal/en/communities/others/mrsd/statistics/Employment.html
5. http://www.mom.gov.sg/publish/momportal/en/communities/others/mrsd/statistics/Unemployment.html
6. http://www.mom.gov.sg/publish/momportal/en/press_room/press_releases/2008/20080131-employment.html
7. http://www.singstat.gov.sg/stats/themes/economy/hist/cpi.html

Noted: [a]Year 2000=100

When looking at employment by sector, the available statistics suggest that four main sectors that have been generating employment opportunities. These are services producing industries; community, social and personal services; manufacturing; and wholesale and retail trade (Table 1.14). All economic sectors are doing well as employment levels have been increasing over the years. In fact, it is interesting to observe that manufacturing is still playing a significant role in the Singapore economy, which is the smallest in term of population size among the selected countries in this book.

Table 1.14 Total Employment by Industry in Singapore, 2001-2007

Industry	2001	2002	2003	2004	2005	2006	2007
Manufacturing	430.1	424.7	419.7	446.7	475.9	517.5	566.8
Construction	287.2	252.9	235.4	226.3	235.0	255.5	295.9
Services Producing Industries	1,438.8	1,455.3	1,465.2	1,520.1	1,593.8	1,706.5	1,849.6
Wholesale and Retail Trade	325.2	325.1	322.8	333.8	346.4	365.0	384.9
Transport and Storage	161.0	164.5	163.9	166.6	173.0	179.0	184.0
Hotels and Restaurants	118.1	121.4	123.3	127.5	133.2	145.8	162.1
Information and Communications	64.8	62.7	60.2	63.0	66.6	73.1	79.4
Financial Services	101.9	99.9	102.1	108.2	116.0	127.3	149.2
Real Estate and Leasing Services	46.5	46.9	46.1	45.9	48.4	52.9	61.5
Professional Services	106.1	102.4	102.3	106.9	114.6	128.4	150.5
Administrative and Support Services	66.6	71.5	76.4	87.3	97.4	113.2	124.1
Community, Social and Personal Services	448.6	461.0	468.1	480.8	498.3	522.0	554.1
TOTAL	2,171.0	2,148.1	2,135.2	2,206.6	2,319.9	2,495.9	2,730.8

Source: http://www.mom.gov.sg/publish/etc/medialib/mom_library/mrsd/yb_2008.Par.81639.File.tmp/2008YearBook_EHWtable3_1.xls

Looking at industrial action and union growth (Table 1.15), the statistics available suggest that the number of strikes, lockouts and disputes have decreased in recent years. However, the number of unions and members has increased. This suggests greater union strength to some extent. The minimum wage has also increased steadily. The wage indices suggest that real wage rates have increased significantly in recent years, but are still lower than that experienced in 1997. As the Singapore economy depends largely on the service industries, the issue of wages and productivity will certainly be of concern to its government.

Table 1.15 Workers and Employers' Industrial Actions and Union Organizations in Singapore, 1997-2007

Year	No. of Strikes, Lockouts and Disputes	No. of Union	No. of Union Members
1997	253	1,522	260,130
1998	291	1,780	272,769
1999	246	1,807	289,707
2000	231	1,827	314,478
2001	266	1,971	338,311
2002	260	2,047	389,676
2003	252	2,052	417,166
2004	182	1,981	443,893
2005	163	1,950	450,004
2006	163	2,258	463,384
2007	133	2,308	494,746

Sources:
1. http://laborsta.ilo.org/STP/do
2. http://www.mom.gov.sg/publish/etc/midialib/mom_library/mrsd/yb_2007.Par.31361. File.tmp/2007YearBook.LRtable5_1.xls.
3. http://www.mom.gov.sg/pulish/etc/medialib/mom_library/mrsd/yb_2008.Par.65254. File.tmp/2008YearBook_LRtable5_11.xls.
4. http://www.mom.gov.sg/publish/etc/medialib/mom_library/mrsd/files.Par.75584. File.tmp/2005YB_LRtable5_3.xls
5. http://www.mom.gov.sg/publish/etc/medialib/mom_library/mrsd/yb_2007.Par.54760. File.tmp/2007YearBook_LRtable5_7.xls

Table 1.16 Average Minimum Monthly Wage in Singapore, 1997-2007

Year	minimum wage per month /dollar	Wage Indices
1997	2,480.30	5.80
1998	2,740.00	2.70
1999	2,813.00	2.10
2000	3,063.00	4.90
2001	3,134.00	2.90
2002	3,158.00	1.80
2003	3,213.00	1.20
2004	3,329.00	2.70
2005	3,444.00	3.10
2006	3,554.00	3.60
2007	3,773.00	4.30

Sources:
1. http ://laborsta.ilo.org/STP/do
2. http ://www.mom.gov.sg/publish/etc/midialib/mom_library/mrsd/ts300508. Par.93612.File.dat/17_Basic_wage_change_30May08.xls..
3. http ://www.mom.gov.sg/pulish/etc/medialib/mom_library/mrsd/row_2007. Par.51300.File.tmp/2007Wages_OWS_Highlights_Findings.pdf.

6.   THAILAND

For Thailand, economic growth plunged after 1997 and then picked up in 1999 (Table 1.17). Since then the economy has been fluctuating in the range of 2.17% and 7.03% and then seems to decline slightly in 2007. The consumer price index was high at 8.07% in 1998 but has reduced significantly in the following years and increased sharply again in 2004 to 6.17% and then decreased gradually to 2.11% in 2007. Unemployment rates were at 3.0% and over during 1998-2001 but declined steadily to 1.38% in 2007, when it could be said that the country achieved full employment. When looking at the employment rate, the figures suggest that employment rates have been high over 90%, i.e., from about 94.1% to 98.8%.

Table 1.17 Thailand's Economy at a Glance

Year	Real GDP ($ U.S.bil.)	GDP Growth Rate	CPI	UE ('000s)	UE Rate	Empl.	Empl. Rate
1997	125.34	-1.37	5.60	292.5	0.9	33,162.3	98.81
1998	112.17	-10.51	8.07	1,137.9	3.4	32,138.0	94.14
1999	117.16	4.45	0.30	985.7	3.0	32,087.1	96.58
2000	122.73	4.75	1.57	812.6	3.6	33,001.0	97.60
2001	125.39	2.17	1.64	896.3	3.3	33,483.7	94.94
2002	132.05	5.32	0.62	616.3	2.4	34,262.6	96.50
2003	141.34	7.03	1.80	543.7	2.17	34,677.1	96.96
2004	150.06	6.17	6.17	548.9	2.07	35,711.6	97.26
2005	156.76	4.46	4.54	495.8	1.8	36,302.4	97.59
2006	164.59	4.99	4.64	499.9	1.51	36,344.5	97.97
2007	171.33	4.10	2.11	442.2	1.38	37,122.0	98.13

Sources:
1. http://www.ers.usda.gov/Data/Macroeconomics/Data/HistoricalRealGDPValues.xls
2. http://www.ers.usda.gov/Data/Macroeconomics/Data/HistoricalCPIsValues.xls .
3. http://laborsta.ilo.org/STP/do
4 Yearbook of Labor Protection and Welfare Statistics 1997-2007
   Department of Labor Protection And Welfare, Ministry of Labor

Notes: [1] Year 2000 = 100

When we look at the employment by sector, it is observed that the agricultural sector is still the largest in generating employment opportunities for the labor force (Table 1.18). Although it seems to decline after 1997, the sector is still significant and this could be due to government policies to strengthen the agricultural sector so that the country can be the 'World's Kitchen'. Manufacturing employment growth rates slowed down after 1997, but picked up again from 2002 to 2007. It shows high potential still in term of employment generation. Another sector which is significant in term of employment generation is wholesale, retail, restaurants and hotels industries, which have been growing steadily since 1997 in employment growth. Other sectors that show sign of growth include public administration and defense, education, financial intermediation, real estate, renting and business activities; other communities, social & personal services; and households with Employed Person (family businesses). In effect, most economic sectors have experienced growth and expansion after 1997. When we look at the industrial relations statistics, it is found that the numbers of industrial action (i.e., labor disputes, strikes, and lockouts) declined after 1997 (Table 1.19). However, in recent years, particularly in 2007, the number of labor disputes increased substantially, although the number of workdays lost is much less than that of 2006, when fewer number of firms were involved. Similarly, it is found that the number of strikes and lockouts are very few and the number of workdays lost has been lower than previous years. This could suggest that employers and employees have been able to resolve conflicts in a more effective manner either by the assistance of the government agencies related to labor relations or by their own approach. Minimum wages in Thailand have also been fluctuating, but seem to decrease in terms of real growth rate in 2007.

Table 1.18 Employment by Sector* in Thailand, 1997-2007 ('000s)

Industry	1997	1998	1999	2000	2001
Agriculture, Forestry, Hunting and Fishing	16,691.20	16,471.70	15,563.50	16,095.50	15,409.00
Mining and Quarrying	46.90	41.30	51.90	38.90	39.60
Manufacturing repair and installation service	4,291.90	4,189.40	4,394.60	4,784.80	4,750.40
Electricity, Gas, Water and Sanitary service	178.40	177.20	158.00	172.50	101.00
Construction	2,020.70	1,279.60	1,285.60	1,280.00	1,409.20
Wholesales, Retails, Restaurants and Hotels	4,601.10	4,463.60	4,736.10	4,801.50	6,595.60
Transport, Storage and Communication Include Financing, Insurance and Real Estate	980.30	922.70	989.20	951.20	977.30
Total	33,162.30	32,138.00	32,087.10	33,001.00	33,483.70

Table 1.18 Employment by Sector* in Thailand, 1997-2007 ('000s) (contd.)

Industry	2002	2003	2004	2005	2006	2007
Agriculture, Hunting and Forestry	15,311.30	15,146.10	14,719.40	15,007.70	14,887.10	15,081.80
Fishing	488.00	415.40	396.00	440.90	428.20	410.00
Mining and Quarrying	36.90	39.60	35.20	40.10	54.60	53.90
Manufacturing	5,039.80	5,086.30	5,313.30	5,350.10	5,306.60	5,593.00
Electricity, Gas and Water Supply	95.40	105.20	98.70	106.80	99.30	104.90
Construction	1,619.50	1,614.10	1,878.10	1,853.00	2,038.90	1,938.70
Wholesales & Retail Trade, etc.	4,739.40	5,057.20	5,451.60	5,297.00	5,401.90	5,525.40
Hotels and Restaurant	1,988.10	2,103.30	2,206.40	2,300.10	2,214.90	2,302.50
Transport, Storage and Communication	964.60	987.50	1,067.50	1,075.90	1,052.90	1,026.50
Financial Intermediation	263.20	279.30	303.40	339.70	349.70	350.20
Real Estate, Renting, etc.	498.70	567.40	633.70	651.70	659.30	717.40
Public Administration and Defense	956.70	902.80	1,015.00	1,095.60	1,170.10	1,286.90
Education	946.70	957.10	1,082.50	1,122.30	1,079.90	1,085.00
Health & Social Work	471.30	518.00	535.10	611.00	602.80	647.20
Other Communities, Social& Personal Services	602.30	621.10	712.70	718.80	710.30	718.00
Households with Employed Person	221.60	254.80	239.00	241.50	221.90	229.10
Extra-Territorial Organization and Bodies	4.90	0.90	0.90	2.20	0.40	1.10
Households with Employed Person	221.60	254.80	239.00	241.50	221.90	229.10
Extra-Territorial Organization and Bodies	4.90	0.90	0.90	2.20	0.40	1.10
Not classifiable by economics activity	14.50	21.00	23.10	47.70	65.80	50.60
Not classifiable by economics activity	14.50	21.00	23.10	47.70	65.80	50.60
Total	34,262.90	34,677.10	35,711.60	36,302.40	36,344.60	37,122.20

Source: http://laborsta.ilo.org/STP/do
*The classification changed from 2002 – 2007.

Table 1.19 Number of Labor Disputes, Strikes and Lockouts and Unions in the Whole Kingdom, 1997-2007

Year	Estab-lishment	Labor Disputes	Strikes	Workdays Lost	Lockouts	Workdays Lost	Union
1997	162	187	22	117,196	17	102,738	968
1998	109	121	4	161,856	4	84,688	999
1999	162	183	3	8,422	13	134,491	1,056
2000	126	140	3	192,845	10	57,403	1,084
2001	136	154	4	4,527	1	1,540	1,123
2002	100	110	4	18,691	2	5,211	1,160
2003	87	97	1	5,100	4	18,951	1,239
2004	110	123	1	372	1	100	1,340
2005	78	87	3	2,112	6	43,745	1,369
2006	75	80	2	24,000	-	-	1,313
2007	87	100	2	1,323	3	10,278	1,243

Source: Yearbook of Labor Protection and Welfare Statistics 1997-2007, Department of Labor Protection and Welfare, Ministry of Labor

Table 1.20 Minimum Monthly Wage in Thailand

Year	Minimum Wage per month (THB)	Wage Rate Growth (%)
1997	6,742.00	n.a.
1998	7,002.00	3.86
1999	6,972.00	-0.43
2000	5,536.00	-0.21
2001	5,562.90	0.49
2002	6,445.70	15.87
2003	5,839.60	-9.4
2004	5,741.26	-1.68
2005	6,053.18	5.43
2006	7,978.70	31.81
2007	7,357.40	-7.79

N.A. = not available

Sources:
1. http://laborsta.ilo.org/STP/do
2. http://www.mol.go.th/download/moldata/past_wagesnew.xls
3. Yearbook of Labor Protection and Welfare Statistics 1997-2007
   Department of Labor Protection and Welfare, Ministry of Labor.

7.   THE PHILIPPINES

Overall, from the available statistics, the Philippines' economy plunged in 1998 to a negative growth rate due to the Asian financial crisis (Table 1.21). However, the country has been growing steadily since then and remarkably well during 2005-2007. The cost of living has been rather high when compared to other countries presented in this book. However, in 2007, the consumer price index dropped to 2.90%, which is much lower than previous years. Thus, it seems that the country has done very well recently in these terms.

Table 1.21 Philippines' Economy at a Glance, 1997-2007

Year	Real GDP ($ bil.)	GDP Growth Rate	CPI %	UE ('000s)	UE Rate %	Empl. ('000s)	Empl. Rate %
1997	69.69	5.19	5.59	2,377	7.7	27,888	92.34
1998	69.28	-0.58	9.27	2,933	8.4	26,968	91.60
1999	71.64	3.40	5.95	2,931	9.0	27,762	91.00
2000	75.91	5.97	3.95	3,133	9.3	27,775	90.70
2001	77.25	1.76	6.80	3,269	11.4	30,085	88.60
2002	80.59	4.34	3.00	3,423	10.3	30,251	89.70
2003	83.48	3.58	3.45	3,567	10.6	31,553	89.40
2004	88.55	6.07	5.98	3,888	11.0	31,741	89.00
2005	92.95	4.97	7.64	2,619	11.3	32,875	88.70
2006	98.01	5.45	6.20	2,625	8.1	32,886	91.90
2007	103.70	5.80	2.90	2,246	7.8	33,672	92.20

Sources: (Noted: [1] Year 2000=100)
1. http://www.ers.usda.gov/Data/Macroeconomics/Data/HistoricalRealGDPValues.xls
2. http://www.ers.usda.gov/Data/Macroeconomics/Data/HistoricalCPIsValues.xls.
3. http://laborsta.ilo.org/STP/do
4. http://www.census.gov.ph/data/pressrelease/1999/lf9903bc.html
5. http://www.census.gov.ph/data/pressrelease/2001/lf0103tx.html
6. http://www.census.gov.ph/data/pressrelease/2002/lf0203tx.html-date
7. http://www.census.gov.ph/data/pressrelease/2003/lf0303tx.html
8. http://www.census.gov.ph/data/pressrelease/2004/lf0403tx.html
9. http://www.census.gov.ph/data/pressrelease/2005/lf0503tx.html
10. http://www.census.gov.ph/data/pressrelease/2006/lf0603tx.html
11. http://www.census.gov.ph/data/pressrelease/2007/lf0703tx.html
12. http://www.nscb.gov.ph/secstat/d_labor.asp
13. http://www.census.gov.ph/data/sectordata/tscpimon.html

When looking at unemployment (Table 1.22), it is found that the unemployment rate in the Philippines is high. The figures vary between 7.7% and 11.4% in spite of the employment rate of between 88.60% - 92.34%. Thus, it seems that the country will need to expand further its economy to absorb the available workforce.

The statistics on employment by sector (Table 1.22) *suggests* that most of the economic sectors are experiencing growth. The sectors that have been the source of significant employment opportunities are agriculture; wholesales & retail trade, repairs of motor vehicles, motorcycles, personal & household; manufacturing; transport, storage and communication respectively. Other sectors that also employ large numbers and are expanding include construction, public administration and defense, and households with employed persons.

In term of industrial relations, the available statistics suggest that the number of strikes, lockouts and disputes decreased significantly from 1997 (Table 1.23). The workdays lost also decreased substantially when compared to that of 1997. Although the number of union organisations is not available for the last few years, the statistics on union members show that increased numbers. In term of wage rates, the minimum wages in the Philippines have been fluctuating, but on the average have been increasing around 2.60% per year (Table 1.24).

Table 1.22 Employed Persons by Industry in the Philippines, 2001-2007 ('000s)

Industry	2001	2002	2003	2004	2005	2006	2007
Total	30,085.00	30,251.00	31,553.00	31,741.00	32,875.00	32,886.00	33,672.00
Agriculture, Hunting and Forestry	10,102.00	10,175.00	10,341.00	10,420.00	10,763.00	10,619.00	10,768.00
Fishing	1,151.00	1,136.00	1,400.00	1,365.00	1,408.00	1,423.00	1,393.00
Mining and Quarrying	103.00	101.00	101.00	96.00	116.00	134.00	135.00
Manufacturing	2,892.00	2,855.00	3,046.00	3,020.00	3,043.00	3,010.00	3,060.00
Electricity, Gas and Water Supply	116.00	124.00	113.00	121.00	108.00	122.00	141.00
Construction	1,571.00	1,589.00	1,688.00	1,643.00	1,616.00	1,626.00	1,740.00
Wholesales&Retail Trade,Repairs of Motor Vehicles,Motorcycles,Personal&Household	5,526.00	5,621.00	5,661.00	5,788.00	6,215.00	6,152.00	6,176.00
Hotels and Restaurant	700.00	713.00	793.00	798.00	871.00	907.00	907.00
Transport,Storage and Communication	2,171.00	2,171.00	2,352.00	2,446.00	2,471.00	2,460.00	2,600.00
Finacial Intermediation	314.00	318.00	329.00	298.00	337.00	366.00	384.00
Real Estate, Renting and Business Activities	534.00	560.00	716.00	702.00	736.00	799.00	881.00
Public Administration and Defence	1,385.00	1,461.00	1,382.00	1,450.00	1,494.00	1,518.00	1,569.00
Education	955.00	939.00	915.00	958.00	989.00	997.00	1,043.00
Health&Social Work	339.00	347.00	370.00	361.00	362.00	370.00	396.00
Other Communities,Social&Personal Services	890.00	847.00	851.00	809.00	781.00	761.00	779.00
Households with Employed Person	1,334.00	1,289.00	1,494.00	1,465.00	1,561.00	1,619.00	1,699.00
Extra-Territorial Organization and Bodies	3.00	5.00	2.00	1.00	3.00	2.00	3.00

Sources:
1. http://laborsta.ilo.org/STP/do
2. http://www.census.gov.ph/

Table 1.23 Workers and Employers' Industrial Actions, Workdays Lost and Union Organizations

Year	No. of Strikes, Lockouts, and Disputes	Days not Work	Workers Involved	No. of Union	No. of Union Members ('000s)
1997	93	672,730	51,531	n.a.	8,822
1998	92	556,796	34,478	n.a.	9,374
1999	58	229,248	15,517	n.a.	9,850
2000	60	319,233	21,142	3,788	10,296
2001	43	206,493	7,919	1,910	14,606
2002	36	358,152	18,240	1,855	11,365
2003	38	150,465	10,035	1,873	11,796
2004	25	53,434	11,197	3,298	11,601
2005	26	123,329	8,496	n.a.	17,132
2006	12	43,519	1,415	n.a.	16,778
2007	6	12,112	915	n.a.	16,810

Sources:

1. http://laborsta.ilo.org/STP/do
2. http://www.nscb.gov.ph/ncs/10thNCS/papers/invited%20papers/ips-22-02.pdf
3. http://gw.kli.re.kr/emate-gw /seminar.nsf/0/625b4200fb78d73c49256d1600353042/$FILE/philippines.doc
4. http://www.press.uillinois.edu/journals/irra/proceedings2004/06b_amante.html
5. http://www.bulatlat.com/news/3-46-unemployment.html
6. http://www.apl.org.ph/APLPrimer/aplprimer_part3.pdf(page8)
7. http://www.nscb.gov.ph/ru5/genderstats/gender2.html
8. http://www.dole.gov.ph/

Table 1.24 Minimum Monthly Wage in the Philippines, 1997-2007

Year	minimum monthly wage (Peso)	% Annual wage
1997	7,283.00	90.43
1998	7,734.00	89.24
1999	8,347.00	89.90
2000	7,300.00	87.00
2001	6,922.20	82.02
2002	7,029.90	126.11
2003	7,131.60	126.30
2004	7,099.50	124.28
2005	7,583.10	119.86
2006	8,244.30	122.19
2007	8,295.60	121.15

Sources:
1. http://laborsta.ilo.org/STP/do
2. http://www.da.gov.ph/wps/portal/!ut/p/kcxml/04_Sj9SPykssy0xPLMnMz0vM0Y_QjzKLN4 g3NAoFSYGYjvqRMJEgfW99X4_83FT9AP2C3IhyR0dFRQDI5f8B/delta/base64xml/ L0lDU0lKQ1RPN29na21BISEvb0VvUUFBSVFnakZJQUFFaENFSVFqR0VBLzRKRm lDbzBlaDFFpY29uUVZZHaGGQtc0lRIS83XzBfMU1LLzE!?WCM_PORTLET=PC_7_0_1MK _WCM&WCM_GLOBAL_CONTEXT=/wps/wcm/connect/Subj6_Stat/Statistics+on+Agric ulture+and+Fisheries/Macroeconomics+%26+Agri+Sector+Stats/
3. http://countrystat.bas.gov.ph/selection.asp

8. CONCLUSION

In summary, it is clearly evident that Japan, Korea, Taiwan, Singapore, Thailand and the Philippines have all experienced economic growth again after being hit hard or affected by the 1997 Asian financial crisis. Among these countries, Korea may be the only one that is experiencing slow growth in many industrial sectors as suggested by the level of employment growth rates. In addition, Korea also is experiencing aging population which may explain this phenomenon to some extent. However, it is observed that in terms of industrial relations situations, all these countries are experiencing decline in disputes, strikes and lockouts. This is likely resulted from the fact that employers and employees in these countries are now learning to negotiate and resolve conflicts at the workplace more effectively.

Chapter 2

INDUSTRIAL RELATIONS IN THE TURBULENT TIMES

Sununta Siengthai

1. INTRODUCTION

It is evident that industrial relations during the post-financial crisis period in some selected Asian knowledge-based economies are being transformed. All of the selected economies in this study are experiencing rapid economic and societal changes. Much of this is evidently a consequence of the globalization process which comes with increasing foreign competition, deregulation and advanced technologies, particularly, information and communications technology (ICT). Knowledge is becoming more essential to maintain a country's competitiveness in the new ICT environments (Tushman and Nadler, 1986). Some scholars also argue that firms are increasingly dependent on knowledge workers as they compete through their employee know-how (Reich, 1991). In fact, in such an environment, fluidity and flexibility in the organization of work, employment relationships and a highly skilled force all become necessary for firm operations. In our view, what will follow in the decades to come would be then dependent on how these economies learn to cope with change.

The intense competition that these selected economies are faced with requires that firms become more productive and innovative in their operations. Improvements in productivity requires, among other things, superior productive techniques and a more creative and motivated force that is committed to product quality and hard work in pursuit of national and organizational objectives (Bahrami, 1988). It also requires an organizational framework that allows for innovative management that is not only concerned with long-term growth, efficiency, and competitiveness of the organization, but also believes that by fulfilling employee psychological needs, resources can be utilized to their ultimate potential (Bahrami, 1988, p.167). It is likely that from industrial relations concern, the high level of unemployment that might result from organizational restructuring in the economy will further weaken trade union (institutional factor) strengths and hence their role in protecting their members. Naturally, a worker who is dissatisfied with his/her employment terms and working conditions may decide to quit the job. But this action by individuals alone will unlikely lead to the changes in the employment terms and conditions of the workers in the workplace, as the employer can easily find a replacement for such workers. However, if workers (we can include all levels of employees who work in return for their pay or remuneration collectively engage in such action, then this combines the power of individual workers and the sum is more powerful than its parts. This concerted effort may lead to some negotiation and hence improvement in the terms and conditions of employment. In the reality of globalization and the more frequent experiences of world economic recession, this type of concerted action will not be able to induce positive effect on this objective of trade unions. The market model stresses the way in which recession (or other factors leading to unemployment, such as -saving new technology) affects the bargaining power of trade unions (Batstone and Gourlay, 1986). First, it is claimed that employers have less need for output, since demand is slack. Consequently, a work stoppage imposes fewer costs upon them in a period of recession (and indeed may even be profitable) than when demand is more buoyant, thus they will be less ready to concede to union demands backed up with sanctions. Secondly, the bargaining power of the union is weakened by the availability of alternative, when unemployment is high. This means that if unions try to impose demands when general unemployment level is high, employers can more easily sack union members and replace them. Third, reduced bargaining power means that union membership become less attractive to workers. According to this view, workers join a union when the gains thereby achieved are thought to exceed the costs. If unions are less able to win wage increases, and if employers are able to adopt a more hostile approach towards union members, then the gains of membership fall relative to the costs. Accordingly, union density declines. It is therefore possible to imagine a vicious circle of declining union strength whereby unions lose their bargaining power, with the result that membership declines. This reduces the union influences of both 'threat' effect and 'spillover' effect in the markets. These arguments are also plausible and applicable to Asian unions where most unions are enterprise-based unions. In fact, it is even more difficult for Asian enterprise-based unions to really claim their influence since they cannot exclude the non-union members from the benefits gained from the collective bargaining. Thus, the phenomenon of 'free-rider' is very high when unions operate as enterprise-based unions. Not many studies have substantiated this pattern of union growth and decline in the Asian context.

With the concern for the viable economy at large, we therefore have proposed a system model of -management relations for innovation and productivity improvement in the workplace to cope with continuously changing environments (see Figure 2.1). Specifically, it is our assertion that human resource management practices can have a two-pronged effect on -management relations within firms, namely, -management cooperation or -management conflict. However, if these relationships of both parties namely management and are effectively managed and balanced through effective human resource management practices, it is hypothesized here that it will lead to organizational learning and better -management relations which eventually lead to innovation and productivity improvement in the workplace.

Figure 2.1. HRM and -Management Relations for Innovation and Productivity Improvement

In the course of our investigation, we trace the development of industrial relations system in these selected Asian countries which experienced globalization. Years of observation of surviving firms in the financial crisis seem to suggest that they have a resilience ability in that they can renew their organization in a reasonably short period of time. Innovation and productivity are among the key factors enhancing their competitiveness. In fact, even without the financial crisis, some firms have already started to downsize or re-engineer to build up their capabilities to compete in the global environment. For some firms, the decisions to restructure such as downsizing or re-engineering maybe undertaken by the management solely. In some others, the situation requires that the management will have to consult with the union or employees' organizations. Therefore, we may observe industrial strife in the case of inability to negotiate and agree on the condition of such action.

Oftentimes, the industrial strife in Asian countries has been acknowledged and reconciled by third parties, which can be relevant government agencies such as the Ministry of , appointed arbitrators, etc. However, the study by Siengthai (1994) on tripartism or tripartite system in ASEAN countries (ILO, 1994) and in particular, Thailand, suggests that the system itself is not functioning effectively. The study points out that in order to enhance the effectiveness of the tripartism, bipartism has to be strengthened at the firm level as well. 'Bipartism' here does not mean specifically "collective bargaining", which is a bipartite relationship at the enterprise level and legalized by laws in various countries. Here, it includes all types of mechanisms designed by the two social partners at the workplace, such as conflict resolution, problem-solving and productivity improvement mechanisms.

Relationship building takes time to develop into a long and sustainable trust and commitment among the parties involved. The process may involve industrial strife and antagonistic attitudes toward each other for some organizations but peaceful throughout the change process for others. However, since both parties are not static, each experiences changes within its own entities such as change of leadership, policies, or pressures from the external environment. Organizational learning can take place in the interaction of both parties within the enterprise. Over time, firms which experience growth tend to adjust and adapt or adopt new approach to management. On the workers' side, they also learn more about the firm's business and the management, they too can become more cooperative. These are, however, cases of those organizations where communication channels have been designed in such a way that information sharing and learning take place and eventually the organization's objectives are achieved.

2.   BUSINESS STRATEGY AND HUMAN RESOURCE MANAGEMENT (HRM)

As HRM activities are becoming a more and more essential component of the strategy implementation process, traditional descriptions of HR activities in terms of operational direction become less relevant. Organizational effectiveness reflected in innovation and productivity has been found to be influenced by the firm's human resource management practices (Boudreau, 1991; Huselid, 1995; Jones &Wright, 1992; Kleiner, 1990; Siengthai & Bechter, 2001). Chang and Chen (2002) investigate the links between human resource management (HRM) practices and firm performance of Taiwan's high-tech firms and find that HRM practices such as training and development, teamwork, benefits, human resource planning and performance appraisal have significant effect on employee productivity. Although in practice, the effectiveness of management practices on organizational performance may be difficult to measure, Ichniowski et al. (2008) assert that empirical evidence suggests that innovative workplace practices can increase performance, primarily through the use of systems of related practices or bundle of management practices that enhance worker participation, make work design less rigid, and decentralize managerial tasks.

This article discusses why it is difficult to measure the effects of management practices on organizational performance. In spite of these difficulties, a collage of evidence suggests that innovative workplace practices can increase performance, primarily through the use of systems of related practices that enhance worker participation, make work design less rigid, and decentralize managerial tasks.

In order to enhance innovation and productivity, large firms need a different concept of organization and different attitudes and behavior in top management (Doz, 1990). In large firms, particularly manufacturing, it is very likely that if they have been long established, workers' organization such as unions can be one of the legal entities established within firms to act on behalf of their employees. In such an environment, the significant role of HRM in firms is clear (Cutcher-Gershenfeld, 1991). The human resource management practices of the firms can facilitate or hinder the ability of middle level executives and technical specialists to sustain multiple perspectives and appropriate channels for resource allocation, as well as the flexibility of the organization. Organizational resistance to changes and innovation processes in production and services can also be reduced or enhanced by effective HRM practices.

3.   UNIONIZATION AND PRODUCTIVITY

One of the distinct functions or roles of a union is its existence as a 'voice mechanism'. Most likely, if there is no 'voice mechanism', the only viable alternative for workers is to quit in search of an employer of choice. In so doing, the employer risks of losing good and skilled employees which may not be easily recruited from the market at the going wage rate. Quitting is regarded as the 'exit mechanism'. However, the benefit of the union as a 'voice mechanism' does have its limitation, as such benefits rest implicitly on the belief that the jobs concerned are in the 'core', or upper segment, of the market where there are elements of skill and progression. For workers, in low skill, usually part-time jobs, the 'voice mechanism' can do little, as it cannot alter job content. Thus, in that case, unions will need to use other means to satisfy member needs or protect and bring about better working conditions for their members.

Union-management cooperation means that the union and company together actively work to make production as efficient as possible. The concept has come to mean joint action to improve worker and technological efficiency.

In the study undertaken by Rosenberg and Rosenstein (1980), the effects on productivity of a worker participation plan in a unionized foundry was appraised. The authors analyzed detailed records of 262 meetings of workers, supervisors, and managers that were held from 1969 to 1975 to discuss means of increasing productivity. An index of participative activity measuring factors such as the frequency of meetings, the relevance of the subjects discussed, and the number of interchanges in a meeting, was compared with an index of productivity through step-wise multiple regression and other techniques. The authors conclude that an increase in the level of participative activity was associated with an increase in productivity and was more important in this respect than a group bonus plan tied to productivity.

4. LABOUR -MANAGEMENT CONFLICT

To some people, conflict is regarded as undesirable. But to others who regard conflict as a natural outcome of human interaction, conflict is believed to be manageable. The way a conflict is managed will determine to a great extent the degree to which the negative impact can be minimized and the positive aspects maximized (Robbins, 1978; Tjosvold, 1985; and Rahim, 1986). On the contrary, conflict that is not identified, understood and managed effectively can lead to inefficient use of organizational resources, stress on the conflicting parties, and misdirection of the energies of those affected by the conflict situation. When conflict is effectively managed, it can result in increased creativity and innovation, a rethinking of goals and practices, and a better informed work group (Burke, 1970; Folger & Poole, 1984; Tjosvold, 1985; Rahim, 1986).

Organizational researchers typically consider conflict in terms of bargaining and negotiation, and consider conflict to be based on opposing interest and preferences; conflict occurs in mixed-motive situations and defining conflict this way has been useful. Conflict is a relationship characteristic which is regarded as deriving from interdependence (Tjosvold, 1989:45). Conflicts and oppositions in complex modern societies in which exist many intersecting organized collectivities and interlocking memberships are a continual source of social reorganization and change.

Dunlop (1958) has recognized the rule-making processes in industrial relations system which is interrelated to other socio-economic system in the society and hence the significant roles of the three main actors in developing a web of rules in the system. However, in spite of many studies undertaken in the past decades on industrial relations, Delaney and Godard, 2001) suggest from their study that more understanding is needed on the underlying conflicts at work, and the implications of new forms of work for workers, as well as the roles the cultural forces, unions, and governments play in shaping the workplace.

5.   CONFLICT AND ORGANIZATIONAL LEARNING

In the classical or functional approach, conflict resolution implies the reduction or elimination of conflict. However, as conflict is a natural process that can take place in the interaction among individuals or group, so the notion of elimination of conflict will not be creative for firms. On the contrary, firms should try to best manage the conflicts so that learning can take place and become beneficial for the organization. A moderate amount of conflict may in fact provide necessary activation or stimulation in order to optimize job performance of the organizational members or to enhance their adaptive or innovative capabilities (Rahim, 1985).

Argyris (1976, 1980) and Argyris and Schon (1978) have contended that an intervention for managing conflict should promote double-loop rather than single-loop organizational learning. In their studies, organizational learning was defined as the process of detection and correction of error. Learning that results in detection and correction of error without changing the underlying policies, assumptions, and goals is regarded as single-loop learning. Double-loop learning only occurs when the detection and correction of error requires changes in the underlying policies, assumptions and goals (Argyris, 1980:291).

Organizational learning is observed to be stratified (Weick and Ashford, 1995; Weick and Ashford, 2000). Whose meaning will be accepted will be partially a function of the hierarchical and inclusionary boundaries defined by Van Mannen and Schein (1979). For example, old-timers' definitions of reality will be more influential than those offered by newcomers and the power to define reality will be loosely correlated with one's place in the organization's hierarchy. This suggests that certain 'voices' will be lost in the organizational learning process and it allows us to specify the likely focus and direction of persuasion and influence attempts. Thus newcomers will be particularly interested in influencing old-timers (and will need to do so in order to have their voices heard) and lower-level employees ought to be particularly interested in influencing higher-ups regarding how to interpret changing "realities." Hence, it can be clearly expected that in order that union members or the union as a subsystem in the organization can influence the decisions affecting union members, they will need to influence through the hierarchical system and incorporate the organization's cultural values to create an effective communication and learning process between groups of different sets of goals interact and mutually are interdependent of each other.

In the currently rapidly changing business environment, companies are implementing restructuring, and replacing vertical hierarchies with horizontal networks, linking together traditional functions through inter-functional teams and forming strategic alliances with suppliers, customers, and even competitors. Many companies are now becoming or trying to introduce flexible work organization where work roles are no longer defined by the formal organizational structure. However, this does not mean that differences in authority, skill, talent, and perspective simply disappear. In the corporation without boundaries, such as multinational enterprises or those that heavily use information technology in their customer services functions, creating the right kind of relationships at the right time is the key to productivity, innovation, and effectiveness (Hirschhorn and Gilmore, 1993). Opportunities for confusion and conflict abound in a flexible organization. Flexibility depends on maintaining a creative tension among widely different but complementary skills and points of view. This need for organizational flexibility affects the job security of employees to a large extent. If employers do not provide training and skill development programs, employees may not be able to cope with change and hence vulnerable to the numerical flexibility practices.

When organizations strike the balance of the need for flexibility and organizational commitment of employees, people feel loyal to their own groups and also maintain a healthy respect for others. In the context of -management relations, if the organizational design processes are built in such a way that these relationships are considered, it may facilitate the productive relationship leading to innovation and productivity of the organization as a whole. It can be clearly drawn from the discussion above that effective communication is an important factor that enhances organizational learning and eventually productivity improvement.

But why would organizations need to promote organizational learning and at the same time encourage the management of conflict so that it becomes a positive-conflict organization? According to Rahim (1985), the reason is that firms would need to increase its level of organizational and systems models. Whereas the goal attainment model attempts to assess organizational effectiveness in terms of the ends, the systems models focuses on the means for the achievement in the goal attainment model, the effectiveness of an organization is assessed in term of ends as opposed to means. One of the advocates of this model is Etzioni (1964), who defines organizational effectiveness as the ability of a social system to achieve its goals or objectives. The measures of goal attainment very often take the form of productivity or efficiency. Another common measure of goal attainment is profitability or return on investment. In the system resource model, Yuchtman and Seashore (1967) have proposed a 'system resource' approach to organizational effectiveness which builds on Katz and Kahn's (1966) view of organizations. This approach is concerned with an organization's ability to secure an advantageous bargaining position in its environment to obtain scarce and valued resources.

6. ORGANIZATIONAL LEARNING AND PRODUCTIVITY IMPROVEMENT

It has been asserted that most companies tend to make two mistakes in their efforts to become learning organizations (Argyris (1993). On the one hand, most people define learning too narrowly as mere 'problem solving,' so they focus on identifying and correcting errors in the external environment. However, if learning is to persist, managers and employees must also look inward. On the other hand, effective double-loop learning is not simply a function of how people feel. It is a reflection of how they think - that is, the cognitive rules or reasoning they use to design and implement their actions. Defensive reasoning can block learning even when the individual commitment to it is high. In another study, Argyris and Schon (1978) define organization learning as the increased process capacity to innovate in the future within that same organizational setting. A different definition of 'organizational learning' is given as the acquisition of new knowledge by actors who are able and willing to apply that knowledge in making decisions or influencing others in the organization (Miller, 1996). Learning is to be distinguished from decision making. The former increases knowledge while the latter need not. Learning may in fact occur long before or long after, action is taken. Of course, methods of decision making may well influence learning processes, and vice versa.

Organizational learning cannot be purchased. It is embedded in people and can be developed only through experience and training. It is because of the human element that the HR practices play such an important role in acquiring and enhancing organizational competencies. To some people, what human resources have acquired over time is implicit knowledge (Nonaka and Johanssen 1985; Nonaka, 1993). Organizations will not gain competitive advantage if they cannot develop organizational learning into a system. The core value of organizational learning itself is the enhancement of the long-term strategic capability of the organization. It is believed to foster creativity, entrepreneurship, and autonomy. Its essential building elements support proactive and flexible global competitive strategies. However, an organization's capacity to learn is much greater than the collective capacity of all of its members to learn. It primarily reflects its collective capability to act and to implement what was learned.

The objective is to move beyond knowledge accumulation towards knowledge creation. To develop an organizational capability to learn and to create new knowledge means to focus on the quality of interactions among organizational members and subunits. Organizational learning has its focus on the long-term survival and growth of the firm. At the same time, for a firm to maintain its competitiveness, long term vision has to be balanced with constant attention to short-term tasks. Organizational learning requires slack resources both human and capital, and only a continuous improvement in products and processes can allow the organization to accumulate sufficient means to learn. Organizational learning and continuous improvement are therefore the two sides of the same competitive strategy (Pucik et al., 1992).

Effective continuous improvement programs are those that are integrated into the routine activities of the firm, including planning, accounting, and human resource management (Pucik et al, 1992). From the HRM perspective, the selection, skills development, and recognition of employees must take into account their accomplishment as champions of continuous improvement. Since dynamic firm strategies cannot rest only on cost cutting, HRM practices must address the need for competencies development of the firm (Pucik et al., 1992, ibid.; Huselid, 1995; Becker and Huselid, 1998; Ichniowski and Shaw, 1999). Organizational effectiveness reflected in innovation and productivity seems therefore dependent on the human resource management practices in developing appropriate culture and organizational learning.

However, to implement the best practices transfer to enhance its competitive advantage through organizational learning is not without difficulty. Just as a firm's distinctive competencies might be difficult for other firms to imitate, its best practices could be difficult to imitate internally. Szulanski (1996) analyzes internal stickiness of knowledge transfer based on empirical dataset of 271 observations of 122 best-practice transfers in eight companies. Contrary to conventional wisdom which blames primarily motivational factors, the major barriers to internal knowledge transfer are found to be knowledge-related factors, such the recipient's lack of absorptive capacity, casual ambiguity, and an arduous relationship between the source and the recipient. The latter certainly could be attributed to the relationship between the employer and employees in the case of technological change and technology transfer in the old existing plant. Another factor that can also cause organizational learning failures is culture (Schein, 1996). This can be due to the lack of communication among three dominant cultures: 1) executives, 2) engineers, and 3) operators. The culture of operators evolves locally in an organization or unit and is based on human interaction. Executives and engineers are task focused and tend to assume that people are the problem. Executives and engineers cannot agree on how to make organizations work better while keeping costs down. Therefore, enough mutual understanding must be created among the culture to evolve solutions that all groups can commit to. For executives, Tushman and Nadler (1986) articulate that one of the most important and demanding executive tasks is the continual management of innovation and change. In order for a company to remain competitive, innovation must become a way of life. Sustained innovation requires both stability and change. The stability permits scale economies and incremental learning, whereas change and experimentation produce changes in products, processes, and technologies. In general, there are two kinds of innovation: 1) product innovation, involving changes in the product a company makes or the service it renders, and 2) process innovation, involving changes in the way a product is made or the service provided. Each category has three degrees of innovation within it – incremental, synthetic, and discontinuous.

Organizations need sufficient internal diversity in strategies, structures, people, and process in order to facilitate different kinds of innovation and to enhance organizational learning. In the information and communication technologies (ICTs) environment, the work teams have gradually replacing the traditional hierarchies in the organizations. D. Andrea – O. Brien and Buono (1996) found in their field study that as networks of teams replace traditional hierarchies, knowledge becomes the main organizational resource. As part of the rapid change in the global business world, organizations will, therefore, have to speed up their learning processes to adapt even ever faster to the world around them. Technological change, diffusion and shortening product life cycles are fundamentally altering the nature of competition in many industries such as computers, bicycles and automobiles (Kotha, 1996). In such industries, the dominant paradigm is mass-production. Whereas the emerging literature has focused on highlighting the differences between mass-production and mass-customization, it is proposed that the interaction between the systems can be an effective source of knowledge creation and organizational learning.

Thus, it is our assertion that to ensure the sustainable competitive advantage, firms will need to develop their competencies through effective HRM and industrial relations system and practices. One of the most important requirements for cooperation of employers and employees is a long-term perspective. Cooperation is a long-term and continuous process, and it does not pay off in a short period of time. One of the principal factors for cooperation is human resource development through continuous and extensive on-the-job training and retraining programs (Bahrami, 1988). In fact, employment security is necessary to induce worker's creative thinking, and willingness to accept technological and work rule changes, gainsharing programs, commitment to product quality, and the objectives of the enterprise, which are at the heart of any attempt to improve long-term productivity and efficiency. To enhance or maintain employment security, practices such as inter-plant transfers are an alternative to termination and work-sharing arrangement help avoid layoffs. As a last resort, when adjustment is necessary by firms, the early announcement of plant closings, pre-layoff assistance (i.e., counseling) job search assistance, retraining by employers in cooperation with unions, can play a significant role in easing the burden of displacement. Adoption of the "Attrition Principle," an agreement to reduce jobs through deaths, voluntary resignations, retirements, and similar events, is another option that gives maximum job security to the present job holders (Bahrami, 1988:171).

7. CONCLUSION

In the industrial relations system, the understanding of the concerned parties of the effect of conflict on organizational effectiveness, and the ability of the organization to manage it, is in fact the rationale for our study of -management relations or bipartism and organizational learning for productivity improvement in any industry. The discussion and the model proposed above suggests that effective human resource management will have a positive relationship on -management relations within firms which will eventually lead to productivity improvement. Secondly, effective human resource management will have a positive impact on organizational learning which will also lead to productivity improvement. Thirdly, cooperative management relations has a positive impact on productivity improvement. Fourthly, -management conflict will have a negative impact on productivity improvement. However, on the feedback response as the consequence of these relationships, we will also expect that when -management cooperation and conflict occur, there can be a positive impact on organizational learning given that certain factors as discussed above are present in the particular firm's context. This organizational learning will eventually lead to productivity improvement. Finally, when firms experience -management conflict, such phenomena can lead to firm innovation by bringing in new technologies of production which eventually have a positive impact on productivity. In sum, we assert that -management relations in whichever form can increase organizational learning and productivity improvement.

ENDNOTES

This paper is based on the earlier version the first author developed during her visit to the University of Michigan Business School as a Senior Fulbright Fellow in 1998. She is grateful to the Fulbright Program for the financial support. Our thanks and appreciation are extended to Linda Y. C. Lim; Karl Weick; John J. Lawler and several other colleagues who have contributed to our thinking in various interactions.

Chapter 3

GLOBALIZATION OF JAPANESE FIRMS AND HUMAN RESOURCE MANAGEMENT

Hiromasa Suzuki and Katsuyuki Kubo

1. INTRODUCTION

In the past 25 years, in terms of globalization, Japanese firms have experienced a dramatic change due to increasing international competition and also to domestic economic slumps. At the beginning of the 1980s, a few large Japanese firms had overseas production plants, but none of them could be compared to leading western multinationals such as IBM, GM or Nestlé. But, today many large and medium Japanese firms have established production plants in China, Southeast Asian countries, the EU or in the USA. In some sectors like the automobile industry, a large proportion of group profits are drawn from overseas sales, in particular from the U.S.A. In less than three decades, Japanese firms have come a long way from the "reluctant multinationals" of the early 1980s to an efficient network of many factories and subsidiaries spread out around the world.

In this chapter, we will overview the transformation of Japanese firms and their HRM system. Indeed, the traditional function of HRM/IR was central to organizational building and control of Japanese firms. In general, the top management relied on a personal network of managers to control the different departments and activities, in contrast to the American firms, which tend to stress financial controls. With increasing overseas production, Japanese firms try to set up new ways of communication and controls with or without the central HRM department.

This chapter is structured as follows. In the first part, we look at the long-term changes in the Japanese economic and social context. This part will also examine structural elements like demographic trends. The second part describes changes concerning the actors of industrial relations and HRM. Finally, the third part reviews human resource management in practice in Japanese firms, in particular recent changes in pay policies and a case study of a global firm.

2.   THE CHANGING CONTEXT

2.1   Economic Environment (1980-2006)

In terms of the stage of globalization of Japanese firms, the beginning of the 1980s marks a turning point. Many Japanese firms had to take a decisive step towards overseas production and globalization. Illustrative of this move is the Toyota Automobiles. This firm was renowned for its careful and conservative attitude in Japan. It was based in the Nagoya region, shielding off the influence of political and business circles. It perfected the famous Toyota flexible production system (Just-in-Time at the core) with the affiliates to the Toyota group concentrated in that area. However, Toyota became by that time too big to stay away from international frictions.

The first step towards globalization was to create a joint venture with the giant G.M., NUMMI, which was a model factory, in order to transfer to the U.S.A. the know-how of the Toyota production management system (in 1984). At the same time, Toyota created a large factory in the Tennessee, following other Japanese carmakers from a distance. Indeed, Toyota was the last big weight to decide to offshore its production in the U.S.A. This move was to echo international trade frictions between U.S. and Japan, exemplified by the stand of the U.A.W. (International Union, United Automobile, Aerospace and Agricultural Workers of America) asking to Japanese car-makers for direct investment in the U.S.A.

At the beginning of the 1980s, the international economic context surrounding Japanese firms changed drastically. Two oil crises put an abrupt end to the high growth period and brought about persistent unemployment and trade imbalances with most industrialized countries. Japan fared relatively well with its competitive manufacturing (electric appliances, machines and cars) and its exports. This success triggered trade fictions, particularly with the U.S.A. At this time, mainly due to international political pressure, the appreciation of the yen against the U.S. dollar was accelerated in this period. Under these circumstances, many Japanese firms had to weigh increasing labor costs (appreciation of the yen and wage rise) and political pressure of trade frictions (particularly with the U.S.A.).

As mentioned earlier, Toyota's decision to transfer major production to the U.S.A. was emblematic of the change of strategy of the Japanese firms in the early 1980s. Noteworthy to mention in this connection is the fact that many Japanese part makers had already come to the U.S.A. or other industrialized countries prior to the car makers themselves (they are a kind of assembler of parts). We shall see later the process of globalization in a case study.

During the latter part of the 1980s, overseas investment continued to rise, due to the appreciation of the yen and the buoyant, speculative mood in the Japanese economy. It was at this time that Rockefeller Center in New York was purchased by Japanese investors. Overall, in the 1980s, Japanese investment was directed towards industrial countries.

The economic context of Japanese firms changed at the beginning of 1990, when the speculative "bubble" economy burst. The end of speculation resulted in slumping domestic consumption together with plummeting asset values (real estate, stocks). In fact, a long series of recessions and the deflationary spiral were set in and it is only from 2003 that economic recovery has been persistent and domestic investment has picked up. In this long recession period, many features of the Japanese economic system fell apart. For instance, the main bank system collapsed, due to huge bad loans in most banks and financial institutions. Some of large banks could only survive thanks to mergers and zero interest policies kept by the Bank of Japan.

One example was the major bank, Sanwa. It was one of six traditional Zaibatsu groups before World War II. The group included some big names such as Kobe steel, Ohbayashi Construction and Nisho Iwai Trading Company. However, the bank itself in difficulty, could only survive with several mergers of banks and eventually ended up being partially absorbed by the Tokyo Mitsubishi Bank (Mitsubishi Tokyo UFJ Bank). It is without saying that the financial and industrial group Sanwa was completely eliminated.

In relation to globalization, most Japanese manufacturing firms continued their move to overseas production in the 1990s. However, the motive behind overseas expansion was different. It aimed at cost reductions by transferring the labor intensive assembly process to mainland China.

At first, apparel and electric/electronic appliances undertook to transfer production or part of the production process to China (in particular the Shanghai and Dalian regions). Then, more technologically advanced processes were transferred to China, to make the most of the cheap and abundant labor there. By the turn of the century, many large firms such as Toshiba and Matsushita set up several dozens of plants and subsidiaries in China. From the middle of the 1990s, China became the factory of the world, from textile products to electronics. Because the Japanese domestic market was slumping all through the 1990s, many heavy industries came to rely on demand from China (steel, chemicals, heavy and light machinery).

Since the turn of the century, a new economic environment has been put forward for Japanese firms. This period roughly coincides with the Koizumi government (2001-2006). It is in terms of policy orientation that the present époque is different. The Koizumi government strongly espoused a neoclassical orientation (market mechanisms) by curbing public spending and by promoting market competition. Maybe more than what was done as deregulation, attitudinal change brought about by the Koizumi government seems important. As in the case of the banking sector, governmental protection could not be afforded automatically, even for regional governments and public corporations.

In regard to labor market regulations, there has been some relaxation of the legislation as to agency work and hours of work (possibility of discretionary working hours for white collar workers). But most of the institutional framework has not been altered so far.

However, a recent trend is noticeable in terms of globalization. Some Japanese firms seem to give a preference to domestic production with higher value added content. This is the case with Canon, which has somehow renewed investment in Japanese plants (cell production for colour-printers, copiers, digital cameras). Given the development of the automated production process and the flexibility of production facilities (possibility of investment), overall production costs of Japanese plants may well be equivalent or more cost-efficient than overseas production, at least in some high valued product segments.

2.2   Changes in the Japanese Labor Market

In the past 25 years, a number of demographic and institutional changes have been brought to the Japanese labor market. We hereafter summarize some of the most significant changes which affect Japanese HRM. Demographic changes in the workforce could be summarized by:
1)   aging working population
2)   increasing female participation
3)   growth of atypical employment

The aging of the Japanese population has been accelerated during the period under review. The proportion of the older population (65 years and above) increased from 8% in 1980 to 20% in 2005. According to an official estimate, this ratio will go up to 25% by 2025. The aging demographic trend poses many difficult problems for the Japanese HRM In the traditional HRM, the entry to large enterprises is limited to new school/ university graduates. The number of new recruits is determined each year by the assessment of the future needs of workforce and also by the performance of the enterprise at the moment.

Because of the long recession in the 1990s, most enterprises restricted the number of new recruits to the minimum, so that the age structure of the workforce often shows a high concentration of elder workers (50 years old and up) and few in the young bracket of 25-35 years old. In addition, the generation of baby boomers (born between 1945 and 1947) is now at the point of retiring without the possibility of transmitting their technical know-how to the younger generation (this is the case in the steel industry, machinery, etc.).

The mandatory retirement age is generally fixed at 60, even though the new legislation requires enterprises to continue to offer employment up to 65 years old by 2013 (today, most workers are reemployed under a fixed-term contract with a substantially reduced wage rate). In fact, Japanese enterprises are quite reluctant to modify their HRM practices in regard to entry (recruitment of new school/university leavers) and exit (mandatory retirement age) for their core workers.

As in many countries, the participation of female workers is increasing, albeit slowly. Female workers represent around 40% of the total labor force. However, female workers have difficulty getting into get into the pool of core workers (career employment) and they very often occupy "female jobs" (clerical jobs, medical or paramedical staff or part-time jobs).

On paper, the Equal Employment Opportunity Law of 1985, amended several times, makes it unlawful to discriminate women in employment. In fact, the number of female employees on career track is very limited. For instance, female employees in managerial positions were only 9.9% in 2003, most of them in lower managerial positions [1].

Closely related to female participation is the growth of atypical employment. The proportion of atypical employment has gone up from 16.6% in 1986 to 33.5% in 2007 of total employment (Figure 3.1). The bulk of atypical employment is constituted by part-time workers. It also involved temporary workers supplied through employment outside agencies. Part-time work is mostly an arrangement of short-time work, which automatically means a lower wage rate and no career prospect. In many cases, part-time workers are a kind of lower status worker executing routine jobs. Part-time workers are in great numbers in the growing service sector.

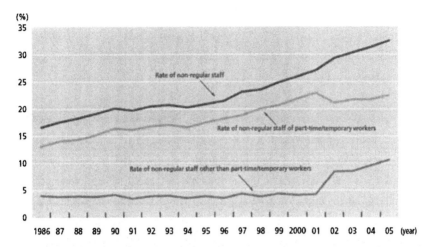

Sources: *Special Survey of Labour Force Survey* (February survey) (1986-2001) and *Labour Force Survey (Detailed Tabulation)* (2002-2005), Statistics Bureau, Ministry of Internal Affairs and Communications
Notes: 1) Rate includes employees other than directors.
    2) A reason for the drop in the rate of part-time workers in 2002 is that the survey questionnaire for the "Labour Force Survey (Detailed Tabulation)" was different from that of the prior "Special Survey of Labour Force Survey," and therefore, that some people who respond-ed until 2001 that they were part-time workers may have answered in 2002 that they were, contract employees or entrusted employees.

Figure 3.1 Breakdown of Employees by Status at Work

3.   CHANGING ROLES OF INDUSTRIAL RELATIONS ACTORS

Responsive to external as well as internal pressures, the major actors of the industrial relations system – government, business organizations and trade unions – have had to undergo considerable changes in the past 25 years. In certain areas, they have changed gradually and in some others only relatively recently. Nevertheless, if Japan could be described by some scholars in the 1980s as a "neo-corporatist" nation, it seems that such a label is today very much outdated.

a)   Government
Prior to the 1990s, the Japanese government was an important player in the industrial relations field. It was the employer of a relatively large business sector (public

corporations and public services). The government (bureaucracy) was often the initiator and executor of labor and social policies, for instance towards equal opportunity between men and women or for the reduction of working hours (e.g., the Equal Employment Opportunity Law of 1986 and amendment of the Labor Standard Law concerning working time in 1987). Moreover, the government used to act behind the scenes as a mediator for the annual wage negotiation cycle called the "spring wage round" (*Shunto*).

These roles now are much more restricted. Firstly, there were a series of privatizations of large public corporations like telecommunications (N.T.T.), railways, aviation (J.A.L.), and tobacco (Japan Tobacco). Although the public services sector (education, health, etc.) is still considerable, the government has ceased to be a major actor in determining the conditions of work and wages. The scope of labor policies has also become limited to the maintenance of a safety net (unemployment insurance, keeping records of minimum labor standards).

Illustrative of this change is the merger of the former Ministry of Labor with the Ministry of Health, which took place in 2001. During the Koizumi Administration (2001-2006), stress was placed on market mechanisms, relaxing certain labor regulations such as agency work and exemption from working hours regulations. Today, it appears that the government has withdrawn from the role of a major actor in industrial relations and labor issues.

b)   Business Organizations

Unlike the European system of collective bargaining, Japanese employer' federations have never been directly involved in negotiations. Collective agreements are always concluded at the enterprise level between the management and the enterprise unions (with very few exceptions such as the seamen's union). However, national federations of employers used to play a role of coordinator. Four major employer federations existed at the national level: 1) the Japanese Federation of Business Organizations, which grouped large enterprises; 2) the Japanese Federation of employers, which specialized in labor matters with a similar composition; 3) Keizai Doyukai was an association of independent (progressive) managers of large enterprises (it is rare that this association intervened in labor matters) and 4) The Japanese Chamber of Commerce represented medium and small enterprises. In many tripartite bodies, both at national and regional level, it had a seat and voices for their members (minimum wage councils, labor tribunals, etc.)

Two major changes occurred in business organizations in the period under review. Firstly, the merger of two major employer federations (Keidanren and Nikkeiren into Nihon Keidanren, Japan Business Federation, in 2003) means that labor issues ceased to be a matter important enough to need a separate organization, since Nikkeiren was created to specifically deal with labor matters (in 1948). Another major change has been the shift of power from established enterprises (zaibatsu groups and quasi-public corporations like the New Japan Steel or the electric power corporation) to more dynamic new-comers. Illustrative of the latter was the nomination of two presidents of Toyota at the head of the influential Nihon Keidanren (Shoichiro Toyoda and Okuda). Toyota used to be considered as an outsider to the core business networks, which were formed around former zaibatsu groups (Mitsui, Mitsubishi) and public corporations. The zaibatsu groups lost their cohesion and influence during the 1990s due to the ailing banking and insurance sector.

c) *Trade Unions*
The changes in union density and total union membership are summarized in Figure 3.2. Union density stayed at around 30-35% up to 1982 but then after, it has been declining of roughly 0.5% per year. The decline in total membership only began in the middle of the 1990s but the movement accelerated after the turn of the century. Roughly two million members were lost between 1998 and 2006.

As is well-known, most Japanese trade unions are organized at the enterprise level (sometimes at the establishment level). This means that the resources and activities of unions are concentrated at the enterprise union level. In large corporations, a union may group 40 to 50,000 members who contribute on average 1~2% of their pay. These big unions often adhere to the industrial federation and to a national confederation. Industrial federations or national confederations are coordinating bodies in most cases without real power of negotiation. Only some industrial federations such as U.I. Zensen or Denki Roren have sufficient power and resources to formulate policy objectives in time of wage negotiation rounds.

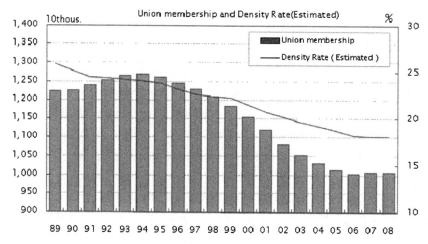

Source: MHLW "Basic Survey on Labour Unions"
Note : 10thous. = 10,000

Figure 3.2 Number of Unions and Estimated Union Membership Density

At the national level, the unification of four national federations into one confederation (Rengo) in 1989 did not produce the expected momentum for the Japanese labor movement. The creation of Rengo meant virtually the end of the ideological rivalry between moderates and radicals in favour of the former. Maybe because most militant radicals were excluded from key positions, the Japanese labor movement has lost its their teeth and become tame counterparts of big business. Today industrial conflicts largely disappeared from the scene of annual wage negotiations (*Shunto*). At its creation, the Rengo could boast more than 7. 6 million members, but it had lost some one million members by 2005. Probably much more damaging for the Japanese labor movements than the loss of membership is the fact that this loss occurred in the sectors which used to play a leading role at the national level.

One could attribute the cause of union decline to several events or factors. Firstly, the wave of privatization was partly aimed at dismantling the stronghold of union movements; this was the case with the national railways and telecommunications. These public corporations, once privatized, had to reduce substantially the number of employees. Secondly, heavy industries such as steel, shipbuilding and machinery had to restructure their activities during the recession in the 1980s and 1990s, so the once powerful industrial federation of steel industry merged with that of shipbuilding in 2003. Thirdly, the delocalization of production sites to China and other countries has accelerated so that the number of employees (particularly production workers) has been reduced greatly. Lastly, the increase of atypical employment (part-time workers, fixed-term, or agency workers) also has accounted for the loss of membership. In enterprise unions, membership is usually limited to "permanent" employees of the enterprise concerned. Atypical workers are excluded from the group of "permanent" employees, hence excluded from union membership. Today, the number of part-time workers is over 12 million, of which only 4.8% are effectively organized in trade unions, in spite of some success of unionization in the distribution sector (2007).

Does the above-mentioned decline of trade unions mean that they have really lost their economic or social role? The answer should be qualified. Indeed, in large enterprises and in the public sector, labor unions are well established with their mechanisms of consultation and collective bargaining. Even today, unions are present in half of the enterprises with more than 1,000 employees. In these unionized sectors, the conditions of employment and work are still determined through consultation and negotiations. Thanks to union shop agreements, labor unions generally have almost 100% of the organization rate of permanent employees (managerial positions are excluded from the scope of unionization by law). This also means that employment protection for permanent employees is still strictly observed in large enterprises. However, problem areas are numerous for the Japanese labor unions. Very few employees actually participate in union activities. Unions are having difficulties finding active members and union officials. Accustomed to satisfactory wages and working conditions, the bulk of employees are distant supporters of union activities. This may well be the price of the end of the ideological rivalries which dominated the Japanese labor union movement before 1980.

4.   HUMAN RESOURCE MANAGEMENT IN PRACTICE

The objectives and functions of HRM may differ considerably from one firm to another according to the history of the firm and sector. Newly created firms such as Internet businesses like Softbank or Rakuten, have little in common with manufacturing firms established, a long ago. The former rely on young and mobile software technicians and engineers, whereas many "old" firms, always stressed development of the potential of their employees through career within the firm. However, if we restrict ourselves to large firms (generally in business for a long time) and compare their HRM to other countries', then we could identify some characteristic traits which might be called "Japanese HRM".

Before going to the case study, several characteristics of Japanese HRM could be summarized here:

1.   The basis of Japanese HRM is no doubt the long-term attachment of permanent employees to the firms, popularly known as lifetime employment (up to mandatory retirement age). Different tools of HRM have been developed and adjusted to the long-term attachment of employees. From the initial recruitment in large firms after graduation from high-school or university, employees are expected to stay in the same firm. In the vast majority of cases, the recruitment of permanent employees is restricted to new graduates (below 25 years old) without occupational experience. Once recruited in a large firm, employees follow a series of internal training and job rotation within the firm. Performance appraisal and internal promotion are congruent with a long-term perspective. Similarly, all the management posts are filled with internal promotion. There is no room for professional managers as in the U.S.A. Mandatory retirement is important in Japanese firms because it puts an end to the long-term employment contract. The system of staffing is now changing, since young Japanese workers generally aspire to be mobile in their careers and lifestyles. In some sectors, such as financial dealers or I.T. engineers, worker mobility has increased greatly, partly due to the development of labor markets for foreign firms. However, this is the exception rather than the rule.

2. Human resource management is generally centralized to the headquarters and plays a much more influential and strategic role in Japanese firms than in the U.S.A. The main reason is that in American firms, organizational controls are by and large carried out by the financial department, whereas in Japanese firms they are entrusted to the human resource department through personal relations and nominations (the financial director has little power in Japanese firms). In large firms with many quasi independent divisions and related firms, it is through personal networks that organizational controls are exercised. This is the main reason why the human resource department is always pivotal to top management. In American firms (and in those many other countries), human resource functions such as recruitment and promotion are often decentralized to a specific division or department and the HR department plays a coordination or mediating role. In most Japanese firms, the human resource department is still at the centre of decision-making in regard to recruitment and internal promotion.

3. Large Japanese firms still operate very much under closed internal market without real connection to the external labor market, which scarcely exists. For instance, there is no market rate for experienced engineers in Japan, because no experienced engineer would quit a large firm unless he is obliged to do so (restructuring of the firm or personal problems). Professional skills are developed within the firm by training, regular rotation of jobs (every 3~5 years) and job content (more responsibility) all through an employee's career. In many cases, the HR department has the last word, over division chiefs, as to the transfer and promotion of an employee.

4. Congruent with this internalization of employees' career is the enterprise union. As in many industrialized countries, union density is decreasing but in the majority of large firms, the enterprise union, whose membership covers all permanent employees, is still active for the protection of workers' employment and career. In fact, unions and the human resource department are mutually supporting in many points.

5. The Japanese HRM is always geared towards permanent employees, excluding other contractual part-time workers. As is well-known, large firms like Toyota are at the top of the pyramid of subcontracting firms (in the case of Toyota, there are 3 or 4 layers of subcontracting firms). Workers in subcontracting firms are excluded from the internal labor market or the scope of HRM. Thus, the HRM in large firms applies only to a small portion of highly selected workers. Workers who are excluded from the internal labor market will have to content with less favourable conditions of work, employment, and career opportunity.

6. Because the Japanese HRM has been developed for a homogenous group of employees with long-term attachment to the firm, overseas production and globalization pose new problems for Japanese firms. A particularly difficult point is that technology and know-how are accumulated through experience and training on production sites and that much know-how is not standardized and explicit, hence difficult to transfer into a non-Japanese environment. It seems that many Japanese firms have tackled this issue pragmatically through trial and error. We will see the process in the case of a large Japanese ball bearings firm.

5.   CHANGES IN PAY POLICIES

In response to stagnant performance, many Japanese firms have changed their wage systems. One of the first companies that introduced performance-related pay was Fujitsu, which introduced it in 1994 for white-collar employees. After Fujitsu, many companies trying to strengthen the link between individual performance and wages revised their pay system. Although the definition of performance-related pay has varied across firms, evidence suggests that more and more firms have been trying to introduce some kind of new compensation system to strengthen the link between pay and performance.

It has been often said that one of the characteristics of Japanese style management is 'Seniority based pay'. Typically, workers receive relatively low salary when they enter the firm after graduation. Their salary increases as they continue working in the firm. Typically, wages are determined by competence-rank. The basic idea is that employees with higher skills receive higher wages. Those who acquired higher skills are promoted. Wage increases are associated with promotion. This wage structure is said to encourage employees to accumulate skills, in particular firm-specific ones.

However, several changes make it difficult for firms to keep this system. These are aging employees and changing technology. Steep age-wage profile implies that wages of young workers are less than their productivities. In contrast, wages of older workers tend to be higher than their productivity. Young employees have strong incentives to keep working for the same firm and to acquire firm-specific skills. This system works effectively only when the number of young employees is larger than that of older employees to compensate the difference between the productivity and wages of older employees. However, because of the aging workforce, firms cannot continue transferring wealth from young worker to older employees.

The second reason why firms cannot keep seniority-based pay is changing technology. Traditionally it is considered that workers with longer experience are more productive. This may not be the case in high-tech industries where young workers are likely to have higher skills. Therefore, many companies have revised their pay system, trying to weaken the link between experience and wages. Instead, they try to strengthen the tie between individual performance and wages by introducing performance related pay.

Figure 3.3 shows the age-wage profile of male graduate workers for the years of 1990, 2000 and 2004. Wage rates are calculated based on the average wages of a 22-year-old worker. The figure shows that the slope of the age-wage profile has become flatter. For example, in 1990, 52-54 year old workers typically received five times the wages of those workers who were 22 years old. In contrast, in 2004, they received four times the wages, showing that the age-wage profile has become flatter. The correlation between age and wage has become weaker. This figure has been consistent with the notion that the seniority-wage system has been collapsing.

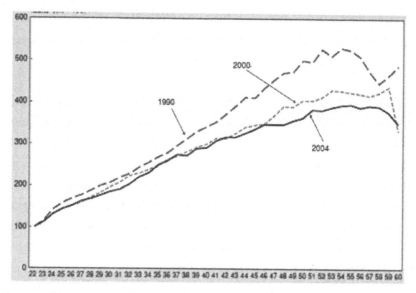

Source: *White paper on the Labor Economy 2005* (the Ministry of Health, Labor and Welfare);
Calculated from the Basic Survey on Wage Structure

Figure 3.3 Age-wage Profile of Male Graduate Worker in 1990, 2000 and 2004

(100 = average wages of 22 years old worker)

A wage survey by Japan Institute for Labor Policy and Training in 2006 revealed that more and more firms emphasize on performance. About 62% of firms in the survey said that performance has become more important in determining wages than before. About 59.5% said an employee's ability has become more important. In contrast, more than 30% of firms said the importance of age, education, and length of service was decreasing. Less than 10% of firms said they put more emphasis on age, education, or length of service than before. Similar results have been reported in other surveys. For instance, when human resource managers were asked whether wages varied substantially due to individual performance, about 37% of the firms strongly agreed and another 49.2% agreed. According to the survey, 219 (86.2%) out of 254 firms have introduced performance-related pay.

Larger firms were more likely to introduce performance-related pay systems. According to the 2004 General Survey on Working Conditions mentioned earlier, about 53.2% of the firm respondents reported that "individual performance is reflected on wages."

Among large firms with more than 1000 employees, about 83.4% of respondents said that individual performance was reflected in wages.

Several studies based on surveys have been undertaken to examine employee response to performance-related pay. The objectives of these studies included investigating whether firm managers believed that performance-related pay had improved employee motivation. According to a 2006 survey by the Japan Productivity Centre for Socio-Economic Development, not all firms were satisfied with the results. In fact, among firms that introduced performance-related pay, about 70% of the firms in the survey said that the system needs to be modified. The most important problem with performance pay, according to the survey, was the performance appraisal. About 65.5% of firms said that it was difficult to have standardized appraisal criteria. About 51.6% of firms agreed that performance-related pay should not be introduced without a detailed performance appraisal system.

The 2004 General Survey on Working Conditions asked firms how firms evaluated the introduction of performance-related pay; 15.9% said "good," 45.3% said "good but needs to be modified," and 30.4% said "needs major revision." The survey also showed that the main problem with performance-related pay was the performance appraisal.

About 50.5% of the firm respondents thought that managers do not have enough skills to evaluate their subordinates. In addition, 54.5% said that it is difficult to compare the appraisals of employees who worked in different divisions of the firm.

6. CONCLUSION

In the past 25 years, Japanese firms have experienced a dramatic change in terms of globalization. Japanese global players today such as Honda, Toyota, Matsushita and Canon were in the 1980s big manufacturers targeting mainly the domestic market. But they were far from being multinational firms. Trade frictions in the 1980s and the depression of domestic markets in the 1990s often compelled these firms to develop overseas activities, by creating new plants in the USA and in European countries. In addition, Japanese firms took full advantage of the opening of the Chinese economy to invest overseas, particularly in the 1990s. This movement toward global markets, together with a slumping domestic market, means that traditional Japanese HRM based on long-term employment has been under pressure for change.

Many Japanese firms have tried to restrict to a minimum level the number of core employees, by making most of the increase of atypical workers (part-time workers, agency workers). Even for core permanent employees, the wide use of performance-related pay is a sign of change in HRM practices so as to reflect costs consideration of human resources.

Finally, we can point out that the speed of globalization in many Japanese firms has outpaced the formation of skilled staff or stock of human resources capable of managing overseas staff in foreign countries. Japanese firms are now groping for ways to preserve many aspects of the traditional HRM, based on long-term employment relations and to adopt it so as to create a necessary flexibility to cope with the fluctuation of global markets.

7. CASE STUDY

The case under study is an old ball bearings firm founded in 1916. Today it employs around 8,000 employees in Japan and 14,000 in overseas factories. The total turnover of the group was around 628 billion yen in 2005. It is an independent manufacturer, well-established in the world market. Its main products range from basic ball bearings for different industries (electric appliances, automobiles, etc.) to higher value precision machinery for automatic transmissions. The main clients of the firm are by far automobile firms (Toyota, Honda, Nissan, Denso, Bosch, etc.). Within Japan, this firm operates a dozen plants mainly concentrated near the Tokyo and the Kyoto regions. Large plants, each specialized in a particular line of products, are found in three locations, each with around 1,000 employees. These three plants act as the "mother plant" for overseas production.

The different steps of globalization of the firm are summarized in Table 3.1. In the 1970s, the firm had already set up production sites in Brazil (1970), the U.S.A. (1973), the U.K. (1974), Singapore (1975), and Canada (1977). It is remarkable that these overseas extensions precede the movement of Honda, which is the most outward-looking Japanese car maker. For instance, Honda set up a major factory in Ohio in 1978 and Toyota only in 1986 in Kentucky. In fact, being a parts-maker, this firm probably went overseas simply because it knew that bigger clients (car-makers) would come later. Even today, overseas Japanese auto makers rely on Japanese parts makers at least for essential elements (motors, brakes, electronic devices, transmission, etc.).

Table 3.1 Chronology of Globalization (major steps)

1916	The firm was founded
1962	Opened a subsidiary in New Jersey
1963	Opened a subsidiary in U.K. and Germany
1970	New plant in Brazil
1973	Joint venture in Michigan (U.S.A.)
1975	Joint venture in Singapore
1977	Opened a subsidiary in Toronto (Canada)
1987	Joint venture in Iowa (U.S.A.) Joint venture in Bangkok (Thailand) Joint venture in Korea
1989	Joint venture in Taiwan
1990	Extension of the U.K. plant
1993	New firm in Malaysia
1995	Beginning of operations in China
1997	Joint venture in India
1998	Acquisition of a large plant in Poland
2003	Extension and creation of new plants and offices in China

Unlike electronic products, machinery to produce ball bearings is rather an old one, which necessitates a lot of practical adjustment and know-how. Equipment introduced some forty years ago can produce relatively low standard products, albeit lower productivity. The transfer of technology and know-how is carried out by the so-called "mother plant system" in this firm. The "mother plant" system designates the flow of transfer of know-how to overseas plants.

From the start-up period and after, the mother plant is responsible for sending the necessary staff (engineers, top management) and training the overseas technical staff. This transfer of know-how implies not only technical aspects but also management processes (cost reductions for purchases, reduction of labor costs, and improvement of workers' involvement). This means that the "mother plant" should accumulate the necessary human resources in order to provide Japanese technical staff and managers to overseas plants.

Table 3.2 shows how a mother plant has dealt with the responsibility (specialized in products for automobiles). In this plant, in 2004 the major target was a Chinese factory near Shanghai. It had a large team of overseas project staff (some 40 technicians and engineers). Of course, the transfer of know-how means that, once the start-up period is finished, the overseas plant should be self-sustaining (with some Japanese expatriates). For the mother plant, these tasks of helping overseas plants are combined with the day-to-day production for the Japanese markets. This is to underscore the needs of human resources in a very competitive segment of the market.

Table 3.2 Mother Plant A and Supporting Overseas Plants

	America	E.U.	Asia
1970s	Brazil	U.K.	
	Michigan		Korea
1980s	Extension Brazil	U.K.	
1990s	Extension U.S.A. (Transmission)		Indonesia
			Malaysia
			China
2000s		Poland (mainly mother plant B)	Thailand China

An example of a vast factory in Poland – acquired in 1998 in the wave of privatization – will illustrate the process of transfer of know-how. In 1998, this Polish plant had 3,500 employees producing 4 million ball bearings. In 2004, with new equipment and an upgraded product line, it employed 1,900 employees, of which 1,400 worked in the old factories. These stringent cost-cutting measures were made possible through long-term training: most Polish managers and key staff trained from several months to one year in Japan.

The process of transfer of technology involved not only technical training (quality controls) but also inculcation of cost consciousness. For this purpose, many graphics showing other factories in Japan or in China are put on the wall of the plant. Japanese managers seem to be convinced that the transition from public corporation to a competitive plant will require attitudinal changes of Polish employees.

Human Resource Management of this firm in Japan is typically a very traditional one. Recruitment on entry level (mostly technical background) is always restricted to new school/university leavers; high schools leavers for production workers and university graduates (including master degree levels) for engineering and future management. Mid-career recruitments are nonexistent. For several years, these new recruits are given on-the-job training under the supervision of experienced employees/engineers. What is most remarkable in this firm is the tendency to specialization in one line of products (simple ball bearings for general use or quantity production, precision ball bearings – sometimes with order-made models – and new transmission devices for automobiles). Skill acquisition for the technical staff is made within one particular line of products.

Periodical job rotation, which is frequent in Japanese firms, is limited to a specialized field (often within the same plant). This relatively narrow specialization is strengthened by the shared feeling of a "family" among technicians and engineers. Most high-ranked engineers or managers know each other and remember from which plant they came. It is in this line of specialization that the "mother plant" system functions smoothly, since overseas managers (generally engineers) personally know their collaborators from the "mother plant".

With a rapid globalization of the firm, it appears that several bottlenecks or problem areas are looming large in the near future. Firstly, the chase for qualified engineers is becoming severe, because the pool of experienced technicians and engineers is dwindling. For instance, in some cases, overseas staff cannot be replaced by new Japanese technicians and engineers for many years. Communication ability and the family status of Japanese employees narrow the already limited pool of experienced staff. This firm tries to make overseas plants self-sustaining through a quick transfer of technology. This process very much depends on the availability of competent local staff. In one case, in view of expanding Chinese plants, the firm has succeeded in recruiting some qualified Chinese engineers who had studied in Japan. In other cases, overseas plants appear to still rely very much on the practical know-how of Japanese expatriates.

Secondly, within Japan, cost pressures are so severe that the firm tries to extensively use agency workers or a sub-contracting system. Indeed, there is a huge differential of overhead costs for permanent employees who receive generous benefits and allowances. However, if such a tendency to outsource some process of the production continues in the future, it may well prove to be detrimental to the human "resources" of the firm.

8. QUESTIONS FOR DISCUSSION

1. From the discussion above, what do you think are the impacts of globalization on Japanese labor market?
2. What can be the government and private sector firm strategies to cope with changes in the labor market? Would the government and the business firms act differently in view of an anticipated recessionary economic period?
3. What should be the role of labor unions? How can they increase their membership? Can their strategies used in the Asian financial crisis be effective in this new round of financial crisis originating in the U.S.?
4. With respect to the case study, what should be the firm's HRM strategies to cope with the anticipated changes?

ENDNOTES

[1] Basic Wage Survey of 2003

[2] S. Jacoby, (2005) "The Embedded Corporation"

[3] Nonaka and Takeuchi "The knowledge-creating company"

[4] Tayoka *suru syugyo keitai no motodeno zinzisenryaku to rodosya no ishiki ni kansuru cyosa* (Human resource strategy and workers' sentiment in various employment forms), Japan Institute for Labor Policy and Training, 2006.

[5] *Nihonteki Zinzi Seido no Henyo ni kansuru chosa* (Survey on the change in Japanese style human resource management), Japan productivity Centre for Socio-Economic Development (JPC-SED), 2006.

[6] *Nihonteki Zinzi Seido no Henyo ni kansuru chosa* (Survey on the change in Japanese style human resource management), Japan productivity Centre for Socio-Economic Development (JPC-SED), 2006.

[7] H. Suzuki and N. Kawabe (ed) (2007) *Ikou Keizai ni okeru Nikkei Kigyo,* Waseda University, I.R.B.A. Series No. 41

Chapter 4

GLOBALIZATION AND INDUSTRIAL RELATIONS IN KOREA

Young-bum Park

1.   INTRODUCTION

Since 1987 Korea has seen the promotion of labor rights, reduced state intervention into union activities and the establishment of a system of collective bargaining to determine wages and working conditions in Korean workplaces. However, the price of this transformation has been substantial. Consecutive wage rises, often surpassing productivity gains, have become a heavy burden on the competitiveness of Korean companies. The Korean economy has also had to pay a high price due to the frequent strikes and work stoppages that occurred during this period.

Hence, the debate over labor law reform as a measure (particularly in the area of expanding union rights and extending labor market flexibility) for the stabilization of Korea's industrial relations system has been at the forefront of industrial relations for many years. There were also many attempts to change the labor laws. Finally, in March 1997, a new set of the labor laws was passed. However, even before the most controversial provision of the 1997 labor law amendment became effective, Korea was hit by a severe financial crisis. The Korean government decided to approach the International Monetary Fund (IMF) for a rescue plan. As the IMF offered a relief fund, it demanded that further steps should be taken to improve labor market flexibility. Korean labor law was amended accordingly.

Globalization has meant opportunities as well as challenges for Korea's union movements. As Korea has made its labor regulations meet with global standards, the union movement's institutional base has been strengthened. Korea's unions have also had difficulties in adjusting under the globalized world. Labor market flexibility measures had to be introduced in order to boost Korea's international competitiveness. As Korea suffered from the financial crisis in the late 1990s, union movements had to accommodate employment adjustment programs that took place nationwide.

This chapter examines the impact of globalization on Korea's industrial relations by looking at the case of Hyundai Motor Company. Hyundai had to dismiss many of its employees during Korea's financial crisis. Through serious conflicts over these dismissals, the company's industrial relations system became even more adversarial and confrontational. The Hyundai Motor Company regained its strength after some years and recalled most of its dismissed workers. However, the labor and management at Hyundai has not yet been able to find ways to work together for productive industrial relation. Industrial relations in the automotive industry have had a strong influence on the country's overall industrial relations, given that the Hyundai union has the largest union membership among private manufacturing companies in Korea.

2.   BASIC FEATURES OF KOREA'S INDUSTRIAL RELATIONS SYSTEM

Korean trade unions are represented on three levels. There are local unions based on a plant, an enterprise level, a region or an occupation, most commonly at the plant or enterprise. Thus all union members at a particular plant or enterprise, regardless of their occupations, join the one local union. The members directly elect local union leaders and the union leaders bargain collectively with their employer. The consequence of the local enterprise union structure is that collective bargaining issues tend to be firm specific. Although the local unions make up occupational federations and regional councils, and these in turn form a national center, the right to negotiate is vested in the local unions with regional councils and industrial federations having only the right to consult and discuss.

However, in recent years the trade unions have been trying very hard to move up the bargaining table from the local to the regional or industrial level and they have some success. There are a few unions, such as the Korean Federation of Communications

Trade Unions (KFCTU), Korea Federation of Metal Workers' Unions (KFMWU) and the Federation of Korean Taxi Transport Workers' Unions (FKTTWU), which are structured on an industrial basis and collectively bargain at regional and national levels. Currently wages and working conditions of some 10 % of the Korean trade union members are determined by industrial level bargaining. This figure has increased since in 2006 some major trade unions, such as the Hyundai Motors Workers Union, have decided to change from the enterprise unions to industrial unions.

As of the end of 2004, there were 1.5 million union members who belonged to some 6,100 local unions, as shown in Table 4.1. About 10.5 % of the total employed workers in Korea were union members. However, the power of the Korean trade unions is much bigger than this figure. Three fourths of the large establishments with five hundred or more employees have unions and the Korean economy is heavily dependent on large companies.

Korean unions are dominated by male production workers in heavy industries. Male members constitute about 72.2% of the total membership (the proportion of male workers in the total employment is about 40%). Local unions belonging to big companies, such as Hyundai Motor Company, play a key role in setting the country's employment relations climate.

3. DEVELOPMENTS IN KOREA'S INDUSTRIAL RELATIONS SINCE 1987

The 1987 was a landmark year for political liberalization in Korea, and was also a turning point for Korean industrial relations. The policies, the institutional framework, and the practices encompassed in Korean employment relations have undergone a significant change since 1987. For example, from June 1987 to December 1987 alone, the number of unions increased from 2,725 to 7,883 and union membership rose from 1 million to 1.9 million. During the same period the number of labor disputes also increased (Table 4.1).

Table 4.1 Selected Industrial Relations Indicators in Korea

	Unions			Industrial disputes		Unemploy-ment rate (%)
	Member-ship ('000)	Density (%)[1]	Number of unions	Number of strikes and lockouts	Workers involved ('000)	
1970	473	12.6	3500	4	1	
1975	750	15.8	4091	52	10	
1980	948	14.7	2635	407	49	5.2
1985	1004	12.4	2551	265	29	4.0
1986	1036	12.3	2675	276	47	3.8
1987	1267	13.8	4103	3749	1262	3.1
1988	1707	17.8	6164	1873	294	2.5
1989	1932	18.6	7883	1616	409	2.6
1990	1887	17.2	7698	322	134	2.4
1991	1803	15.9	7656	234	175	2.3
1992	1735	15.0	7527	235	105	2.4
1993	1667	14.2	7147	144	109	2.8
1994	1659	13.5	7025	121	104	2.4
1995	1615	12.6	6606	88	50	2.0
1996	1599	12.2	6424	85	79	2.0
1997	1484	11.5	5733	78	44	2.6
1998	1402	11.5	5560	129	146	6.8
1999	1481	11.8	5637	198	92	6.3
2000	1527	11.6	5898	250	178	4.1
2001	1569	11.5	6150	235	89	3.8
2002	1538	10.8	6506	321	94	3.1
2003	1550	10.8	6257	462	137	3.4
2004	1537	10.5	6107	285	185	3.5

Note: 1) With respect to total employees
Source: Korea Labor Institute (various issues), *Quarterly Labor Trends*

Out of this development, trade unions became a powerful institution in Korea's labor-management relations, and collective bargaining became an important institution for improving the working conditions of both union members and general workers. Most importantly, the major Korean manufacturing firms in the auto, steel, and shipbuilding industries that were the engine of Korea's remarkable economic growth became unionized. Before 1987, unionization was prevented through strong government intervention. After 1987 these newly organized unions in large firms became the power base for Korea's new union movement. Large-scale industrial actions continued after 1987 on issues related to union recognition, the improvement of wages and working conditions, and issues concerning union security. Violence often accompanied the industrial action and in certain cases confrontation with police followed. An important development in Korean trade unionism since 1987 is the rise of an independent trade union movement, separate from the Federation of Korean Trade Unions (FKTU), that had been the only officially recognized national center until 1999. There were many attempts to organize a separate independent national center by union activists who did not follow FKTU policy lines (The Korean law allowed only one national center until 1997). The Cheonnohyup (Korean Council of Trade Unions: KCTU) was formed in January 1991. The Cheonnohyup and other non-recognized unions formed the Minjunochong (Korea Confederation of Trade Unions: KCTU) in November 1995. In November 1999, the Korean government officially recognized the KCTU. The leaders of the new union movement were critical of the FKTU that had the history of closely working with the government and the management under the authoritarian regime.

The KCTU claimed only a membership of 400,000 in 1995 (Park, 1996). It continued to increase its membership after its birth. In 2004, the KCTU claimed a membership of 668,000, while the FKTU had 780,000 members. Although the number of the KCTU members is smaller than that of the FKTU, the power of the KCTU is much stronger than that of the FKTU since its member unions include big chaebol companies in key sectors of the Korean economy. Minjunochong affiliated unions, are based in the large manufacturing firms that were unionized after 1987. The average size of the KCTU unions is more than twice larger than that of the KFTU's. Its unions, in tune with contemporary developments, tend to be more assertive and independent.

Another important development is that white-color workers began to be unionized in the late 1980s. The white color unions, which represented only some workers mostly in the banking sector before 1987, grew to 15 % of the total union membership in 1989. The white color unions continued to grow in the 1990s. Since teachers obtained the legal right to organize into unions, and the public sector and banking industry were subject to severe structural adjustment after the country was hit by the financial crisis, Korea's white-collar union movement gained momentum. The KCTU is strong because of the white-collar union movement.

However, the trade union membership peaked to 1,932,000 in 1989, and then continued to decrease until very recently (Table 4.1). The decline of the union membership is attributed to a number of factors. First, the drop in union membership reflects the changes in Korea's industrial structure. In the past ten years, under industrial restructuring, labor intensive manufacturing industries rapidly disappeared and the share of manufacturing employment declined significantly. As a result, the share of manufacturing in total employment declined from 27.5% in 1990 to 21.2 % in 1997. The proportion of large companies with more than 300 employees, which is a strong base of Korea's new union movement, also decreased from 35% in 1990 to 28 % in 1995.

The second contributing factor to declining union power is that the union movement as a whole has not managed itself well with respect to changing environments. The union movement has not been able to unify its strengths. Instead, as discussed above, it has been divided into two competing group: the traditional FKTU and the new KCTU. The only major joint action which the two national centers could manage was a general strike against the government unilateral trial of the 1996 labor law amendments. In addition, the enterprise bargaining structure, under which collective bargaining issues tend to be firm specific, has failed to strengthen solidarity among all union members regardless of their occupations or companies. Local unions in large companies emphasized only the interests of their local members, such as annual wage increments that resulted in a wider gap in wages and working conditions between union members belonging to large companies and small ones.

Third, a large-scale employment adjustment nationwide, which followed the financial crisis in the late 1990s, was another blow to the declining union power. After the financial crisis took place, manufacturing and regular jobs, which are two traditional power bases of the union movement, lost their share in employment substantially. From 1997 to 1999, employment in manufacturing declined from 4,482,000 to 4,006,000. Regular workers also decreased from 7,151,000 to 6,050,000 during the same period.

However, this does not necessarily mean that union influence in the collective bargaining process is insignificant. Korea's growth strategy in the manufacturing sector until recently has been to promote large-scale industry for low-cost competition. Even though Korea is trying to move toward a high-value, technology-based economy, the manufacturing industry still plays a key role in Korea's industrial structure. Unions are very strong in manufacturing, particularly in large firms. The Korean unions proved their strong power with a general strike against the state's unilateral labor reform trial in 1996. On the other hand, the recent increase in union membership is mainly attributed to the labor law amendment giving teachers union rights.

In the 1990s, before the financial crisis started, the number of industrial actions declined substantially dropping from 3,749 in 1987 to 322 in 1990 (Table 4.1). In 1995 and 1996, less than 100 cases of industrial action took place. The large drop in the number of disputes was due to a combination of factors. First, the Korean economy suffered a recession in 1989, which made worker, and trade unions realize that their hard-line stance would not win support from the general public. Second, employers and unions gained experience in resolving conflicts through dialogue. Both parties realized that lock-outs or strikes should be the last resort in the process of collective negotiation. Third, the government, which remained indifferent in major industrial disputes after 1987, made it clear that law and order should be established in the workplaces. More unions and employers, as they encountered difficulties in their collective negotiations, began to follow the procedures outlined in the labor laws.

However, after December 1997, labor disputes increased sharply as the threat of job losses mounted with Korea having implemented a serious reform program, which aimed to overcome the economic crisis. Labor disputes in 1998 were 129, which was up 65% compared to the 78 recorded in 1997. Workers who took part in the labor disputes numbered 146,000, three times as many as the 44,000 who participated a year earlier. This trend continued in 1999, too. The number of lost production days reached 1,452,000 in 1998, compared with 444,000 days a year earlier.

A neo-corporatist approach has been experimented in Korea in the process of economic restructuring which started with the IMF bailout, as the newly installed national leadership of DaeJoong Kim emphasized a social agreement among the three parties which would assure that structural reform measures be implemented quickly and decisively. A tripartite commission was established on January 15, 1998. It was this Tripartite Commission that fostered the process of structural reform and some additional amendments to labor laws by reaching the landmark agreement on January 20, 1998. However, the KCTU did not participate in the Tripartite Commission, except for a short time.

4.   DISCUSSIONS ON AMENDMENTS ON LABOR LAWS IN KOREA

In 2007, two major changes in labor laws were to be implemented. First, payment to full-time union officials by employers was supposed to be prohibited. Second, multiple unions at the enterprise level were to be allowed. However, the FKTU and employers agreed to postpone barring the payment of full-time union officials by employer and allowing multiple unions at workplace for another three years (until 2009) without the consent of the KCTU and the National Assembly decided not to change the labor law accordingly.

If payment to full-time union officials by employers is prohibited many small unions will not be able to survive financially. This change is expected to hit the FKTU hard since its unions are small. Given Korea's enterprise bargaining structure, even if multiple unions at enterprise level are not barred, all unions are not expected to have collective bargaining rights. The Korean government aims to make some sort of arrangements concerning bargaining representation. The KCTU would suffer from this change since most of its unions are large and the second or third union will be organized in the large unions. Likely, this change could create fragmentation in union organizations, unless the newly formed unions make clear their organizational goals and objectives in serving their member and manage their structural relationship at the larger scale well.

These expected changes have been observed to influence the bargaining structure. Some trade unions have been promoting an organizational shift from enterprise union to industrial one and they achieved their goal in 2006. Large unions in the automotive and metal industry chose to shift to the industrial unions. These unions believe that establishing an industry-based bargaining structure will also be a way to prepare for the expected labor law changes.

At this moment of writing this manuscript (December 22, 2009), the National Assembly is discussing about whether it should revise and/or (if needed) how to change the labor law related to these issues. If the National Assembly decides not to change the current labor law, multiple unions will be allowed at workplace without proper bargaining representation and employers will not pay wages to union officials from 2007.

Another important impact which globalization has brought on the Korean society is that the number of irregular workers has increased substantially. The proportion of the irregular workers to the total wage earners rose from 45.6 % in 1997 to 51.5 % in 1999 after Korea was hit by a financial crisis in late 1997. Their wage and working conditions are inferior to the regular workers. Their jobs are insecure since many of them are on a fixed-term labor contract.

Reflecting society's concerns about the irregular workers problems, a specific labor protection law for this group of workers was proposed at the National Assembly. However, some unions, including the KCTU, have opposed the proposed labor law demanding more protection of the irregular workers than the law has intended. The KCTU basically insists that irregular workers should be allowed only for exceptional cases and the scope of the temporary work agency should be limited. On December 2006 the National Assembly passed a law prohibiting using contract workers more than two years and discrimination against irregular workers.

5. CONCLUSION

Globalization has meant opportunities as well as challenges for Korea's union movements. As Korea has made its labor regulations meet with global standards, the union movement's institutional base has been strengthened. However, Korea's union movement has also suffered due to globalization. The unions had to accommodate employment adjustment programs that took place nationwide following the financial crisis in the late 1990s.

In recent years the trade unions have been trying very hard to move up the bargaining table from the local to the regional or industrial level which proved to be successful to some extent. Korean unions are dominated by male production workers in heavy industries. Trade unions became powerful institution in Korea's labor management relations, and collective bargaining became an important institution for improving the working conditions of both union members and general workers. However, the trade union membership peaked to 1,932,000 in 1989, and then continued to decrease until very recently. The decline of the union membership is attributed to about three main factors. First, the drop in union membership reflects the changes in Korea's industrial structure. Secondly, the union movement as a whole has not managed itself well with respect to changing environments. Third, a large-scale employment adjustment nationwide, which followed the financial crisis in the late 1990s. However, this does not necessarily mean that union influence in the collective bargaining process is insignificant. Another important impact which globalization has brought on the Korean society is that the number of irregular workers has increased substantially.

It seems that the management has not come up with a strategy to have the labor and management work together in order to cope with the increasing competitive environment brought by globalization. It may take much time and may be very difficult for management to induce cooperation and participation from the union. But, there is still a chance for labor and management at the enterprise level to establish productive labor-management relations. Both labor and management at the enterprise level have common interests to protect. The union members understand that the union will not be able to protect their jobs in a globalized world despite strong job protection clauses in their collective agreement through their experiences during the financial crisis. Management also understands that having a strong production site at home is strategically important for a world-class company, even though it has many production sites elsewhere in the world.

In the sections that follow, the overview of the Korean automotive industry and the case study of Hyundai Motor Company will be given.

6.   OVERVIEW OF THE KOREAN AUTOMOTIVE INDUSTRY

The automotive industry has been one of the key engines contributing to the sustained growth of the Korean economy. The industry is structurally important within Korea, producing upstream and downstream effects on a number of related industries. Korea is one of the few countries that possesses independent R&D capabilities and, among newly industrializing countries, has a massive manufacturing capacity. In the mid 1990s Korea was already positioned fifth in the world in terms of the volume of automotive production. Despite soaring labor costs and a number of disputes following the emergence of a more militant labor movement since 1987, Korean auto companies grew steadily until the mid-1990s, as illustrated in Table 4.2.

The Korean auto industry was also confronted with unprecedented hardship during Korea's foreign exchange crisis of December 1997. In 1998 the total volume of production dropped by 30.6 % and domestic sales dropped by 48.5 %. Kia Motors, the country's second largest automaker, went bankrupt in the summer of 1997 whilst Samsung, Ssangyong and Daewoo fell into a deep financial crisis. When the crisis was over, nearly all of the Korean car companies had been acquired by new foreign owners. Daewoo, Samsung and Ssangyong went to GM, Renault and Shanghai (a Chinese company) during the reconfiguration period. The two exceptions are Hyundai Motor Company (HMC), Korea's largest automaker, and Kia Motors, which was acquired by the Hyundai Group in November 1998. A number of auto parts manufacturers were also taken over by foreign multi-national companies.

The Korean auto industry regained its strength from 1999 as domestic sales increased by 68.5% as shown in Table 4.2. In 1999 the industry's production volume rose by 45.5% compared to the previous year. In recent years the export performance has been remarkable. For example, in 2004 export volume increased by 57.6%. The Hyundai Motor Company, which, with Kia Motors, is the only locally-owned manufacturer, has been vigorously seeking a globalization strategy. It already operates large plants in China and India, and will also establish plant in the USA.

Table 4.2 Production and Sales Trends in Korean Automotive Companies

	Production		Domestic Sales		Export Sales	
	Unit	Change %	Unit	Change %	Unit	Change %
1990	1,321,630	17.0	954,277	25.1	347,100	-2.5
1991	1,497,818	13.3	1,104,184	15.7	390,362	12.5
1992	1,729,696	15:5	1,268,374	14.9	456,155	16.9
1993	2,050,208	18.5	1,435,967	13.2	638,557	40.0
1994	2,311,663	12.8	1,555,602	8.3	737,943	15.6
1995	2,526,400	9.3	1,555,902	0.0	978,688	32.6
1996	2,812,714	11.3	1,644,132	5.7	1,210,157	23.7
1997	2,818,275	0.2	1,512,935	-8.0	1,316,891	8.8
1998	1,954,494	-30.6	779,905	-48.5	1,362,164	3.4
1999	2,843,114	45.5	1,273,029	63.2	1,509,660	10.8
2000	3,114,998	9.6	1,430,460	12.4	1,676,442	11.0
2001	2,946,329	-5.4	1,451,450	1.5	1,501,213	-10.5
2002	3,147,584	6.8	1,622,268	11.8	1,509,546	0.6
2003	3,177,870	7.9	1,318,312	-9.2	1,814,938	20.9
2004	3,469,464	10.2	1,094,652	-32.5	2,379,563	57.6

Source: Korea Automotive Manufacturer Association

The recent restructuring of the Korean automotive industry has not only resulted in intensified confrontation between labor unions, management and sometimes the government, but has also produced some salient changes in employment relations practices. Industrial relations in the automotive industry (particularly at Hyundai Motor Company: HMC) have had a strong influence on the country's overall industrial relations, given that the Hyundai Motor Workers Union (HMWU) has the largest union membership among private manufacturing companies in Korea.

7. CASE STUDY: GLOBALIZATION AND INDUSTRIAL RELATIONS AT HYUNDAI MOTOR COMPANY [1]

With Korea's democratization in 1987, there immediately followed a revival of the labor movement that manifested in increased numbers of unions and disputes. In 1987 there were 4,000 strikes. The HMC also experienced severe labor disputes. Confrontational collective bargaining practices, conflict between unions and company management, and intensified internal union politics resulted in heavy losses in productions and exports. Lost production due to the strikes from 1987 to 1995 came to over hundreds of thousand of automobiles.

The company made great efforts to stabilize industrial relations by offering high wage increases, improving fringe benefits plans and expanding education and communication programs for employees. Some of these efforts were effective and some of them were not. Industrial relations appeared to have stabilized between 1993 and 1995, but had become unstable again with the re-emergence of the militant union.

As discussed above, after December 1997 labor disputes in Korea increased sharply as job losses mounted with the implementation of a serious reform programs that aimed to overcome the economic crisis. The HMC also experienced a severe dispute during the summer of 1998, which represented a proxy of nation-wide confrontation over the enforcement of massive layoff plans in other companies. The HMWU held a 36-day-long strike and the company reacted with plant closures. This dispute ended with the involvement of the unofficial government mediation team, concerned that the prolonged dispute at the HMC would have a critical impact on the nation's troubled economy. Whilst the lengthy dispute caused serious damage to both management and the union, the company damage was more serious due to the government's involvement. The company was compelled to give up its dismissal plan to expel many union activists. Instead, the HMC had to rely on early retirement package, unpaid leave and cutting the size of the subcontracted workforce. In 1998 the HMC undertook a sizable downsizing of over 12,000 employees through various methods, such as dismissals (277), unpaid leave (1,968), early retirement packages (6,451), regular retirements (1,420), and cutting its subcontracted workforce (1,722) (Lee, 2003). Since demand within the domestic auto market has recovered rapidly from the second half of 1999 (the Korean government officially announced that the financial crisis was over in 2000), The HMC recalled workers on unpaid leave as well as the permanently dismissed workers in early 2000.

The HMWU regained their organizational power in the context of the economic recovery and put its prime concern became employment security. The HMWU obtained management's full guarantee of employment security in the 2000 collective agreement. This agreement set out three principles of employment guarantee: prior information sharing, joint union-management decision, and complete employment security. It also made clear the prohibition of dismissals and early retirement. The 2003 collective agreement between the HMWU and management included contractual language (provisions) to provide even stronger employment protection, which mainly reflected the rank-and-file's growing concern with the company's level of overseas investment. According to the agreement, all production workers (union members) are fully guaranteed of their employment until the retirement age at 58 years old, and the company should maintain production volume at the minimum level of 1.8 million units [2] in domestic manufacturing plants, regardless of its overseas production.

Interestingly, even though the HMWU gained various ways to guarantee employment security, the rank and file remains concerned about job insecurity. A survey conducted by Korean Metal Workers Federation (KMWF, 2005a) reports that 83.9% of the production workers at Hyundai maintain some feeling of employment insecurity. Another workplace survey, conducted in 2005, shows a similar result that 74 % of Hyundai workers feel threatened by employment insecurity (Park 2006) [3].

This can be explained by several factors. First, the 1997-1998 experience of downsizing has made the workers realize that the union's protective power cannot overcome the market power driven by the globalized world. Second, the HMC has aggressively expanded the overseas production capacity. The Hyundai Motor Group, including HMC and Kia Motors, manufactured 28.7 % (860 thousand units) of total production volume at overseas plants in 2005 and plans to expand overseas manufacturing capacity up to 40 percent (1.2 million units) of its production volume by 2010. Expanded overseas production is regarded as a key reason for employment insecurity at the HMC, even though the labor union implemented regulatory contract language to prevent overseas investment from threatening member employment. The 2005 worker survey at the HMC showed that 77% of production workers opposed the company's plan to build overseas plants, because 83.3% of the same respondents believed that overseas plants would result in employment insecurity (Park, 2006). Third, the company has implemented modular production, which has a crucial impact on work organization. With the establishment of the Hyundai MOBIS the level of modularization had grown from 10% in 2001 to 30% in 2005 through change of vehicle models. The corporate group plans to lift the overall level of modularization from 30% in 2005 to 40% by 2006. The modularization is accompanied by outsourcing of parts sequencing jobs, automation of modular parts assembly, ergonomic improvement of working environment, and work load balancing of main production lines. At the same time, the modularization has created surplus labor by simplifying the production line.

An emerging employment practice after the HMC was hit by the crisis is the growing use of non-regular labor, particularly contract workers. Prior to the economic crisis, the company used contract workers, who were hired by subcontractors to cover sub-assembly lines of auto plants. However, the number of contract workers has increased sharply in the post-crisis period, since the HMC have expanded their use of subcontractors in their productive operations in face of the rapid recovery of market demands, rather than recruiting new regular workers. The number of the regular workers at the Korean automakers including the HMC had remained more or less the same after Korea's financial crisis was over, as illustrated in Table 4.3. On the other hand, between 1998 and 2004, the number of contract workers grew from around 4,000 to nearly 10,000. The proportion of those workers in relation to the total production workforce in the HMC plants soared from 16.9% (the ratio agreed between the union and management) to over 30%. All production shops and production support departments (mainly auto parts handling), but not maintenance and quality control requiring highly skilled labor, precipitously expanded the use of contract labor in this period. The growing use of contact labor in the production line is common at other automakers, although there is some variation in the share of contract workers.

Table 4.3 Employment of Regular Workers in the Korean Automakers

	1996	1997	1998	1999	2000	2001	2002
Hyundai	47,098	46,254	37,752	50,984	49,023	48,831	49,855
Kia	29,619	18,151	17,652	29,937	29,857	29,489	30,070
Daewoo	17,243	17,500	18,599	18,059	17,235	13,555	13,238
Total	93,960	81,905	74,003	98,980	96,115	91,875	93,163

Source: Korea Automotive Research Institute (2004)
Note: Hyundai and Kia merged their affiliate of sales and car repairs in 1999. Daewoo was acquired by General Motors in 2002.

The increased use of contract labor at the HMC is explained by a number of factors. First, contract labor is much cheaper than regular workers. Controlling for the tenure of both workers groups, the contract workers' wage is still two thirds of the regular workers'. Second, management at auto plants are able to flexibly utilize contract labor in terms of job transfer and redundancy, in contrast to regular workers, whose job re-allocation and layoff are strictly constrained by labor unions. At the HMC a worker cannot be transferred within the same plant without the worker's consent. Third, it is more difficult to organize contract workers into labor unions. Even if they are able to organize labor unions, the company is immune from the legal responsibility of undertaking collective bargaining with those contract workers unions and can replace unionized subcontractors with non-union ones. Fourth, contract workers are accepted as a buffering resource. They usually take over the difficult and dirty jobs that are avoided by regular workers (Lee & Frenkel, 2004). According to Ha (2005), contract labor was mainly deployed to dangerous or difficult work stations through workplace-level negotiation. Moreover, they can be easily dismissed in times of economic difficulty. Haunted by massive downsizing during the financial crisis, the HMWU and the HMC's regular workers recognize the need of non-regular workers. About 70% of the regular workers believe that non-regular workers are necessary, and 65% of regular workers feared that the regularization of the non-regular workers would dampen their employment security (Woolsan Maeil Simun March 31, 2005). This is a reason for the HMWU accepting that the share of non-regular workers be 16.9% of the total workforce in 1998.

As discriminatory employment conditions of contract workers were exposed as a social issue, the HMWU has pressed the company to improve economic and working conditions on behalf of those non-regular workers. The HMWU has demanded wage increases and the improvement of fringe benefits and working conditions for contract workers as part of its bargaining agenda from 2000 on. In September 2002, the labor union and management at the HMC reached an agreement that 40% of new regular workers be recruited from the existing contract workers. The 2003 collective agreement stipulated that extra points be given to contract workers applying for the recruiting process of new regular workers. Management at Hyundai applied these agreements to the recruiting of new regular workers in October 2002 and October 2003 thereby respectively selecting 200 and 120 contract workers out of 500 and 300 recruiting jobs.

The extensive use of contract labor at auto plants has been challenged by the Labor Ministry and faced with the growing resistance of contract workers. In September 2004, the Labor Ministry made an official charge that the use of contract workers at the HMC plants violated the Act of the Protection of Dispatched Workers, which prohibits dispatched labor on the production line. According to this charge, contract labor at auto plants was a sort of illegal dispatched work, because their work was carried out independently under the direct supervision of automakers' shop-floor management (not the subcontractors). The Labor Ministry's charge was also applied to other Korean automakers, including Kia Motors, and GM Daewoo. Influenced by the charges, contract workers at most automakers organized their own labor unions (at Hyundai, Kia, and GM Daewoo) and demanded that contract workers at the job positions that the government ruled as illegal dispatched work would be transferred to the status of regular employee as illustrated in Figure 4.1. The management at the HMC, however, disregarded the Labor Ministry's charges as well as contract workers unions' demands, and insisted that the court overturn the Labor Ministry's ruling. In fact, the Prosecutor's Office decided that most of the Labor Ministry's charges (more than 90%) against the illegal use of non-regular workers at the automakers had no grounds. However, acrimonious controversy among concerned parties regarding the use of contract labor on assembly lines will continue.

Issues related to irregular workers at Hyundai Motor Company	•Hyundai Motor Worker Union and related unions filed complaints again Hyundai Motor Company (HMC) and its 127 subcontractors for violating the Protection of Dispatched Workers Act. - It claimed that 9,122 workers of the subcontractors at the three factory sites violated the law •The Ministry of Labor regarded the union claim appropriate and sent the case to the prosecutor's office.
Arguments supporting the union claims	•Subcontractors' workers worked together with the HMC workers at the same lines, even alternated each other, the performance evaluation of the subcontractors' workers were done by the HMC management. •When the HMC workers were injured for work-related accidents or absent, spent paid leave or reject holiday work, the subcontractors' worker were called to do the job of the HM workers •The subcontractors did not have the authority to decide on the working hour, holidays, overtime work on their own. They had to consult with the HMC. •When a subcontractor was replaced with another one, the HMC decided about who will stay out of the previous subcontractors' workers. •The HMC decided about the number of production workers of the subcontractors at factory site, recognized the managerial staff of the subcontractor up to 7% of the production workers and paid the their wages without regard to the work performance of the production workers.
Management's arguments for using subcontractors' workers at factory site	•It was not a matter of the Protection of Dispatched Workers Act. •Labor Ministry's decision did not reflect automotive industry' production characteristics. •Labor and management at HMC had the agreement about the proportion of the contracting out within factory and the management abided by that agreement. •The subcontractors at factory site had the authority on the personal matters of their workers. •Lack of flexibility of using workforce caused excess use of irregular workers. •Wages and working conditions of the subcontractors within factory site' workers were fair compared to the other subcontractors at HMC.

Figure 4.1 Arguments Concerning the Use of Irregular Workers at the Hyundai Motor Company

The growing use of non-regular labor, or contract workforce in specific, at auto plants has created a "mixed" production process, combining regular and contract workers together. In the past, contract workers were mainly deployed in separate work areas of sub-assembly lines. In the post-crisis period, however, those non-regular workers have been located along the main production line, particularly by filling in empty positions of laid off regular workers or taking dangerous and difficult jobs. The mixed composition of regular and contract workers in the production line is the main source for the Labor Ministry's charge of illegal dispatched work, although the two workers groups have separate supervisory structures at the workplace. This mixed work organization, embracing a number of contract workers, offers a contradicting picture of operational performance. On one hand, units per (regular) employee improved from 18.6 in 1998 to 29.6 in 2002. However, this remarkable improvement of productivity cannot be properly understood without considering the increasing presence of 'invisible' contract labor. On the other hand, the massive inflow of contract labor into the main production lines has worsened the line efficiency down from 78.4% in 2001 to 66.6% in 2004 at the HMC auto plants. The number of contract workers to be deployed into production lines is determined as part of work standards negotiation between department managers and union shop stewards.

Collective bargaining at the HMC takes place at the company level like most other industries in Korea. The union and management conduct wage bargaining every year and negotiate other content within collective agreements every two years. The unions are affiliated with the Korean Metal Workers Federation (KMWF), which belongs to the Korean Federation of Trade Unions (KCTU). In February 2001, the KMWF was converted into an industrial union, named the Korean Metal Workers Unions (KMWU). However, only in 2006 (as discussed in the above), the unions of all the automakers joined the KMWU.

In June 2006 the HMWU decided to join the KMWU, which was followed by the unions of other automakers. As discussed above, in 2010, payment to full-time union officials by employers will be prohibited. Then, even large unions, say ones with 1,000 members, might face tough times without the wages of their officials being paid by the employers. The HMWU seems to believe that establishing an industry-based bargaining structure be a way to prepare for the expected labor law change. Allowing multiple unions at enterprise level seems to be another factor. As discussed earlier, it is hard to say that allowing multiple unions at workplaces will be only good for unions. There will be the second or third union at the HMC. The company might take advantage of the divided power of the labor. This consideration seems to influence the HMWU's decision to shift from enterprise union to industrial union. Through this shift the HMWU will strengthen solidarity with other unions belonging to the same federation, thus overcome structural weakness of enterprise-based bargaining structure.

There are some employment practices at the HMC that have remained the same despite the external shock brought by the economic crisis. The work organization is one of them. The work organization structure which consists of work team (*cho*), operational unit (*ban*), and Department (*kwa*) had remained unchanged There is also Taylor-inspired labor control on the shop floor. Given the hierarchical structure of work organizations, work order flows from the department to work teams in a top-down manner. There is little room for worker participation. The HMC adopted quality circles and suggestion programs in the late 1980s, however those Japanese-style employee involvement techniques are not active, due to few incentives for those activities and high production workloads. Multi-skills and job enrichment are also very limited. Job rotation within an operational unit or at the departmental level is relatively active, while job transfer across departments or plants is quite rare. Job rotation is not determined by foremen or department managers, but by workers themselves as a means of balancing workloads and avoiding the monotony of simple production jobs. Workers' avoidance of job transfer has, to a large extent, limited functional flexibility of regular employees, and, as a result, encouraged management to further rely on flexible contract labor. This structure of work organization has remained intact over several decades.

The compensation scheme at the HMC has also not changed. In Korea, individual worker's wages are basically determined according to seniority. Qualifications, characteristics of jobs and ability to undertake work, are taken into consideration, but their influence is minor. This is the same for workers at the HMC. Wages increase with workers' tenure, as displayed in Table 4.4. The ratio of basic wage payment (which is paid regardless of worker's working hours) to the total wage bill was 33.7 percent (January 2004). The employers have responded to the unions' wage demands by providing various allowances rather than increasing basic wages. The proportion of overtime allowances and/or night-work allowance is also high. At the HMC this ratio was 26.5 percent (January 2004). The performance achievements of individuals are not reflected in the determination of annual wage increases. Before 1987, the HMC had a performance evaluation scheme for production workers. The evaluation system was abolished as a result of complaints by the union. The company has sought to re-introduce an individual incentive scheme, but the re-introduction of the system has not been possible due to the dissatisfaction of the union and workers. While the proportion of bonus allowances is very high, there are no linkages between wages and company performance. The achievement target for bonus allowances has been very low and/or the companies have paid the bonus allowances even though the workers failed to meet the goals with the presence of the strong unions.

Table 4.4 Wages and Tenure at Hyundai Motor Company (2003)

Tenure in years	Average age in years	Wage compared to that of 14 years of tenure
34	54.2	127.8%
29	52.8	129.6%
24	48.2	114.0%
19	42.9	109.7%
14	37.8	100.0%
9	33.2	88.1%
4	29.1	76.1%
Less than 1	26.1	65.6%

In brief, through serious conflicts over the dismissals during the financial crisis period, industrial relations in Korea have become even more adversarial and confrontational. The automotive industry is no exception. At the HMC a massive downsizing was implemented by the management during the financial crisis, however the union has regained power and been able to achieve strong employment protection schemes for its members after the country recovered from the financial crisis.

The only compromise that labor and management at the HMC could reach was the increased use of irregular workers. Management needed to use more irregular workers for a more flexible and cheaper workforce. The union and workers recognized the need of the irregular workers as a buffer in times of economic difficulties. However, this arrangement has also generated complex labor-management confrontations as the extensive use of irregular workers at the production lines has gained social attention. A law to protect irregular workers was passed in December 2006 (as discussed above) and the use of irregular workers has been limited at the HMC accordingly.

Very rapidly the HMC has been losing its major comparative advantage. The average labor cost of the HMC workers is over 50,000 US dollars per year. The proportion of the labor cost to total cost is already as high as other automakers in the world. The HMC management will no longer be able to buy the industrial peace by agreeing with the union's high wage demand. Transforming the HMC's industrial relations to one based on participation and cooperation will not be an easy task for both the union and management.

The union has been proposing an option to the management at the HMC. It claims that establishing an industrial bargaining structure will solve problems in HMC workplaces. It will reduce the gap in wages and working conditions between regular and irregular workers at HMC since their wages and working conditions are discussed together. The management and union at the company level (i.e. HMC) will be able to discuss productivity improvement since the union and employer's representative negotiate on conflicting issues at industry level. However, the management is not likely to take the union's proposal of doing industrial bargaining with the union. It is afraid of having dual bargaining structure. They might have bargaining at the enterprise level together with one at the industrial level.

It is yet to see that the HMC management comes up with a clear strategy to enhance labor and management cooperation to cope with even tougher competition brought by globalization. It may take much time and may be very difficult for management to induce cooperation and participation from the union. But, there is still a chance for labor and management at the HMC to establish productive labor-management relations since both the labor and management at the HMC have common interests to protect.

8.   QUESTIONS FOR DISCUSSION

1.   With more severe competition due to globalization process, what should the three actors in the Korean industrial relations system do? How could labor-management relations at the workplace level be strengthened?
2.   What are the factors that influence the decline in union membership?
3.   What has been the factors that have reduced the number of strikes and lockouts in recent years?
4.   In your view, how could Korean labor unions serve their members better in the globalized economy?

ENDNOTES

The author is grateful to Hansung University for the financial research support in the year of 2010. The author also would like to thank Professor Sununta Siengthai for her helpful comments.

1.   This part is largely taken from Lee and Park (2006).
2.   The level is based upon the total number of vehicle units produced in Hyundai domestic plants in 2003.
3.   According to Park (2006), only 1.6% of union members in the 1988 HMWU survey showed a concern over job insecurity. This is quite contrasting to the recent survey results.

Chapter 5

INDUSTRIAL RELATIONS IN A KNOWLEDGE-BASED ECONOMY: THE CASE OF THE BANKING INDUSTRY IN TAIWAN

Joseph S. Lee

1.   INTRODUCTION

Taiwan has enjoyed enormous success in its ongoing economic development for over fifty years, and as a result, the island has gained international recognition for this 'economic miracle'. Furthermore, due largely to the extraordinary transformation of Taiwan over a period of less than two decades, from an authoritarian state to an open and democratic society, this 'economic miracle' has subsequently been developed into a 'political miracle'.

Although Chen Shui-Bian, the former president of the ROC, failed to live up to the expectations of the general public during his administration from 2000 to 2008, Taiwan is still, nevertheless, one of the most democratized societies in Asia, with its citizens enjoying freedom of speech and the freedom to directly elect their political leaders at both the national and local government level. Taiwan has continued to liberalize its economy in recent years in its attempts to remain competitive, and is now rapidly moving towards establishing itself as a knowledge-based economy (KBE); thus, the share of employment has been steadily shifting from the industrial sector to the service sector and from production jobs to professional, technical, clerical and service jobs.

The shift in the Taiwanese economy towards services and the establishment of a KBE has also led to a corresponding shift in Taiwan's industrial relations system, away from collectivism towards individualism. This is essentially because, within a KBE, it is not just the number of workers that is important, but also the individual worker performance and the innovative and creative abilities that these workers possess which are the new important factors determining the rate of economic growth.

This chapter begins with a brief description of the industrial relations system during the former industrial era in Taiwan. Then, we examine the new developments within the emerging KBE. The banking industry is then used as a case to illustrate the changing face of industrial relations within a KBE. We select the banking industry as our case because this industry has traditionally accounted for a substantial share of white collar workers enjoying high employment stability and good levels of pay and benefits in Taiwan.

Currently, the banking industry is experiencing a rapidly changing economic structure and environment. This has greatly reduced the position of economic superiority previously enjoyed by workers within this particular industry, essentially as a result of the privatization of banking in response to growing international competition. The result of this is that both the higher levels of pay and the notion of lifelong employment within the banking industry are now fading rapidly. Workers within the banking industry must today face similar problems to those faced by workers in other industries, including the risk and uncertainty arising from constant mergers and acquisitions, as well as new developments in information and communications. Banks are now required to innovate constantly and develop themselves, coming up with new products and new business models on a regular basis; should they fail to do so, they will be unable to meet the constantly changing demands of their customers within the global economy. The banking industry is therefore regarded as an appropriate case study for investigating the impact of globalization and the establishment of a KBE on the industrial and employment relations system within an economy.

2. THE EMERGENCE OF A KBE AND CHANGES IN INDUSTRIAL RELATIONS IN TAIWAN

Over the past two decades, Taiwan has been moving rapidly away from an economy dominated by labor-intensive industries, towards an economy dominated by service and knowledge-intensive industries. Alongside these changes, there has also been a rapid shift in employment from the agricultural and manufacturing sectors to the service sector (Table 5.1) and from blue collar production work to white collar professional, technical and clerical occupations (Table 5.2).

Table 5.1 Employment, by Industry, 1980-2007

Year	Agriculture	Mining	Manufacturing	Utilities	Construction	Services
1980	19.50	0.85	32.87	0.42	8.38	37.98
1985	17.45	0.47	33.67	0.46	6.96	40.98
1990	12.85	0.24	32.03	0.43	8.12	46.32
1995	10.55	0.17	27.08	0.40	11.09	50.71
2000	7.79	0.11	27.97	0.38	8.76	54.98
2001	7.54	0.10	27.57	0.38	7.95	56.46
2002	7.50	0.10	27.11	0.37	7.66	57.25
2003	7.27	0.09	27.05	0.36	7.33	57.90
2004	6.56	0.08	27.30	0.35	7.48	58.23
2005	5.93	0.07	27.48	0.90a	7.96	57.66
2006	5.48	0.07	27.47	0.87	8.20	57.93
2007	5.27	0.07	27.61	0.90	8.22	57.92

Source: DGBAS (2008), Yearbook of Manpower Survey Statistics.
a: change of classification of utility industries in 2005

Table 5.2 Employment, by Occupation, 1985-2007

Year	Admin.	Professional	Technical	Clerical	Services	Agriculture	Production
1980	3.74	3.86	7.60	6.35	14.78	19.18	44.49
1985	3.86	4.15	8.46	6.88	16.49	17.26	42.9
1990	4.72	5.15	11.63	7.98	16.69	17.73	41.11
1995	4.82	5.53	14.79	9.70	16.35	10.41	38.40
2000	4.34	6.43	16.77	10.82	18.04	7.65	35.96
2001	4.33	6.56	17.21	10.93	18.59	7.41	34.97
2002	4.49	6.87	17.58	11.01	18.94	7.39	33.73
2003	4.46	7.09	17.92	11.09	18.98	7.14	33.33
2004	4.56	7.42	18.13	11.30	18.89	6.42	33.27
2005	4.51	8.00	18.45	11.39	18.77	5.81	33.08
2006	4.47	8.22	19.08	11.26	19.05	5.35	32.57
2007	4.49	8.41	19.62	11.00	19.08	5.16	32.24

Source: DGBAS (2008), Yearbook of Manpower Survey Statistics.

Prior to the lifting of martial law in 1987, industrial relations in Taiwan had been a very simple matter, largely because trade unions were very tightly controlled under the authoritarian government; thus employers had full control of matters relating to personnel, and paternalism was widespread within the workplace.

Of the legislation that had been enacted, most of the labor laws had not been enforced prior to 1984, because many of the labor laws that were in place had been enacted in the 1920s and 1930s when the nationalist government was still on the mainland; at that time, the economic environment was totally different from the situation that existed in Taiwan in the 1960s, 1970s and 1980s.

Given that Taiwan has always been dominated by small and medium sized enterprises (SMEs), with workers being able to move freely within the labor market, wages and benefits were more or less determined by market forces (Lee 1988; Lee 2000a). However, as the economy continued to develop, and as the educational attainment of the workforce improved, workers became more aware and concerned about their working environment, and there was a growing desire for participation in the decision-making processes which affected not only their pay and benefits, but also their working conditions, occupational safety and health, and general welfare. Under growing public pressure, the government enacted a comprehensive Fair Labor Standards Law (FLSL) in 1984, and established the cabinet level Council of Labor Affairs (CLA) in 1987 with a mandate to enforce this law. Since then, the government has also been updating many of the old and outdated labor laws and enacting new laws with the purpose of bringing Taiwan's labor law system up to date with the new industrialized and globalized era.

The lifting of martial law legalized other political parties in opposition to the ruling Kuomintang (KMT), and with the growing pressure from these opposition parties, the ruling party began to enforce the labor laws on the island much more vigorously. At the same time, workers were becoming more concerned, not only about the rate of economic growth vis-à-vis the rate of increase in their pay, but also about their job security in general. Given the rapid relocation overseas of many of the island's labor-intensive firms in search of lower labor costs, there was a consequent and continuing rise in the number of displaced workers.

As Taiwan was becoming more industrialized, there was rising concern among its affluent workers, not only with regard to higher pay and benefits, but also with regard to the growing desire to participate in the sort of decisions that impacted their working environment and their occupational health and safety. Thus, workers began to form unions that were independent of the influence of the ruling party, with the leaders of these independent unions demonstrating much greater militancy and being much more independently minded. Although many of these independent unions were illegal under the Trade Union Law that existed at the time – since the law prohibited dual unionism, i.e., one workplace was allowed to have one union, and only one industrial federation was permitted within any single industry – many workers have, nevertheless, intentionally gone on to form overlapping unions for the purpose of competing with the ineffectual government-controlled unions.

The independent unions that were developed between 1987 and 1995 invariably had very common characteristics, i.e., they were workplace based, oriented towards local issues, self-reliant and rather *ad hoc* in nature. These unions were also invariably formed to deal with one or two particular issues arising in their immediate workplace, such as disputes over year-end bonuses, pay increases, or the unfair treatment of employees, and it is precisely for this reason that the unions tended to admit only those employees within the same workplace who were faced with the same labor problems. These unions were usually totally reliant upon their own efforts in resolving their problems; seldom did they seek help from external sources, such as government officials or local/national legislators, and only on very rare occasions would they engage in mass demonstrations on the streets as a means of publicizing their cause. These unions have therefore had to come up with various creative and effective tactics to pursue their aims, including short-term slowdowns, short-term work stoppages and 'collective vacationing' (a situation where large numbers of employees take their entitled vacation simultaneously, with the ultimate aim of placing significant pressure on their employers).

The unions that were formed between 1995 and 1996 were concerned with issues which differed significantly from those of their predecessors that had been formed between 1987 and 1995. The newer arrivals came on the scene because, at that time, many of the island's labor-intensive firms were in the process of relocating their production facilities abroad, while the economy was also in the throes of a brief recession; thus, the major concerns of the trade unions at that time were layoffs, severance pay, pensions and the right to work.

Nevertheless, the collective actions that the trade unions took against employers within the private sector during this period were largely ineffective, essentially because such actions succeeded only in accelerating the employers' deployment overseas, resulting in the loss of significant numbers of jobs. Another significant issue which occurred involved large numbers of bus drivers and conductors who took strike action for overtime payment and shorter working hours; their concerted actions were met by the government's deregulation of the bus routes which totally undermined the bargaining power of the unions.

Within such an unfavorable economic and political climate, the power and attraction of the independent unions dwindled for a brief period. However, a new wave of unions started to appear within many of the island's public enterprises in 1996, as the government announced its five-year plan to privatize all public enterprises in Taiwan. As a result of this announcement, many of the employees within these public enterprises became quite alarmed, and, in response, started joining the existing unions, or forming new unions, and through their concerted efforts were able to halt, or at least delay, the process of privatization. There were also growing numbers of employees starting to join existing unions, or to form new ones, within the public sector. In 1998, there were only 52 public sector workers who were union members; however, by 2004, union membership had risen to a total of 9,081. It should be noted, however, that most of these union members were technicians and janitors; this was essentially because, with the exception of janitors and low-level blue collar workers in non-essential service areas, the Civil Service Law prohibited employees within the public sector to form unions or to become union members (CLA, 2005). Nevertheless, by 2003, the government had enacted a law granting civil servants the right to form and to join unions.

Many of the independent unions formed during this period were reincarnations of the old unions, albeit now through the direct election of union staff and leaders of their own choice, as opposed to the previous method of appointment of union leaders and staff by the ruling party. The Taiwan Federation of Railroad Workers Unions (TFRWU), the

Federation of Postal Workers Unions (FPWU), the Taiwan Telephone and Telegraph Workers Union (TTTWU), the Taiwan Power Workers Union (TPWU), the Taiwan Petroleum Workers Union (TPWU) and the Taiwan Highway Workers Union (THWU) are all examples of old unions having been successfully transformed into independent unions through such direct elections.

As increasing numbers of unions gained independence from the government, they also withdrew from the heavily government-influenced Chinese Federation of Labor (CFL) and began to form their own independent federations. In March 1998, five large unions from the public enterprises, the China Telephone and Telegraph Workers Union (CTTWU), the China Petroleum Workers Union (CPWU), the Taiwan Railroad Workers Union (TRWU), the Taiwan Tobacco and Wine Manufacturing Workers Union (TTWMWU) and the Taiwan Power Workers Union (TPWU), announced that they had withdrawn from the CFL and had formed the Taiwan Confederation of Trade Unions (TCTU). This was quickly followed by the formation of other federations by other groups of independent unions.

By 2005, there were a total of nine national federations in Taiwan; however, only the following five federations could be regarded as being particularly powerful: the Taiwan Confederation of Trade Unions (TCTU), the Chinese General Federation of Workers' Unions (CGFWU), the National Trade Union Confederation (NTUC), the Chinese General Labor League (CGLL) and the Republic of China Federation of Craft Workers Unions (FCWU). The TCTU, along with the government-influenced CFL, are the two largest and most influential federations. Clearly therefore, in recent years, both the government and the trade unions have become more active players in Taiwan's industrial relations system. Details on the total number of unions formed in Taiwan between 1987 and 2007, as well as union membership levels, are provided in Table 5.3.

Table 5.3 Number of Unions and Union Members in Taiwan, 1987-2007

Year	Total No. of Unions	Total No. of Members (1,000 persons)	Union Members as a Proportion of the Labor Force (%)
1987	2,510	2,100	25.7
1988	3,041	2,260	27.4
1989	3,315	2,419	28.8
1990	3,524	2,756	32.4
1991	3,654	2,941	34.4
1992	3,657	3,058	34.9
1993	3,689	3,172	35.7
1994	3,706	3,277	36.0
1995	3,704	3,135	34.0
1996	3,700	3,048	32.7
1997	3,714	2,952	31.3
1998	3,732	2,921	30.6
1999	3,804	2,927	30.3
2000	3,836	2,868	29.3
2001	3,945	2,879	29.2
2002	4,120	2,866	29.3
2003	4,185	2,908	28.8
2004	4,317	2,970	28.9
2005	4,335	2,992	29.0
2006	4,500	2,984	28.9
2007	4,574	3,026	28.4

Sources:

1. Data on union membership is provided by the Department of Labor Management Relations at the Council of Labor Affairs.
2. Labor force figures are taken from DGBAS (2008), Monthly Bulletin of Manpower Statistics.

Although the trade unions have become very active in a wide variety of different areas over recent years, their influence has, nevertheless, remained very limited, due largely to the lack of economies of scale of these unions. This is essentially because, as noted earlier, most of the business units in Taiwan are small and medium in size.

In fact, since 2000, the Taiwanese economy moved away from industrial domination and becomes an economy dominated by services. Better-educated workers have been more aware of what is happening around them and are now keen to participate in the decision-making processes that affect the working environment. Among all white collar worker unions, the ones that have become the most active are those in the finance, banking and real estate industries. Only 22,849 employees in these industries were union members in 1997; however, by 2004, union membership within these industries had risen to 54,782.

Although teachers were not allowed to form or join unions under the Trade Union Law, a Chinese Teachers' Association was nevertheless formed in 1999, and indeed, by September 2002, this association had succeeded in organizing a rally involving more than 80,000 teachers which marched on the streets with a demand that the government should grant them the right to become union members, to engage in collective bargaining, and to form their own unions. However, despite this association performing many functions akin to those of trade unions, even now, teachers still do not have the right to form their own unions.

Aside from the rise in union membership, a different form of employee representation in the workplace has been emerging in the form of management/employee conferences (similar to the works councils adopted in many European countries). In 1999 there were only 1,296 of these employee-management conferences in Taiwan, but by 2007 this had already risen to a total of 16,607 (Table 5.4).

It is not only the unions that have become much more active; since 2000, the government has also been playing an increasingly active role in the industrial relations system in Taiwan, through the updating of employment relations laws so as to meet the needs of modern society. For example, in 2000, the government amended the Trade Union Act, followed by the enactment of the Occupational Safety Protection Act in 2001, and the Equal Gender in

Employment Act and Employment Insurance Act in 2002. There were also numerous amendments in 2002 to the Labor Dispute Act, the Labor Inspection Act, the Occupational Training Act, the Labor Insurance Law and the Fair Labor Standards Act (which shortened the total number of working hours permitted). In 2003, the Massive Layoff Protection Act was enacted, followed in 2004 by the enactment of the new Pension Law (Table 5.5). The government is also considering introducing a new law to regulate and protecting the job security and working conditions of the rapidly increasing number of temporary 'dispatch' workers in Taiwan.

Table 5.4 Total Numbers of Management/Employee Conferences, 1992-2007

Year	Management/Employee Conferences			Growth Rate (%)
	Public Enterprises	Private Enterprises	Total No.	
1992	430	484	914	–
1993	440	492	932	1.97
1994	473	497	970	4.08
1995	457	523	980	1.03
1996	458	536	994	1.43
1997	451	562	1,013	1.91
1998	491	561	1,052	3.85
1999	547	749	1,296	23.19
2000	646	1,297	1,943	49.92
2001	684	1,933	2,617	34.69
2002	630	2,071	2,701	3.21
2003	552	2,364	2,916	7.96
2004	1,260	4,553	5,813	99.35
2005	1,446	5,358	6,804	17.05
2006	429	7,065	7,494	10.14
2007	441	16,166	16,607	121.60

Source: CLA (2008), Labor Management Relations Division.

**Table 5.5 Enactment, Amendment or Abolition of Employee Relations Laws,
1928-2008**

Laws Enacted	Date/Year of Enactment	Date of Amendment/Abolition
Labor Dispute Act	1928	Amended 29 May 2002
Trade Union Act	1929	Amended 19 July 2000
Labor Inspection Act	1931	Amended 29 May 2002
Employees Welfare Fund Act	1943	Amended 29 January 2003
Labor Insurance Law	1958	Amended 29 January 2003
Workers Health and Safety Act	1974	Amended 12 June 2002
Occupational Training Act	1983	Amended 29 May 2002
Fair Labor Standards Law	1984	Amended 27 December 1996, 13 May 1998, 28 June 2000, 19 July 2001, 25 December 2002, 16 May 2008
Employment Service Act	1992	Amended 16 May 2003
Occupational Accident Labor Protection Act	31October 2001	–
Equal Gender in Employment Act	16 January 2002	–
Employment Insurance Act	15 May 2002	–
Public Employment in Service Act	6 February 2003	Abolished 18 June 2004
Massive Layoff Protection Act	7 February 2003	–
Pension Law	30 June 2004	–
Collective Bargaining Law	28 October 1921	Amended December 2007

Source: CLA (2008), Labor Legislation.

The increasing role of the government in the labor market has raised a new type of debate in Taiwan, i.e., whether the pendulum has swung too far, from the one extreme of a 'hands-off' policy, to the other extreme of too much regulation, and whether there is therefore a need for deregulating the labor laws, i.e., a need for greater deregulation along with an increase in labor market flexibility, thereby enabling employers to compete much more favorably in the international market.

Table 5.6 Cases of Industrial Disputes in Taiwan, 1989-2007

Year	Total No. of Cases	Type of Labor Disputes															No. of Issues per Case
		Employment Contracts		Wage Issues		Working Hours		Retirement Benefits		Fringe Benefits		Industrial Accidents		Others		Total		
		No.	%	No.	%	No.	%	No.	%	No.	%	No.	%	No.	%	No.	%	
1989	1,943	710	36.5	489	25.2	29	1.5	234	12.0	64	3.3	206	10.6	211	10.9	1,943	100	1.00
1990	1,860	788	42.4	418	22.5	12	0.6	202	10.9	29	1.6	191	10.3	220	11.8	1,860	100	1.00
1991	1,810	836	40.2	528	25.4	20	1.0	210	10.1	51	2.4	233	11.2	204	9.8	2,082	100	1.15
1992	1,803	848	40.4	557	26.6	9	0.4	185	8.8	52	2.5	224	10.7	222	10.6	2,097	100	1.16
1993	1,878	852	38.9	548	25	43	2.0	207	9.4	61	2.8	234	10.7	246	11.2	2,191	100	1.17
1994	2,061	931	39.6	643	27.4	27	1.1	210	8.9	55	2.3	295	12.5	190	8.1	2,351	100	1.14
1995	2,271	962	38.1	761	30.2	17	0.7	257	10.2	50	2.0	272	10.8	204	8.1	2,523	100	1.11
1996	2,659	1,271	43.1	891	30.2	15	0.5	239	8.1	32	1.1	262	8.9	236	8.0	2,946	100	1.11
1997	2,600	1,172	41.9	738	26.4	18	0.6	251	9.0	24	0.9	367	13.1	228	8.1	2,798	100	1.08
1998	4,138	1,945	43.6	1,321	29.6	36	0.8	306	6.9	67	1.5	493	11.1	297	6.7	4,465	100	1.08
1999	5,860	2,976	46.4	1,953	30.4	28	0.4	363	5.7	56	0.9	656	10.2	384	6.0	6,416	100	1.09
2000	8,026	3,921	42.7	3,127	34.1	63	0.7	512	5.6	100	1.1	850	9.3	603	6.6	9,176	100	1.14
2001	10,955	6,187	49.1	3,895	30.9	117	0.9	613	4.9	93	0.7	814	6.5	893	7.1	12,612	100	1.15
2002	14,017	7,514	42.6	6,190	35.1	185	1.0	643	3.6	280	1.6	824	4.7	2,014	11.4	17,650	100	1.26
2003	12,204	6,427	40.5	5,536	34.9	120	0.8	507	3.2	234	1.5	866	5.5	2,166	13.7	15,856	100	1.30
2004	10,838	4,851	35.4	5,289	38.6	169	1.2	461	3.4	236	1.7	922	6.7	1,771	12.9	13,699	100	1.26
2005	14,256	6,732	38.7	6,456	37.1	204	1.2	762	4.4	258	1.5	1,144	6.6	1,851	10.6	17,407	100	1.22
2006	15,464	6,669	34.9	7,584	39.7	235	1.2	610	3.2	221	1.2	1,221	6.4	2,571	13.5	19,111	100	1.24
2007	19,729	8,668	33.2	10,034	38.4	380	1.5	766	2.9	348	1.3	1,393	5.3	4,549	17.4	26,138	100	1.32

Source: Council of Labor Affairs.
Notes: The causes and results of disputes were reclassified in June 1988 according to the Settlement of Labor Dispute Law, as amended. Within the classification of disputes, two of more dispute issues were permitted for each case from 1991 onwards. The totals do not add up as it is weighted above the total.

As the workplace has become more democratized, and as more formal mechanisms have been put in place to handle grievances, there has also been a significant increase in the number of industrial disputes, where workers are provided with a forum to openly air their grievances; thus, from the previous total of 2,600 labor dispute cases in 1997, by 2002 this had risen to 6,701 cases, and by 2007 there were a total of 19,729 cases of industrial disputes (Table 5.6). Furthermore, not only has there been an overall increase in the total number of labor disputes, but the content of these disputes has also changed, relative to the different economic conditions, away from retirement benefits, industrial accidents and compensation issues, towards disputes over the termination of contracts and other wage-related issues, such as severance pay and wage arrears.

As for employers, they have become more aggressive in adopting the new techniques in human resource management. For example, most of the high-tech firms have expanded their human resource management techniques, such as use of core competencies in recruiting, performance appraisal evaluation, formal- and informal on-the–job training, and incentive-based wages. Large employers in other industries have all converted their personnel departments into human resource management departments and have adopted many of the new techniques in recruiting, training and performance evaluation.

In short, alongside the changes that have taken place in the economic and industrial structure, there have also been significant changes in the roles of the actors in the industrial relations system. As Taiwan continues to develop itself into a truly democratic society, and as it experiences the shift away from its industrial economy towards becoming a service and knowledge-based economy, the roles of employers, employee representatives and the government have all changed. As we have seen from the foregoing sections, these actors have all become much more active.

Employers are now much more aware of the important contributions made by their human resources, and are therefore paying much more attention to human resource management principles. High performance work systems, such as core competence recruitment, performance and incentive pay, job evaluation and on-the-job training, have all become increasingly important practices in the effective management of enterprises in Taiwan. In other words, the trend in industrial relations in Taiwan is moving away from simple paternalism, to a much more diversified system wherein there is simultaneous emphasis on both collectivism and individualism.

3. INDUSTRIAL RELATIONS IN THE BANKING INDUSTRY

3.1 Changes in the Banking Industry Environment

In the past, the banking industry in Taiwan was a very conservative industry, largely because, up until 1992, all of the banks in Taiwan were owned by the government, including the commercial banks, specialized banks, cooperative banks and the financial department of the general post office and its branches. Within such a monopolistic environment, there was no particular need for these banks to provide high quality services to their customers. The situation has now changed, however, because as Taiwan has become more globalized and liberalized, the banks must now be much more customer-oriented in the face of growing international competition.

The government amended the Banking Law in 1989, permitting the establishment of new private commercial banks, with the ultimate aim of enhancing the competitiveness of the banking industry. In 1991 and 1992, as a result of the amended law, a total of 16 new banks were granted operating licenses, whilst three trust and investment companies were also allowed to convert to commercial banks in 1991 and 1999. The Ministry of Finance subsequently encouraged other credit cooperatives those with sound balance sheets to convert themselves into commercial banks, whilst permitting foreign banks to set up branches in Taiwan.

Following the adoption of such a policy of encouragement by the government, the number of financial institutions in Taiwan increased rapidly; an issue which led to some experts arguing that there were now too many banks and financial institutions. Indeed, by 2000, there were a total of 6,075 financial institutions in Taiwan, of which 491 were head offices (including the Central Bank of China) and 5,584 were branches. These financial institutions comprised of 47 domestic banks, 39 foreign banks, 50 credit cooperatives, 314 credit departments of the farmers' and fishermen's association, five banks whose services were targeted exclusively at SMEs and one postal savings system. With such an excessive number of financial institutions, there has been inevitable cut-throat competition in both price items (interest rates) and in non-price items (service charges, guarantee fees, and so on), resulting in low loan prices, poor services, low profits and the inability to compete within the international market.

The government subsequently went on to initiate several policies aimed at enhancing the competitiveness of the banking industry, one of which was to privatize the government-owned banks; consequently First Commercial Bank, the International Commercial Bank of China, the Changhua Commercial Bank, the Huanan Commercial Bank and the Taiwan Small and Medium Sized Business Bank were all privatized in 1998, while in 2000, the Chiao Tung Bank and the Farmers Bank of China were both privatized through a reduction in government holdings. By 2000, private banks had become the backbone of the financial system in Taiwan with the total number of private banks far outnumbering government-owned banks; indeed, the government in Taiwan now retains ownership in just five banks, namely, the Bank of Taiwan, the Land Bank of Taiwan, the Taiwan Cooperative Bank, the Central Trust of China and the Export-Import Bank of China.

In order to help private banks to overcome their deficiencies, in term of their lack of economies of scale, the government enacted the Financial Institutions Mergers Act in December 2000 and the Financial Holding Company Act in 2001, with the overall aim of encouraging the smaller banks to merge so that their capacity could be expanded, thereby enabling them to compete favorably in the international market. Since then, through the integration of a total of 68 related enterprises, 14 financial holding companies have been established. The government also implemented further measures aimed at liberalizing the island's financial markets, as follows:

1. Liberalization of both the qualifications for establishment and the scope of business of the local branches of foreign banks;
2. The lifting of the ceiling of the foreign equity-holding ratio in any given local financial institution;

3. The disposal of the limitation on stock holdings for foreign portfolio investment starting from 1 January, 2001; and

4. The opening up of reinsurance, insurance intermediation and insurance auxiliary services to foreign institutions.

Many of Taiwan's domestic banks have also transformed themselves, adopting a universal banking system which enables them to cover a wide range of business, including banking, securities transactions, investment management and insurance business. Banks have also accelerated the implementation of electronic banking programs so as to provide rapid, low cost and convenient services to their customers.

3.2 Problems Relating to Changes in the Industrial Structure

The changes in the economic environment within the banking industry have led to changes in the characteristics of the workforce, as well as the emergence of new types of labor problems and new forms of industrial and employment relations. The new labor problems can be summarized as follows: increasing employment insecurity, changes in the seniority-based pay system, changes in the pay system, changes in employment standards, erosion of life-long employment for senior managers, increase in employment flexibility, the shift towards job demarcation, and deskilling of the workforce. We will discuss these in the paragraphs that follow.

Increasing employment insecurity – In the past, employment within the banking industry was quite stable, with the banks usually hiring workers who were fresh out of school to work at entry level as bank tellers. As they received more on-the-job training and accumulated experience in their positions, they were gradually and systematically promoted to higher management positions until they finally retired from the bank. Workers in other industries were rather envious of the employment security and high pay enjoyed by those working within the banking industry, resulting in such work being labeled the 'golden rice bowl'. Nevertheless, as the banking industry has become more globalized and liberalized, the economic superiority enjoyed by bank employees has been eroded.

As banks became more customer-oriented as soon as they became privatized and started venturing into other new areas, employees needed to acquire new skills, new knowledge and new attitudes, since the working experience accumulated in the past had become much less relevant to their new jobs. Thus, employers began adopting early separation programs with the aim of removing some of their older employees who had difficulties in acquiring the necessary new skills, knowledge and attitudes. The banks now required younger and better-educated workers who were trained in sales, management information systems, insurance, security, accounting and finance. Hence, the labor turnover rate (the entry rate) within the banking industry expanded from 0.84% in 1991 to 2.06% in 2004, whilst the resignation rate (the exit rate) grew from 0.40% to 1.53% over the same period (Table 5.7).

Table 5.7 Entry and Exit Rates of Domestic Banks in Taiwan, 1991-2004

	1991	1992	1993	1994	1995	1996	1997
Entry Rate (%)	0.84	1.35	0.95	1.11	0.95	0.81	1.27
Exit Rate (%)	0.40	0.30	0.38	0.45	0.41	0.46	0.49
	1998	1999	2000	2001	2002	2003	2004 (Jan-Aug)
Entry Rate (%)	1.13	0.92	1.10	1.10	1.19	1.62	2.06
Exit Rate (%)	0.58	0.61	0.76	0.84	1.13	1.10	1.53

Source: NFBEU (2004), Yearbook of Taiwan Bank Employees.

Changes in the pay system – A seniority-based wage system had previously been commonplace amongst all banks, with employees salaries being raising automatically, along with their seniority, as they accumulated more and more experience in their jobs; today however, as the banks are expanding further into other business areas, and as the technology used in the banks is constantly changing, prior experience has become less relevant, resulting in new types of pay systems, such as skill-based and performance-based pay systems being introduced into the banking industry. For bank employees who had grown accustomed to stability, this constantly changing, highly competitive working environment was now somewhat alien to them.

Changes in employment standards – A long-standing tradition among banks was to recruit employees fresh out of college who had majored in banking, finance, economics or other related fields. They then received on-the-job training and were promoted to higher positions through the internal labor market. In recent years, however, the banks have started recruiting large numbers of new employees with MBA (Master of Business Administration) degrees. These newly-recruited employees usually have specialized training in business administration, business finance, mathematics, statistics, or management information systems, and they are no longer taken on as entry-level bank tellers, but instead, are entered directly into management training programs; in other words, internal promotion is no longer the route to senior management. The American Express Bank, for example, places its newly-recruited MBA holders into 'management associate' positions, whilst the Hong Kong and Shanghai Bank places such MBA holders into management trainee positions from which they can directly achieve management positions after several months of orientation training.

The erosion of lifelong employment for senior managers – In the past, it was invariably the case that the banks' senior managers were promoted from within and generally looked forward to lifelong employment. Today, the situation is quite different, since high-ranking managers can be replaced at any time through external recruitment. These days, it is not unusual for senior managers who had worked extremely hard to successfully complete a merger to suddenly find themselves out of a job and, as a result, finding the need to switch to another bank, or even another occupation or industry for employment. The net result of such changes in management practices has been the loss of loyalty amongst senior managers and staff towards their banks.

The increase in employment flexibility – In order to reduce employment costs, banks are increasingly adopting policies to promote employment flexibility, such as flexible working hours, short-term and fixed-term employment contracts and outsourcing, leading to considerable increases in the numbers of temporary 'dispatch' workers being used. Permanent jobs are now reserved for highly professional core employees, whilst many of the clerical and low-level positions are increasingly being outsourced.

A survey conducted by the Council of Labor Affairs (CLA) in 2001 found that banks were hiring greater numbers of temporary dispatch workers for the purpose of meeting business fluctuations (51 per cent), reducing wage costs (51 per cent), cutting fringe benefit costs (37 per cent), reducing training costs (21 per cent), reducing severance and pension costs (42 per cent) and avoiding labor disputes (23 per cent). Dispatch workers are usually found in administrative work (56 per cent), accounting and financial work (9 per cent), personnel (5 per cent), information management (5 per cent) and repair and maintenance work (2 per cent) (CLA 2001).

The shift towards job demarcation – Jobs within the various banks had, in the past, been characterized by vertical integration, with any experience gained from a lower-ranking job also being of value in a subsequent higher-ranking position; thus, employees continued to be promoted through the internal labor market. However, the various jobs in the banks today have been totally redesigned, and are divided into so-called 'front office' and 'back office' work, with 'front office' workers being in charge of sales, and thereby entitled to performance pay, whilst workers in the 'back office' are regarded as supporting staff, and as such, are not entitled to bonuses or performance pay. Clearly, therefore, employment within the banks is no longer mutually supportive, but instead is characterized by a segmented workforce which includes primary, secondary and temporary dispatch workers.

The deskilling of the workforce – The introduction of e-business programs within the banking industry, as well as automatic telling machines (ATMs) and other automatic banking programs, has rendered many of the previously important skills obsolete; thus, the skills that are required by the banks today have become increasingly oriented towards computer programming, customer relations and sales, skills which are also commonly required in other industries. Bank-specific skills are, therefore, disappearing within the banking industry.

3.3 Responses to the Changes by Employees

In response to the issue of the security threat to their jobs arising from mergers and the reorganization of banks, employees within the banks came together to form their own unions. The first union specifically for bank employees in Taiwan, the Taipei Business Bank Employee Union, was formed in 1988 in direct response to an announcement by the bank of a policy of reducing year-end bonus payments and a delay in promotions. The new policy was specifically aimed at reducing costs; however, there had been no pre-warning of this proposed policy, nor had there been any consultation process with the bank's employees. Five employees within the bank decided that it was necessary to initiate such a union for their own protection, and it was subsequently certified by the Taipei City government in 1989. Other bank employees followed soon afterwards, and by the end of 1989, four unions had been formed specifically for bank employees, with a further five unions being formed in 1990, two in 1991, six in 1993 and three in 1994; all of these were craft unions.

Later on, industrial unions were also formed in 18 other banks, resulting in a total of 38,241 individual union members by the year 2000 (NFUBE 2001). In March 1991, bank employees in Taipei, Kaohsiung and nine other unions together filed a petition to the CLA to form a federation of bank employee unions, which was finally certified by the government in 2001. By 2005, this federation had 22 affiliated industrial unions and 19 craft unions with a total of 50,000 individual members (NFUBE 2008). The federation, and the individual unions within it, together aimed to achieve advances for their members in a number of areas: collective bargaining agreements, Appointment of Bank Employees to the Board of Directors. We discuss these in more detail below.

Collective Bargaining Agreements – Collective bargaining agreements were regarded as an appropriate means of tackling the problems arising from mergers, acquisitions and privatization. For example, when the Fubon Financial Holding Company acquired Taipei Bank in 2003, the First Bank Employees' Union negotiated a collective agreement with Fubon which stipulated both the scope and the conditions under which Fubon could change employees' working rules and conditions, early separation, the transfer of employees within Taipei Bank and the relocation of Taipei Bank employees to other subsidiaries of the Fubon Holding Company without union consensus. Fubon consented to this agreement, and indeed, honored it. However, there is considerable doubt among many observers as to whether Fubon would ever agree to extend this agreement once it expires, and indeed, whether other banks would ever sign up to this type of agreement which is strongly in favor of employees.

Further examples of the use of collective agreements by unions to resolve the problems arising from mergers comes from the acquisition of Kaohsiung Bank by First Bank in 2001 and the acquisition of the General Bank by Chinatrust Bank in 2003. Prior to its acquisition, Kaohsiung Bank employees formed a union and negotiated a collective agreement under which the union recognized First Bank's full right to restructure Kaohsiung Bank, but that First Bank would be required to consult with the union prior to the implementation of any new personnel policies.

Prior to acquiring the General Bank, Chinatrust Bank had reached an agreement with the General Bank union that it would buy back the lifetime employment contracts for laid-off employees (in order to attract good employees from other banks to switch to General Bank during the early stage of its establishment, the owners of the bank had promised all newly-recruited employees that they would be granted an employment contract to the age of 60 or 65). Thus, General Bank employees were concerned as to whether Chinatrust would honor these contracts after the acquisition, and thereby guarantee their employment to the age of 60 or 65. An agreement was finally reached which stated that when Chinatrust did decide to lay off any of the workers with a lifetime employment contract, these employees must be paid a lump sum payment equivalent to the following formula:

> "For those employees with more than 10 years of service, the payment was to be 2N+4 months of the employee's monthly salary prior to the layoff, whilst for employees with 5 to 10 years of service, the formula was N+2, where N is the number of years of service at General Bank. Examples of this in practice were that if Chinatrust Bank wished to lay off any employees with 'lifetime employment guarantees' prior to their 60th birthday: (i) those with 15 years service with General Bank would be entitled to a lump sum payment of 34 months salary (2 x 15 +4 = 34); and (ii) those with 9 years service with General Bank would be entitled to a lump sum payment of 11 months salary (9 + 2 = 11) (NFBEU, 2003)."

The Appointment of Bank Employees to the Board of Directors – In general, collective bargaining has not been very effective in terms of providing protection for union members, largely because the process of negotiation is quite long and because the dominant banks will usually refuse to recognize the union of the bank which they are about to acquire. An alternative tactic for the unions was therefore to have union members appointed, or elected, to the board of directors, so that they could have some influence on the direction of the bank's development, particularly with regard to mergers and privatization issues. In working towards this goal, the unions lobbied very hard for the enactment of laws requiring employers to appoint union members to their board of directors, even though the candidate did not hold any company stock.

After several years of debate, the government finally amended the Public Enterprises Administration Act in 2000, with the new Article 35 of the law permitting employees within public enterprises, with no holdings of any company stock, to appoint representative(s) to the board of directors. Since then, bank employee unions have successfully lobbied Chinatrust Bank, the Cooperative Bank, the Land Bank and the Overseas Chinese Bank to appoint one or two union members to their board of directors even though none of these representatives were holders of any company stock. Additional law was enacted in 2003 in which it was required that, when any public enterprise was being privatized, if the government were to retain more than 20 per cent of the stocks in the new business, one of the government board members must be an employee representative.

Since private banks are not covered by either of these two laws, ownership of company stock remains a prerequisite for election to the board of directors. However, in order to achieve board representation, unions within the private banks can solicit empowerment letters from other stockholders to enable them to garner enough support to be voted onto the board of directors.

In order to ensure that union representatives can perform their roles well on the various boards of directors, the NFBEU has conducted training programs for newly-elected or newly-appointed union board members, with the content of these training programs including bank management, the prevention of hostile takeovers, contract negotiations and issues relating to mergers.

3.4   Acquiring New Skills for Alternative Employment Opportunities

Most of the bank employees in Taiwan today recognize that both employment stability and lifetime employment are gone forever, and that the rapidly changing economic environment and advances in technology are part of everyday modern life; therefore, they realize that the best way for them to protect themselves is to pick up new skills and upgrade their knowledge so as to be able to meet the ever changing requirements of both banks and other financial institutions, or to seek out new careers in different industries or occupations. Thus, many of these bank employees are now attending various occupational licensing classes both on and off the job.

A survey conducted in 2003 showed that most bank employees were attempting to gain certification in various fields including: (i) life insurance licenses (since most of the banks have now expanded their business to include various types of insurance services); (ii) internal control licenses (since banks are increasingly being controlled by holding companies, and, as a result, internal auditing has become an important function of the banks); and (iii) financial planning licenses (given that banks are now more customer oriented, they are providing much more advice to customers on lifetime financial planning matters; this has therefore become a very lucrative area of the business both for the bank, and for the their employees, because the latter receive commission on the financial plans adopted by the customers). There is also growing popularity among bank employees to obtain security management licenses. In 2008 many bank employees are seeking various financial license from mainland China so that they can expand their career choices including working in mainland China due to poor employment condition caused by the 2008 worldwide financial crisis.

4.   CONCLUSION

It is clear from the above discussion that as changes have continued to take place in Taiwan's economic and industrial structure, there have also been corresponding changes in the island's industrial relations system, with each of the three main actors involved, i.e., the government, the employers and their employees (along with their representatives), now playing much more active roles.

For the government in particular, the extremely passive role played in the past has now been superseded by a much more active role through the enactment of labor and employment relations laws aimed at regulating the activities of both management and trade unions (see Table 4). Given the increasing instability of jobs in Taiwan, the government is also playing a much more active role in providing training programs for employees of all types in order to provide them with the new skills and knowledge and hence to ensure their sustainable employability. Indeed, between 2002 and 2004, the government implemented a comprehensive Employment Ability Enhancement Program which involved a cash injection of NT$10.3 billion (US$ 334 million) into employee training; given the success of this program, the government subsequently extended it for a further three years, from 2005 to 2007, and has provided a further cash injection of NT11.9 billion for the extended program (Lee and Hsin 2003).

There is now some debate in Taiwan as to whether the government has become too involved in the labor market, along with a call for labor market deregulation; the general consensus, therefore, is that the government should be somewhat less active in industrial relations. The rapid decline in job security as a result of the globalization of the economy, along with rapid changes in technology as Taiwan moves towards becoming a KBE, has resulted in more workers joining unions in the hope that they may achieve collective bargaining agreements aimed at raising their job security levels.

However, given that the Taiwanese economy is dominated by SMEs, and that the unions therefore suffer from a lack of economies of scale, employees in Taiwan are not yet receiving the level of protection that they desire from their unions. Although this deficiency may be partially remedied through the use of the so-called 'e-union', available on the Internet, a study carried out by Lee and Chen (2005) found that, not only were unions not aware of the benefits of such technology, but there were also numerous technical, financial and attitude barriers that the unions would need to overcome before they could transform themselves into service-oriented institutions, as opposed to political institutions.

While unions may have had some success in the banking sector, their impact has been minimal; indeed, as the leaders of the banking unions have stated themselves, there is a serious leadership problem in the labor movement because so few union staff members are willing to devote their time and effort to union business, not only because of the lack of financial rewards, but also because of their efforts and dedication are not appreciated by union members. There is additional concern that there are too many 'free riders' in the workplaces who are content to stay on the sidelines and allow the union and other employees to fight their battles and then reap the benefits. Many union officials also use their union leadership position as a stepping stone for a career in the political arena; thus, it seems that other forms of employee representation are also required.

As Taiwan moves towards establishing its KBE, employers are much more aware of the important contribution of human resources. Many employers, particularly those in the high-tech industries are paying greater attention to HRM principles and trying hard to develop human capital within their enterprises. Thus, we have seen an emphasis on individualism by employers on one side, while the government and unions strive for collectivism on the other. Clearly, however, employers, unions and the government in Taiwan must search for an optimum combination of individualism and collectivism suitable for a KBE and for Taiwan's special social and cultural background.

5.   CASE STUDY – THE BANK OF OVERSEAS CHINESE

The *Bank of Overseas Chinese* (BOC) was founded in 1961 with funds of NT$100 million provided both by Chinese emigrants living overseas and by local citizens. The creation of the Bank came in response to the call by the government for the encouragement of greater investment in Taiwan by Chinese emigrants living overseas; this was to be facilitated through the provision of better financial services to aid such investment. There are currently over one million Taiwanese business people and their families living in mainland China, where they have invested in excess of NT$150 billion. Thus, in 1999, the Bank set up an additional unit in Hong Kong to provide services to manufacturers from Taiwan who had established their production bases on the mainland; it also set up the *BOC International Leasing Company* in the same year for the purpose of strengthening the services provided to its corporate clients. In October 2003, the Bank founded the *Overseas Chinese Insurance Brokers Company Ltd.* to provide additional services in the insurance field.

Traditionally, BOC's strength has always been in the financing of international trade, a market segment in which it has continually ranked amongst the top ten players; however, in terms of its asset quality, the Bank remains rather weak. As a result of the considerable efforts by the management team to improve the overall performance of the Bank, which did in fact have some significant impact, reducing its impaired asset ratio (defined as official non-performing loans, loans under surveillance and foreclosed properties to total loans) to 15 per cent in 2004, this ratio was, however, still much higher than the average impaired asset ratio for the banking industry as a whole in 2004, at about 6% to 7%. The Bank's capitalization is also weak. Whilst a NT$5.1 billion injection of new equity capital in June 2004 did help to moderate the pressure on the Bank's capitalization level, given that its loan-loss reserves covered only about 25% of its impaired assets in that year, the amount was obviously insufficient in terms of helping to restore the Bank's capital base to a more acceptable level.

Clearly then, the BOC management team has placed considerable effort into rebuilding its business position; however, it is still a long way from establishing the level of operating efficiency enjoyed by most of the island's domestic banks. In 2004, Polaris Securities, the biggest online brokerage firm in Taiwan, acquired 22.1% of the Bank's holdings, making it the biggest single shareholder. In March 2005, Polaris took over the management of BOC and began implementing a series of plans aimed at revitalizing the Bank.

As a result of the efforts of a strong team, the financial position of the Bank improved significantly; and indeed, by 2007, it had become sufficiently attractive for the world's largest financial institution, Citigroup, to make an offer of purchase. However, it was not BOC's underlying assets that attracted Citigroup to make the purchase offer for the Bank, but rather its substantial number of branches and its well established network. Indeed, whilst Citibank currently has just 11 branches in Taiwan, following the acquisition of BOC, there would be an immediate increase in its overall presence in Taiwan, to 66 branches. The potential immediate benefits from the proposed acquisition are:

1.   It would immediately become the largest bank in Taiwan; in addition to the six-fold expansion from its 11 branches to a total of 66 branches in 2007, its total assets would increase to US$22.8 billion, whilst the total number of customers would climb to more than one million.

2.   Citigroup has pledged to completely dispose of BOC's bad debt problem which currently stands at NT$5 billion.

3.   Polaris Securities has pledged to set aside NT$2.8 billion to buy the seniority in BOC, so that Citigroup would have no responsibility for BOC's pension costs.

4.   Along with all other local banks, BOC is prohibited by the Taiwanese government from conducting business directly with mainland China; as a result, all business undertaken by BOC with its Taiwanese customers in mainland China has to be conducted indirectly. Citigroup is an international organization; therefore, the acquisition would immediately help the Bank to bypass the government's restrictions and enable it to expand its business not only into mainland China, but also into numerous other countries around the world.

5.   Citigroup has forecasted that it will be able to repay all BOC's debts within one year, and begin to register a profit in the subsequent year.

There are, however, several labor issues which Polaris Securities must resolve before Citigroup can officially conclude its proposed deal with BOC.

1.   *Job Security*. BOC employs 2,200 staff at its branches in 2007, all of whom have been very concerned about their job security following the acquisition. A demonstration was carried out by the BOC employees' union at which there were

demands for a guarantee of no layoffs as a result of the takeover. Citigroup's response so far has been to pledge a one-year freeze on layoffs.

2. *Clearance of Seniority.* As a result of the purchase of the previous seniority under BOC, Citigroup would become responsible only for the seniority of the Bank after the acquisition. As noted earlier, Polaris Securities has pledged to set aside NT$2.8 billion for this purpose; however, the 1,800 union members have refused this offer and are demanding collective negotiations so that this issue may ultimately be settled by means of a collective agreement. Thus far, Polaris Securities has refused to deal with the union on this matter; however, such intransigence subsequently led to the union conducting a strike vote on 1 May 2007 at which the majority vote for a legal strike required under the law was successfully secured. In other words, the established union at BOC has won the right to conduct a legal strike whenever it chooses to do so, which could of course jeopardize Citigroup's willingness to close the deal, closure which is otherwise expected to occur in September 2007.

3. *Confrontation between Management and the Union.* In January 2007, the BOC management dismissed two union leaders after accusing them of inciting employees to call a strike through illegitimate means. The Bank had argued that this violated its code of conduct and related industrial policies, and posed a risk of potential damage to the company's image and reputation. However, the union argued that these two union leaders had done nothing wrong, and retaliated by accusing the Bank of using such improper layoffs to put fear into the Bank's employees. The union has, in the past, threatened to take industrial action if the BOC management refused to sign an agreement guaranteeing the job security of all bank employees in the event of a Citibank takeover. The Bank responded by saying that manipulation by a few union members had led the union to oppose the management team, regardless of the fact that a survey showed that more than 95 per cent of all employees were in agreement with the Bank's proposed compensation program. Weng Chien, a spokesman for the Bank, said that it had been patient with the two union leaders and had shown them goodwill with an offer of early retirement, which they subsequently turned down. The executive downplayed the union issue, saying that it was not a major problem which would ultimately result in

disrupting the proposed deal, but stated: "we have to do something to stop more damage to the Bank as a whole, or else we will be letting our shareholders and customers down".

Polaris Securities would very much like to see nothing interfering with the successful conclusion of the acquisition because it sees this as an excellent opportunity for them to expand their business, not only into mainland China, but essentially, on a global scale. Indeed, major preparations have been made for the international expansion of the Bank's business; for example, by setting up an international human resource management department and recruiting the former VP of Human Resource Management from one of the most reputable firms in Taiwan, TSMC, as a consultant. Let us therefore imagine what our response might be if we were to be placed in the shoes of either the Polaris Securities or Citigroup management team, or those of the leader of the bank employees' union.

6. QUESTIONS FOR DISCUSSION

1. If you were the management of Polaris Securities how would you handle the thorny issue of the dismissed union leaders? Would you reinstate these two union leaders or regard this as only a temporary threat that, ultimately, will not materialize because the majority of the union members would not wish to jeopardize their employment for these two union leaders (it is well known fact that Taiwanese workers do not like direct confrontation).

2. As the management team at Polaris Securities, how would you handle the seniority issue? Would you be willing to negotiate with the union on this issue, or would it be appropriate to stick to the NT$2.8 billion pledge?

3. As the management of Citigroup, how would you handle the issue of job security one year after taking over BOC?

4. As the leader of the bank employees' union what would you do? There are currently too many banks in Taiwan; thus, there are likely to be many other proposed mergers

and acquisition in the near future resulting in considerable turbulence throughout the banking industry labor market. Should you therefore carry out union's threat and call for the strike, seeking the support of other bank unions? Clearly, the unions of other banks would undoubtedly see this issue as one not just affecting BOC employees, but all banking employees.

Chapter 6

SINGAPORE INDUSTRIAL RELATIONS SYSTEM IN THE GLOBALIZATION ERA

David Wan

1.   INTRODUCTION

This chapter provides a brief introduction to employment relations in Singapore in general and a case study on the various industrial relations issues between Singapore International Airlines (SIA) and its five unions. The case study traces the intense union-management relationship occurring during the period from the September 11 tragedy to crisis management immediately after the Severe Acute Respiratory Syndrome (SARS) outbreak. The SIA group was chosen as the point of focus because it is in this particular industry (the global airline industry) and this enormous organization that the climate of industrial relations attracts the most attention from the government, the labor movement, employers in general and the mass media. Given the significance of Singapore as an undisputable international air hub and SIA as a showcase of the country's (business) success story, good employment relations, mutual acceptance, teamwork and the avoidance of industrial conflict are not only indispensable but also must be maintained at all cost. The case provides a vivid example of the so-called "non-adversarial problem-solving approach" applied to an industry which has been adversely affected by economic slowdown, high oil prices, constant threat of terrorism, emergence of regional budget airlines and the occasional health disaster like SARS.

2.   DEVELOPMENT OF INDUSTRIAL RELATIONS IN SINGAPORE

Industrial relations in Singapore can be understood and studied using Dunlop (1958)'s well accepted framework. It is comprised of three actors (namely, the government, union and management), an environmental context, the mechanisms through which actors interact, the outcomes of the interaction (rules of the workplace) and the feedback mechanism (implications for the actors and for society). According to Wong (1987), the Singapore model is also characterized by cooperative tripartism with features that encompass (i) strong informal and formal networks of communication; (ii) the dominance of the government as policymaker; (iii) primary concern with economic growth, political stability and industrial peace; (iv) a strong centralized union movement (there is only one union federation, the National Trades Union Congress); (v) a symbiotic relationship between government and the unions; as well as (vi) a non-adversarial problem-solving approach.

Tripartism in Singapore carries the philosophy of earnestly forging and promoting co-operation and mutual understanding amongst the government, employers and unions as social partners. It implies the involvement of workers and employers (directly or indirectly) through their organizations, and the government in the formation and application of policies in the economic, social and labor fields (Chew and Chew, 1995). Examples of tripartism at work include, to name a few, the Industrial Arbitration Court (IAC), National Wages Council (NWC), and tripartite representation in statutory boards and other organizations such as the Central Provident Fund Board, Economic Development Board, Vocational and Industrial Training Board, Community Chest, and People's Association. What tripartism in Singapore means to the labor movement is that it allows unionists to participate as an equal partner in nation building. It gives unionists and employers equal stature and provides them opportunities to understand the bigger picture and the practical difficulties of running a government. The successful outcome of Singapore's tripartite processes and practices can be seen in terms of investment growth, economic competitiveness, mutual trust, industrial peace and social justice.

One of the key actors in the tripartite framework is the National Trades Union Congress (NTUC) which was set up in 1961. It is the only national centre of trade unions in

Singapore. As of 2005, there were 63 unions and 6 associations affiliated to the Congress. The role of the labor movement in Singapore is "to help the country to stay competitive, to build a strong, responsible and caring movement, foster good employment relations and actively participate in tripartism." (www.ntuc.org.sg). The unions are tasked to increase productivity, support industrial health and safety, and to enhance members' economic and social status. Hence, in addition to traditional collective bargaining and safeguarding jobs, unions also have a crucial role to play to increase the employability of workers. To carry out its broader role effectively, the NTUC maintains strong symbiotic ties with the government. Several cabinet ministers and Members of Parliament serve/ have served as union leaders at the apex of the labor movement. The NTUC has over the years set up a wide variety of cooperative enterprises (supermarkets, insurance, taxi, dental clinics, childcare, healthcare, food, home services, elderly care) and other related organizations (e.g., Singapore Labor Foundation, Ong Teng Cheong Institute of Labor Studies, Consumers Association of Singapore) to further the wellbeing of Singapore workers.

Employer organizations are generally less homogeneous than union federations. This is because employers are much more diverse in their nature of business and in their forms of representation. In some countries, employer organizations negotiate with unions at the national, local and industry levels. In Singapore, they tend to play an advisory role on employment relations (Tan, 2004). Collective bargaining is still largely determined at the firm level (Chew and Chew, 1995). Within the context of employment relations, the major employer organizations are the Singapore National Employers Federation (SNEF), the Singapore Business Federation (SBF), the Singapore Manufacturers' Federation (SMF), and the Singapore International Chamber of Commerce (SICC). They play important roles in influencing national policy-making (for example, wage reform, employment of women, extension of retirement age, productivity improvement) and ensuring the overall success of tripartism in Singapore.

Recent examples of employer and union involvement at the national level that have significant impact on the industrial relations scene include the Tripartite Panel on Retrenched Workers (1998); Manpower 21 Report (1999); Tripartite Guidelines on Non-discriminatory Job Advertisements (1999); Code of Responsible Employment

Practices (2002); Code on Industrial Relations Practice (2004); National Wages Council Wage Guidelines (yearly); Guidelines on Best Work-Life Practices (2004); Guidelines on Flexible Work Schedule (2004); Guidelines on Family Friendly Workplace Practices (2004); and Tripartite Committee on Employability of Older Workers (2005).

The role of the Singapore government as a key player in the management of employment relations are clearly reflected in the administration of employment laws by the Ministry of Manpower; its assistance in the settlement of disputes; and participation in various tripartite organizations (Tan, 2004). In general, the government's expectations of the Singapore labor movement are manifold: protect the interests of the workers at the workplace; earn the trust and respect of workers and managers; support the nation's development strategies as well as to play an active role in shaping a responsible work ethics. Its expectations on employers, on the other hand, are that management should as far as possible adopt a union acceptance strategy, build trust, provide timely information for collective bargaining purposes as well as encourage union roles in activities such as worker training / retraining, employee consultation, empowerment.

In sum, while the government has to constantly balance the needs and expectations of employees and employers, labor and management representatives must refrain from pressing for short-term gains. Concessions by labor or management should not be viewed as a loss to the other opponent, given the supreme priority of 'national interests'. This principle is especially evident in the case of resolving the disputes between Singapore International Airlines (SIA) and its unions and indeed in sectors (e.g., shipping, transportation, banking & finance, services, telecommunication) that are of critical importance to the growth and survival of Singapore. Since employment relations policies in Singapore are guided by the requirements of national development plans, the government and its agencies must play a central role in the country's social and economic development processes.

The major employment laws governing employment relations in Singapore are similar to many other countries. Examples include the Employment Act, Industrial Relations Act, Trade Unions Act, Trade Disputes Act, Workmen's Compensation Act, Retirement

Age Act, Factories Act, and the Employment of Foreign Workers Act. Collective agreements are enforceable for a specified number of years before the next negotiation. Every collective agreement has to be certified by the IAC and the IAC may refuse to certify on the ground of public interest. The IAC thus registers, certifies and interprets collective agreements. Disputes between labor and management can be resolved by referring the case for conciliation and mediation by the Ministry of Manpower, whereas arbitration is conducted by the IAC. In its decision, the IAC considers not only the interests of the unions, workers, or employers, but also that of the country/economy as a whole. The decision of the IAC is final and cannot be appealed.

The presence or absence of good industrial relations climate in any country depends on (a) its legal structure (employment laws), (b) the roles played by the government, the labor movement and employer organizations, and (c) national shared values or ideology (e.g., consensus, harmony). At the workplace level, employee relations depends heavily on management attitude and commitment, objectives of the unions, inter-relationship between supervisors and union leaders, and the employees' attitude. To foster good employer-employee relations in Singapore, numerous schemes have been tried out and put into practice over the years. These include, for example, labor management committees for joint consultation, quality control circles, grievance handling mechanisms, newsletters, suggestion schemes, safety committees, recreation committees and profit sharing (Dessler and Tan, 2006). Whether the presence of these schemes alone are sufficient to counter adverse economic impact on organizations remain to be seen. Indeed, a relatively long period of industrial peace does not imply that one can take things for granted.

3.   EMPLOYMENT RELATIONS IN TRANSITION

The economic and social development of Singapore has long been and still is heavily shaped by the role of the ruling People's Action Party (PAP) government. It is indeed an indispensable driving force in the strategic utilization of human resources in the country, accomplished through a well-established tripartite framework of government, employers and unions. To propel Singapore's human capital into a world-class workforce, a two-pronged approach has been called for (Committee on Singapore's Competitiveness, 1998). First, Singapore has to fully utilize and develop its domestic workforce. Secondly, the country must continue to attract overseas talent.

The Singapore economy grew from 2004 to 2007 at an average of 7.8% a year. Moreover, annual employment growth averaged 2.8% from 1996 to 2006 (*Business Times*, 25 July 2007). The country's ability to ride on the rise of China and India and to attract foreign investments and expand its service sector should ensure continued growth, barring unforeseen circumstances. Economists generally agree that given Singapore's small open economy, it is crucial to continue to strengthen the country's human capital, which in turn contributes to GDP growth.

While the prospects for the long-term job market in Singapore remains optimistic, labor costs (and business and residential rentals) here are comparatively much higher than elsewhere in Southeast Asia. Globalization, rapid technological innovation, company consolidation as well as outsourcing will continue to have significant impact on industrial relations climate at the workplace. What are some of the implications of these issues and challenges on workplace relations? Firstly, the employment system is fast moving into one that can no longer promise lifelong jobs with frequent career advancement or predictable pay increases. Examples can be seen not only in private enterprises, but also the civil service, the statutory boards and other government agencies. In the face of global competition, organizations will continue to restructure so as to compete and survive. They will have to segregate the revenue earners from the non-performers.

Secondly, balancing the interests of employers and their counterparts will require management and workers alike to adopt a fresh look at employee relations and employment practices. A win-win situation will not be easy to achieve given the constant need for companies to address cost containment and cost effectiveness. As highlighted by Cappelli (1999), the biggest challenge for organizations in this new employer-employee relationship will be how to motivate employees and generate commitment when employers are no longer willing to promise long-term security. Companies that maintain a harmonious relationship with their unions and adopt responsible restructuring strategies/employment practices will have a better chance to secure the morale and commitment of those who remain.

Thirdly, temporary employment will become more important over the years. Organizations are careful not to increase their permanent headcount; and contract/part-time employment provides considerable labor flexibility. Temporary employment offers a viable alternative for desperate job-seekers now that the 'iron rice bowl' has become more or less extinct. It provides them with the opportunity to constantly upgrade their skills and experiences by working in different environments. This employment trend is not restricted to those traditional secretarial and clerical staff but increasingly embrace people trained in higher level of professional field of studies, such as marketing, HR, IT, management, accountancy and engineering.

Given the above changes, the labor movement, employers, ministries and government agencies alike have crucial roles to play in facilitating the adjustment process and to better manage employer-employee relationship. For example, the tripartite partners in Singapore came up with a code of industrial relations practice in April 2004. Among the recommendations are that management and union leaders should: (a) regard each other as partners and collaborate; (b) lead by example, provide direction and take responsibility; (c) build trust, respect and bargain in good faith; (d) share information and engage in constant dialogue; (e) work together to resolve issues fairly and professionally, establish effective procedure to resolve grievances; and (f) identify common objectives, share visions and formulate win-win solutions.

Another example is the tripartite guidelines on managing excess manpower. In essence, it is recommended that (a) companies should look for alternative work within the organization (to redeploy surplus workers); (b) they should take the opportunity and upgrade the skills of their employees under the government's Skills Redevelopment Programme; (c) workers and unions should be consulted when companies decide to implement shorter work-weeks and temporary lay-offs; (d) companies should adjust the various components of their flexible wage systems with the consent of the union or workers; (e) retrenchments should be carried out responsibly and in consultation with the union; (f) early notification to the affected workers and the Ministry of Manpower would reduce anxieties and minimize the job search period; and (g) employers should help the retrenched workers to look for jobs in other companies.

Finally, given that the population growth in Singapore has slowed down and the life expectancy of the average person has increased steadily over the years, the tripartite committee on employability of older workers (set up in March 2005) recommended four key thrusts to enhance the employability of older workers. They are: expand employment opportunities of older workers; enhance cost competitiveness of older workers; raise skills and value of older workers; and shape positive perceptions towards older workers.

4.   CONCLUSION

The economic and social development of Singapore has long been and still is heavily shaped by the role of the ruling People's Action Party (PAP) government. It is indeed an indispensable driving force in the strategic utilization of human resources in the country, accomplished through a well-established tripartite framework of government, employers and unions. To propel Singapore's human capital into a world-class workforce, a two-pronged approach has been called for (Committee on Singapore's Competitiveness, 1998). First, Singapore has to fully utilize and develop its domestic workforce. Secondly, the country must continue to attract overseas talent. Globalization, rapid technological innovation, company consolidation as well as outsourcing will continue to have significant impact on industrial relations climate at the workplace. What are some of the implications of these issues and challenges on workplace relations? Firstly, the employment system is fast moving into one that can no longer promise lifelong jobs with frequent career advancement or predictable pay increases. Secondly, balancing the interests of employers and their counterparts will require management and workers alike to adopt a fresh look at employee relations and employment practices. A win-win situation will not be easy to achieve given the constant need for companies to address cost containment and cost effectiveness. Thirdly, temporary employment will become more important over the years. Organizations are careful not to increase their permanent headcount; and contract/part-time employment provides considerable labor flexibility.

Temporary employment offers a viable alternative for desperate job-seekers now that the 'iron rice bowl' has become more or less extinct. Given the above changes, the labor movement, employers, ministries and government agencies alike have crucial roles to play in facilitating the adjustment process and to better manage employer-employee relationship.

5. CASE STUDY: SINGAPORE AIRLINES

5.1 Background Information on Singapore Airlines

SIA is now an international carrier that serves over 40 countries and 90 destinations. Over the years, it has evolved into one of the leading airlines in the world and indeed one of the most respected travel brands. In 2000, SIA became a full member of the global Star Alliance and with it came the benefit of "seamless" worldwide air travel. The year 2004 witnessed the inauguration of the world's longest non-stop commercial flight to the U.S., which shortened travel time by up to four hours. In late 2007, Singapore Airlines made aviation history again when the world's largest aircraft, the Airbus A380, came into service.

SIA's success can be attributed to its management's vision and strategic choices, core competencies and internal organization, resource deployment, service excellence, innovative offerings and effective people management (Heracleous, Wirtz and Pangarkar, 2006). The company's corporate website also sheds some hint on the reasons for its continued success:

> "Singapore Airlines has grown from a regional airline into one of the world's leading carriers. We have a young, efficient fleet, an educated staff attuned to quality, and a top-ranked travel gateway, Singapore's Changi Airport, at the centre of our extensive route network. Our history, our country, and our customers all contribute to our success and our future."

Since the focus of this chapter is on employer-employee relations, it is in the area of human resource policies and practices that the following case study shall emphasize.

For a company that proudly claims to be a 'great way to fly', SIA relies heavily on state-of-the-art aircrafts, inflight facilities and dedicated employees (pilots, cabin crews, engineers, and front-line staff) to deliver sustained customer care and service excellence. It has invested strategically in the youngest, most advanced, and fuel efficient planes -- the average age of its passenger fleet is 5 years 8 month. Heracleous *et al* (2006: p.148) reported that five interrelated elements seem to underline the company's pro-human resource strategy: (a) rigorous selection and recruitment processes; (b) holistic approach to human resource development; (c) high-performance service delivery teams; (d) empowerment of front-line staff to control quality as well as (e) motivation through rewards and staff recognition.

SIA's subsidiaries include the short-haul carrier SilkAir, the package-travel company Tradewinds, SIA Engineering Company, SIA Cargo and the ground-handling provider Singapore Airport Terminal Services (SATS). Given such a huge organization, it is no wonder that more than one employee organizations represent its very diverse groups of workers. In the SIA group, there are five unions, namely the Air Line Pilots Association- Singapore (Alpa-S); Air Transport Executives Staff Union; SIA Staff Union; Singapore Airport Terminal Services Workers' Union; and SIA Engineering Company Engineers and Executives Union. As expected, the five employee organizations differ in terms of membership profile, union goals and union strategies.

Industrial conflicts in Singapore are relatively rare, compared to many other countries. SIA's relationship with its unions, especially Alpa-S, provides an interesting case study on the occasional uneasiness and tensions created by economic downturn, high oil prices, regional terrorism, and heightened competition brought about by the entry of budget airlines across Asia and the strengthening position of key competitors like British Airways, Emirates, Qantas and Cathay Pacific. When severe cost-cutting becomes a reality, how do the SIA unions respond to the management's demand for pay cut, forced no-pay leave and retrenchment? Given the drastic actions that have to be carried out, how would employees (pilots, cabin crews and ground staff) react to a sudden change in organizational climate? Can the five pillars of SIA's human resource strategy ensure the speedy recovery of staff morale and rebuilding of the company's service-oriented culture that other airlines talked about? The following section offers a glimpse of the intricacies of labor-management tension that calls for immediate and even unprecedented solutions.

5.2   Labor-Management Relations in Singapore Airlines

Amid a possible global economic slowdown in 2001, SIA went through a very difficult period immediately after the September 11th tragedy in the United States. Its half-year profit dropped a significant 88%. The most immediate action required to survive this unprecedented hard time was to cut costs, especially across-the-board pay cuts. Its CEO decided to take a pay cut of 15% and appealed for pay sacrifice. Management staff would take pay cuts of between 7 and 15 percent. In addition, CEO Cheong met with the heads of the five unions in the SIA group to convince them of the need for wage cuts of 5% for all non-managerial staff and 7% for aircraft captains. This was not an easy task, especially when it came to convincing the powerful Alpa-S which represented some 90% of SIA's 1,800 pilots. Getting the support from the pilots' association (which was not affiliated with the NTUC) was crucial. Moreover, though comprising just 12 per cent of the airline's workforce, the pilots' earnings made up 25 to 30 percent of the total wage bill. After much discussion among themselves, the five unions finally gave their in-principle support to the pay-cut proposal but they also wanted management to state at which "trigger points" the wages would be reinstated.

SIA offered staff at all levels with more than 15 years of service the opportunity to take up its golden handshake scheme. Participation in this one-time offer however would be based on "mutual consent". Furthermore, a voluntary no-pay leave scheme was extended to all its employees. They could take leave of between one month and two years. Other cost-cutting measures involved the deferral of aircraft delivery and the cutting of flight schedules. Efforts to reduce costs and an improvement in air travel meant that SIA could restore wage cuts faster. For the year ending March 2002, it made a full-year net profit of $632 million. While the amount represented a drop of 61 per cent over the previous year, the airline kept its 30-year loss-free record intact.

A long tussle between SIA and its pilots erupted in July 2002. The introduction of new and bigger SpaceBed seats created pressure on cabin space. Pilots on these long-haul flights were advised to take their meals and rest breaks in the economy-class when no business-class seats were available. The pilots thought this instruction was a breach of their 1988 collective agreement and threatened to take work-to-rule action. The Ministry of Manpower provided mediation services to both parties while the Transport Minister announced that the government would intervene if necessary to help resolve the dispute. Given that SIA had not experienced any industrial action for 22 years, the conciliation talks undertaken by the Manpower Ministry was crucial. In any case, even if that failed, the ministry could order both sides to go to the Industrial Arbitration Court for its final decision.

After six rounds of talks at the Manpower Ministry, SIA and its pilots finally ended their deadlock and a compromised agreement was reached. Simply put, one business-class seat would be set aside for pilots. If they had to sit in economy-class, the pilots would each time receive S$200 compensation. They would also be given priority to upgrade to business-class ahead of passengers and staff. If business class was full, they could even occupy an empty first-class seat. Moving ahead, it was clear that more open communication, trust building and closer working relationship between SIA senior management staff and the pilots' union officials were very much needed.

The war in Iraq, the Bali bombing and the outbreak of severe acute respiratory syndrome (SARS) in early 2003 again hit the airline industry badly. SIA had to face its worst crisis in its 56-year history. SIA had to reduce flight service by 20 per cent. Capital expenditure was frozen. Plans to buy new planes and new recruitment were cancelled. Some 206 cabin crew trainees were axed. The airline also asked its 6,600 cabin crews to take compulsory unpaid leave (seven days every two months till end-March 2004) and capacity was cut further to 29 per cent. Talks with the Air Line Pilots Association possible no-pay leave of 10 to 12 days went ahead. But the union wanted the company to first release its overseas-based pilots who were seconded to SIA. In the eyes of Alpa-S, they were not SIA employees and they were hired as "extras". These 120 pilots did not live in Singapore but were based in gateway cities like London, Los Angeles, Sydney, Perth and Brisbane. They were employed by a wholly-owned subsidiary called SIA Mauritius. They were not members of Alpa-S and were not covered by the union agreement.

Meanwhile, wage cuts of between 15% and 27.5% were planned across the whole company -- rank-and-file employees, managers, senior management and pilots. Directors would take 50% fee cut. Relations with the pilots remained tense since they were strongly opposed to pay sacrifice of 22.5% for captains and 15% for first officers. A loss of flying hours already meant a drop in flight and meal allowances. However, as pilots' wages formed the largest cost component among staff expenses and there was a surplus of pilots, SIA was ready to go for arbitration if negotiations with the pilots' union on compulsory no pay leave and wage cuts failed. The first round of talks between SIA and Alpa-S ended in a deadlock. While management indicated that they would consider a reduced requirement for the pilots to take compulsory no-pay leave, two sticky issues remained. First, how to deal with the airline's overseas-based pilots and second, whether the wage cuts would be restored.

Indeed, for both immediate and long-term survival, SIA had no choice but to remain lean and competitive. The global aviation industry had been undergoing dramatic structural changes ever since the September 11 terrorist attacks that called for cost reduction and labor flexibility. In addition to SARS, economic slowdown and the constant threat of terrorism, SIA had to face rising competition from the low-cost carriers. The Deputy Prime Minister and the Secretary-General of NTUC both reminded the airline employees that wage reform, productivity improvement and better management of costs in SIA were critical. Prime Minister Goh further added that the company could go into the "intensive care unit" if pilots did not promptly settle their differences with management and accept cost-cutting measures.

In May 2003, SIA indicated that while employee pay cuts would not be restored, it would make a one-off *ex gratia* payment (based on the company's profitability) once the business prospect improved. Furthermore, while the pay cuts were aimed for cushioning its losses due to the SARS outbreak, SIA was determined to revamp its seniority-based wage system and move towards one that is more flexible and performance linked. In line with NWC recommendations, the wages paid should reflect the value of the job. Increases in pay must tie in closely with performance of the workers and the company. Productivity would also be factored into the equation.

Alpa-S however regarded cost-cutting (for immediate relief) and overall wage reform (for long-term competitiveness of the company) were two separate issues. The pilots opposed permanent wage cuts since they felt that the proposed pay reduction of 22.5 percent for captains and 15 percent for first officers were too severe when coupled with the imposition of no-pay leave. They were also unhappy with the need for retrenchment of some pilots even after wage cuts and compulsory unpaid leave were carried out. SIA, in addition, rejected the Alpa-S's counter-proposal that captains take 12% and first officers 7% pay cuts and that the profit threshold for wage restoration be lowered from S$700 million to S$350 million. The second round of talks failed and SIA called in the Ministry of Manpower to mediate. Even then, the gap between the pilots and management remained far too wide for successful conciliation.

After two attempts of mediation failed, SIA decided on 12 June 2003 to send its wage dispute to the Industrial Arbitration Court (IAC) for settlement. The arbitrator's ruling would be final and legally binding. Meanwhile, the SIA group was considering a major retrenchment exercise involving both ground staff and operating crew. This would be the first retrenchment in 20 years. Facing its first-ever quarterly loss and losing S$6 million a day, it had no choice but to retrench 414 ground staff (office and engineering staff, airport workers) or about 1.5 percent of the 30,000 employees in the SIA group, which included regional carrier SilkAir. While this represented the biggest number of job cuts in the flagship carrier's 31-year history, the figure was significantly lower than many had expected. In addition to retrenchment, 145 staff had taken up a voluntary early retirement package (for selected employees with at least 25 years of service). Pilots and cabin crews were not affected at this stage but it was understood that cutbacks in pilots and cabin crews would follow and be considered separately.

To avoid open court confrontation and realizing the urgent need to move on, in-principle agreement on the wage cuts dispute between the Airline Pilots Association and SIA was reached in late June. The pilots agreed to take pay cuts of 16.5 per cent for captains and 11 per cent for first officers. The cuts would be effective till 31 March

2004 by which time a new collective agreement would be hammered out. SIA would also implement no-paid leave of up to two days every month for all pilots for the same period, down from up to six days that the airline initially demanded.

To make up for the wage reductions, SIA agreed to a lump-sum financial compensation plan. If the after tax group profit reached S$200 million, 25% of the wage cuts would be restored. 50%, 75% and 100% of the wage cuts would be restored when the figures hit S$300, S$400 and S$500 millions respectively. These lump sum payments should give the airline a more flexible pay structure. For example, more of the employees' pay could be converted from fixed wages to a variable component of the overall reward package.

Furthermore, a "sweetener" in the form of an additional 15% on top of the full restoration would be given out should SIA made S$600 million after tax group profit. It was noted that SIA's newly appointed chief executive officer was personally involved in the final days of the negotiations and approved the "sweetener". This settlement was timely since it cleared the way for the company and the pilots to move on and at the same time provided a middle ground example for other SIA unions to follow.

6. QUESTIONS FOR DISCUSSION

1. Compare and contrast the Singapore system of industrial relations with that of your country's. What are the differences and similarities? In your view, what are the strengths and weaknesses of each system? Can the Singapore model be applied to your country?

2. With respect to the SIA case, what have you learnt from the case study? Comment on the appropriateness of actions taken by the management and the unions immediately after the SARS epidemic. With the benefits of hindsight, what other actions could have been taken by management, the unions and the government?

3.   (for class debate)

"Tripartism in many developing countries is just a public relations gimmick where leaders of the three actors (parties) put on a show for foreign investors. Relations at the workplace are still sullen and industrial peace is maintained only by the strong arm of the government because managers and workers expectations on how the economic pie should be shared are still miles apart." Do you agree or disagree with the statement? Why?

ENDNOTES

The SIA case as presented in this chapter serves only as a basis for classroom discussion rather than to illustrate effective or ineffective handling of an administration or business situation. The information collected for the writing up of this chapter are based on secondary sources, for example, newspapers, magazines, reports, books and the Internet.

SOME USEFUL WEB ADDRESSES

Industrial Arbitration Court (www.iac.gov.sg)

Ministry of Manpower (www.mom.gov.sg)

National Trades Union Congress (www.ntuc.org.sg)

Singapore Airlines (www.singaporeair.com)

Singapore Business Federation (www.sbf.org.sg)

Singapore Human Resources Institute (www.shri.org.sg)

Singapore National Employers Federation

Chapter 7

GLOBALIZATION AND INDUSTRIAL RELATIONS
IN THAILAND

Sununta Siengthai

1. INTRODUCTION

Thailand has experienced drastic economic changes since July 1997 when it was severely affected by the Asian financial crisis. On reflection, the country had experienced the ups and downs in its economic development process in the last three decades. Whether Thailand will learn from this and develop some system that would allow some economic shock absorbance, particularly now that it is a player in the global market, is still to be seen. The country had experienced peak average economic growth rates about 6-8% during the decade of 1987-1997 before the economy plunged in mid-1997. During those boom years, the manufacturing sector emerged as a leading sector contributing to the economic growth both in terms of value added and export earnings. It was a totally different direction when compared to the earlier decade of 1977-1987. At the time, the source of growth stemmed mainly from domestic demand and the engine of growth was primarily from import substitution. Now, in the decade of 1997-2007, the country has become more affected by the globalization process. This chapter however, focuses on the changes Thailand experienced immediately after the financial crisis and its economic adjustment processes in which industrial relations have been a part. It also provides some case studies on industrial relations in the auto-related industry that describes how cooperative labor-management relations has been able to enable firm's survival and growth.

2.   THE THAI ECONOMY AFTER THE FINANCIAL CRISIS

In 1998, the Thai economy was deeply in recession, contracting by 8.5 per cent. Private sector investment dropped sharply due to the liquidity crunch in the first half of the year. Excess production capacity in many industries, reduced private sector consumption caused by worker layoffs and price increases also played key roles in the recession (Bangkok Bank Annual Report, 1999). Public sector expenditure, especially investment outlay, also dropped due to restrictive monetary and fiscal measures implemented in line with the IMF-supported programs [1]. International trade became sluggish as the crisis spread throughout the world. Exports, in U.S. dollar terms, dropped at the beginning of 1997. Imports also fell sharply, in line with declining domestic demand, resulting in trade and current account surpluses. Meanwhile, inflation averaged 8.1 per cent, which was considered low for an economy undergoing adjustment.

The government policy during the first half of 1998 focused on economic stability (Behrman et al., 2000). This was reasonably successful, resulting in a stable baht (currency), a reasonable rate of inflation and greater international reserves. However, it also resulted in a more severe liquidity crunch and a sharp rise in non-performing loans (NPLs) in the banking system which severely damaged the real economic sectors. A large number of businesses had to terminate operations due to lack of working capital and high interest rates. Statistics available indicate that in 1997, the number of establishments that had to layoff employees increased to 861 compared to 77 establishments in 1996 The number of employees affected jumped from 5,015 persons to a total of 41,927 persons (see Table 7.1). In 1998, the number of employees laid off increased to 51,960 persons and most of these people, i.e., 41,065 persons were from the production activities. In 1999, the number of the employees laid off had decreased to 20,886 which seemed to suggest that many firms had been able to adjust their operations and that the economy started to pick up. Thus, the adjustment seemed to take a few years of economic restructuring. This at least shows the capacity of the country to gain resiliency in a sufficiently short period of time. From the available statistics, the three industries, namely, auto-related industries experienced the highest number of employees laidoff (see Table 7.2) followed by the garment industry as the second highest. Although the total number of laid-off employees was not the largest number, in terms of the organizations affected, the banking, finance and insurance sector experienced the largest number of organizations that had to lay off their employees. It is noted that in the following year (1999), they remained the highest number of organizations affected while in the other two sectors, namely auto-related and garment sectors, the numbers of laid-off employees decreased. In 1999, 802 enterprises had to terminate employment of their employees due to either the following reasons: production reduction (which is the largest number), temporary closure, closure and other unspecified reasons (Table 7.3). From 2000 – 2006, termination of employment cases were significantly reduced. However, it is evident that the economy contracted significantly during this decade of 1997-2007.

Table 7.1 Number of Employees Laid-Off, Whole Kingdom, 1994-1999

Year	No. of Establishments	Total	Production	Service	Administration
1994	177	5,970	5,448	374	148
1995	74	6,936	6,658	236	42
1996	77	5,015	4,862	81	72
1997	861	41,927	30,905	9,596	1,426
1998	1,076	51,960	41,065	7,040	3,855
1999	802	20,886	17,023	2,047	1,816

Source: Labor Studies and Planning Division

Table 7.2 Number of Employees Laid-Off by Industry

Industry	No. of Establishments		No. of Employees	
	1998	1999[a]	1998	1999 [a]
Garment	51	8	8,812	236
Banking, Finance and Insurance	329	49	5,231	302
Auto parts, Assembly, Repair and Equipment 143	24	9,355	284	

Source: Social Security Bureau (establishment of 10 persons and over)
Department of Social Welfare and Labor Protection (establishment of 1-9 persons)
[a] First quarter data (Jan. – April, 1999)

Table 7.3 Termination of Employment in the Whole Kingdom by Cause, 1998 - 2006

Year	No. of Enterprises	No. of Employees	Causes			
			Pdn. Reduction	Temp. Closure	Closure	Others
1998	1,076	51,960	20,205	2,659	17,458	11,638
1999	802	20,886	8,610	1,008	4,891	6,377
2000	372	15,646	3,004	1,504	7,230	3,908
2001	234	18,675	7,411	855	6,930	3,479
2002	207	6,036	1,922	31	3,608	475
2003	58	2,337	1,452	49	378	458
2004	23	948	133	37	753	25
2005	98	1,622	525	-	769	328
2006	38	519	92	-	239	188

Source: Year Book of Labor Protection and Welfare Statistics, 2002

In the following year (1998), the government adopted more relaxed fiscal and monetary measures to help increase liquidity. These included an increased budgetary deficit to allow greater government spending, especially on improving infrastructure, creating jobs in rural areas and strengthening economic communities. Attempts were made to stimulate private sector demand by encouraging commercial banks and financial institutions to extend more trade and housing credits. Meanwhile, the Bank of Thailand (BOT) was successful in pushing down interest rates, resulting in ample liquidity in the money market. Interest rates dropped sharply and rapidly in the last quarter of 1998.

To strengthen the financial system and build investor confidence, the authorities implemented a number of measures to address the problem of NPLs. The rapid rise in NPLs discouraged new bank lending needed for economic recovery. These measures included:

- Promotion of debt restructuring and debt settlements
- Amendment of laws and taxes to facilitate debt restructuring
- Financial sector rehabilitation package to help banks recapitalize

These measures were designed to enable financial institutions to function more efficiently and help other economic sectors recover. However, the economic and financial crisis resulted in unprecedented damage to the commercial banking sector. In addition to the effects of the crisis, banks were required to comply with new rules and regulations, enforcing stricter standards on debt classification, income recognition and loan loss reserves. As a consequence, the whole commercial banking system suffered huge losses in 1998.

Definitely, the public sector was the main stimulator of the economic growth during this period of financial crisis, as it implemented policies regarding savings and consumption (for example, the reduction in savings interest rates and the issuing of the government bonds). The structural readjustment of the manufacturing sector contributed to the economic stability of the country in the following years.

However, with all these attempts for economic recovery and restructuring, it has been observed by the ILO (2000):

> "Although statistics indicate that Thailand is in an intermediate position between high and low technology exports, a closer look at the data shows that the rise in technology-intensive production often only involves minor local contributions and only simple assembly practices required by foreign companies. Thailand has been using a broad range of imported technology rather than developing its own capacity to design and adapt. A number of indicators are a source of concern. Spending on research and development is low. One indicator of the application of technology is the number of International Organization for Standardization (ISO) certificates, and Thailand has relatively few. This suggests that despite its impressive output performance before the economic crisis, Thailand has demonstrated a serious weakness in terms of its technology infrastructure." (ILO, 2000:6).

The statistics available suggest that Thailand has not been attracting investors who use advanced technology and require an educated workforce, but is still attempting to compete with low-wage economies for labor-intensive production. Thus, this seems another urgent agenda for Thailand's development for sustainability in the decades to come.

3.   INDUSTRIAL RELATIONS IN THE 1990s

3.1   Structure of the Social Partners

Workers' Organizations in Thailand

According to the Labor Relations Act of 1975, workers can organize as a trade union if they have no less than 10 members. These workers must be employed in the same undertaking no matter how many employers they have; or they may be employed in different undertakings but have the same employer. The worker organizers must be of legal age and be Thai nationals. Trade unions can be organized as in-house unions or on an industry-wide basis. They can organize on a nation-wide basis. However, there are two important restrictions: (a) the Registrar has the power to register and dissolve unions and (b) outsiders cannot participate in or become leaders of trade unions. Only employees of a given undertaking can apply for registration and be elected as members of the administrative committee of the union. In practice, this means that unions are generally organized as in-house unions, i.e., as unions with membership restricted to employees in the same firm. In Thailand, labor unions can be organized at two levels of employment: lower level and supervisory level employees. The members of the lower level employee unions must be those who do not have the authority to appraise an employee's performance. The supervisory level unions draw their members from the upper level. However, there were only a few of them and these were mainly in the large enterprises.

The structure of the workers' organization in Thailand (herein means the lower level of unions) can be categorized into 3 levels as follows:

1.   *General labor unions* which are labor unions as defined in the Labor Relations Act 1975. Of most of the Thai labor unions, 90 per cent are in-house or enterprise unions. There are only very few industrial unions in the metal and textile

industries. Since most unions are enterprise-based, their internal structure is relatively simple. The rank-and-file elects a committee of representatives which in turn elects an executive. In fact, most unions are faced with the problem of inappropriate organizational structure. Worker organizations are not generally well accepted by their employers. The formation of their organization is therefore a secretive activity. It is consequently difficult for those organizations to be designed appropriately according to the size of membership and size of the firm itself.

2. *Middle-level union organizations.* There are three categories under this level. There are federations of industrial unions, labor union groups (formed by at least two labor unions), and confederations of labor unions. The Labor Relations Act 1975 states that the objectives of the federation of labor unions are to promote good relations among labor unions and workers and dissemination of knowledge about labor to the public.

3. *National centers.* These are the highest level of labor union organizations formed by 15 unions. The Labor Relations Act 1975 defines the objectives of the national center of labor unions to be the education of workers and promotion of good labor relations.

According to the Labor Relations Act 1975, only labor unions or the employees themselves can submit demands to the employer to amend agreements relating to conditions of employment. The labor federations or congress may only serve as advisors at the negotiation. If the labor union or employees and the employer are able to agree on the demands submitted, the agreement has to be written down and signed by representatives of both parties. If there is no negotiation within 3 days from the date the demand is received, or if no agreement can be reached for whatever reason, a labor dispute shall be regarded as having occurred. The labor union or the employees who presented the demand have to notify the conciliation officer in writing within twenty-four hours. The conciliation officer will proceed to effect a settlement between the two parties within five days from the date the conciliation officer is notified. If settlement cannot be reached within the period, the dispute will be regarded as an unsettled labor dispute. In such a case the employees or the labor union and employer may agree to appoint a labor dispute arbitrator. Otherwise, the employer may effect a lock-out or the labor union may go out on strike.

However, if the unsettled dispute occurs in an essential undertaking such as railways, port, telephone or telecommunications, electricity, water works, in the production or refinery of oil, fuel, or in a hospital or medical clinic, the conciliation officers have to refer the dispute to the Labor Relations Committee for consideration. The Committee will notify both parties within thirty days from the date notice of the labor dispute is received. Parties may appeal against the Committee's decision to the Minister of the Interior (see the Labor Relations Act 1975) within seven days from the date the decision is received. The Minister shall consider the appeal and notify both parties of this decision within ten days from the date the appeal is received. When there is an unsettled labor dispute in any undertaking other than in an essential one, the Minister may, if he considers it will affect the economy or public order, direct the matter to be referred to the Labor Relations Committee. The Committee shall decide the matter within thirty days from the date the order is received and such decision will be final. If martial law or a state of emergency is declared, or if the country is facing a serious economic crisis, the Minister shall specify in the Government Gazette that disputes occurring in any locality or in any undertaking which cannot be settled by negotiation or conciliation, shall be decided by any group of persons as the Ministry may determine or appoint.

Employer Organizations in Thailand

The Labor Relations Act 1975 defines the right to organize for employers as follows:

1. An employers' organization at the lower level is a legal entity. Organizations at this level have, as their objectives, the protection and achievement of better terms and conditions of employment, and the promotion of good labor-management relations. Those who organize must be of legal age and of Thai nationality. There also must be at least three persons as organizers.

2. Federation of Employers. According to the LRA 1975, this is a middle-level organization which is composed of at least two employers' organizations in the

same undertaking. Its objectives are to promote good relations among employers and to protect the interests of the employers' organizations and of employers.

3. Council of Employers. This is the highest level of employer organization. The LRA 1975 defines the right of at least 15 employers' organizations or federations to organize or form a council. The main purpose of a council is to promote education and labor relations. Most of the activities of the Councils of Employers have been focused on providing assistance to alleviate social problems and problems in member employers' organizations. These have been in terms of providing training and educational programs on labor relations and labor and management education, and various seminars both in and outside the country.

3.2   Industrial Relations: Before and After 1997

Thailand's pattern of economic development had been influenced and determined by the various military-dominated regimes which had governed Thailand in the last half of the 20th century. The use of cheap, largely uneducated labor as a key element of comparative advantage, particularly for inward investors, had necessitated the promotion and maintenance of an unorganized work force, weak trade unions and dominant employer authority. The lack of "class consciousness" among workers, resulting from reliance on rural labor, and the centrality of Buddhism to the Thai culture, the practices of 'middle-path', that is, no advocation for extremism, has contributed to this industrial relations framework.

Thailand is still far from achieving an effective industrial relations system whereby the two partners are considered equal. The reasons include the lack of effective conflict resolution mechanisms which provide satisfaction to both employers and employees. Often, many manifested conflicts at the enterprise level have extended outside and involved more people and industrial productivity loss than it should have been. Other than this, the employees' organizations themselves still have many problems to be solved (Prasert, 1997)

Previous to 1975, workers associations were formed. However, trade unions in Thailand have only been legal since 1975, and strikes legal since 1981. The trade union movement has been weak, both in coverage and in workplace industrial relations. One explanation may be that most unions are recognized at the enterprise level. Although during the financial crisis period, i.e., during 1997 – 1999, both the number of union organizations and employer organizations decreased, union membership experienced some sharp rise again during 2004 – 2006 and again declined significantly in 2007 (See Tables 7.4, 7.5, and 7.6) There are very few industrial unions but they seem to have increased in number. Hence, it could be said that the threat effect of the union is significant. This leads to the improvement of management practices and styles as well as terms and conditions of employment, in firms locating in the same neighborhood and the possibility of effective union avoidance strategies.

In 1991, there were in Thailand 693 unions of which 36 were public enterprise associations (see Table 7.5). However, in 1997, the number of unions had increased to 1,013 of which 44 were public enterprise associations. Even though the number suggests a substantial increase from 1991, a closer look at the statistics shows that this number in fact decreased from the earlier year (1996), when the number was 1,060. This could be partly explained by the fact that most of the unions are enterprise unions. Thus, when the enterprise closed down, the company union was therefore legally dissolved as well. However, in the following years, the number of union organizations increased again. In terms of the higher level of labor organization structure, the number of labor federations and labor union councils are rather stable (see also Table 7.5).

The low level of union density in the private sector is a reflection of the difficulties faced by unions. Business firms have used various tactics to undermine strikes which were regarded by the organized workers as the only powerful industrial weapon to bargain with their employers for better terms and conditions of employment. These include tactics which are illegal or exploit "legal loopholes" to maintain non-union status, temporary company shutdown, mass terminations, sacking of union leaders and use of temporary workers.

Table 7.4 Union Organizations and Union Membership, 1972-2007

Year	Public Enterprise	Private sector (persons)	Union Membership
1972	2	9	n.a.
1973	4	22	n.a.
1974	11	45	n.a.
1975	28	111	50,000
1976	49	184	70,483
1977	47	164	n.a.
1978	54	174	95,951
1979	62	206	114,349
1980	70	255	150,193
1981	79	334	153,960
1982	84	376	214,636
1983	91	414	221,739
1984	93	430	212,343
1985	97	436	214,359
1986	107	469	241,709
1987	116	514	272,608
1988	118	562	295,901
1989	123	593	309,041
1990	130	713	336,061
1991*	36	657	169,424
1992	37	749	190,142
1993	41	839	231,480
1994	43	888	242,730
1995	44	971	261,348
1996	43	1015	280,963
1997	45	968	270,276
1998	45	999	265,982
1999	44	1056	n.a.
2000	44	1084	n.a
2001	45	1123	n.a.
2002	44	1160	n.a.
2003	46	1340	n.a.
2004	46	1239	497,999
2005	45	1369	494,508
2006	45	1313	566,100
2007	44	1243	501,880

* After the public sector enterprise unions were disbanded by law, they set up their organizations as 'Associations' instead.

Source: Dept. of Labor Protection and Welfare, Ministry of Labor Protection and Social Welfare

Table 7.5 Number of Labor Organizations by Type in the Whole Kingdom, 1991-2007

Year / Type	Labor Organization			
	Public Enterprise	Private	Federation	Council
1991	36	657	17	7
1992	37	749	19	7
1993	41	839	19	8
1994	43	888	19	8
1995	44	971	18	8
1996	43	1016	18	8
1997	45	968	18	8
1998	44	999	18	9
1999	45	1056	18	9
2000	44	1084	19	9
2001	45	1123	19	9
2002	44	1160	19	9
2003	46	1239	21	9
2004	46	1340	21	10
2005	45	1369	18	10
2006	45	1313	16	11
2007	44	1243	16	12

Source: Labor Studies and Planning Division, Dept. of Labor Protection and Welfare

With respect to the employers, the number of employer organizations has also increased substantially. For example, it increased from 19 in 1991 to 180 organizations in 1999 (see Table 7.6). Employer association federations has increased to three in 1999 while that of the employer councils increased from one in1991 to ten in 1999. This suggests more interest of employers to act as a group rather than individually, as they used to. To a certain extent, it may be attributed to the fact that many industries in the manufacturing sector have been exposed to the global market. Therefore, it has led to the necessity to cooperate under the competition.

Table 7.6 Number of Employers' Organizations by Type, Whole Kingdom, 1991 – 2007

Year/Type	Employers Associations	Employers Federation	Employer Councils
1991	19	1	1
1992	20	1	1
1993	51	1	1
1994	108	2	3
1995	128	2	5
1996	140	2	5
1997	143	2	6
1998	151	3	9
1999	180	3	10
2000	226	3	10
2001	256	3	11
2002	282	3	11
2003	342	3	11
2004	377	3	11
2005	420	3	12
2006	413	3	12
2007	411	3	12

Source: Labor Relations Bureau, Dept. of Labor Protection and Welfare

In term of grievances, Table 7.7 Suggests that the number of grievances was high in early 1980s and declined during 1988-1990. However, the occurrences of grievances fluctuated during 1991-2007. There was an increasing trend in the early 1990s up to 1998, e.g. it increased from 3,697 in 1991 to 9,081 in 1998. Then, the numbers decreased gradually to 2002 (i.e., 4,615) and started to increased significantly from 2003 to 2007 (i.e., from 6,421 to 8,785). For these grievances, the number of workers involved also increased substantially particularly in 1997 when it was up to 75,815 persons. This may be attributed to the fact that there were cases of plant shut-downs and relocations of production bases to other countries. Workers were laid off particularly those in textile industry and those in the sport shoes industries. When looking at the grievances received by major issues (Table 7.8), it is found that most of the grievances were about wages and dismissal pay respectively. The available statistics on labor disputes suggest the similar trend to that of grievances (Table 7.9). For strikes, which is one of the most effective industrial actions of workers to bargain with employers, the number drastically declined from thousands (i.e., 5,577) in 1973, which was before trade unions gained their legal status, to only seven in 1977. The number of strikes had maintained at one-digit up until 1997. When the financial crisis took place, this number increased to 22 in 1997 and significantly declined from 1998, although suggesting significant involvement of workers and number of workdays lost. On the part of the employers, the number of lockouts has also increased dramatically. Needless to say, the industrial relations scenario will be much intensified with the country's economic and social restructuring process. In the past decades, Thai unions have been faced with various obstacles both in terms of employer recognition and their own union administration management. More than 90 per cent of the unions are faced with financial difficulties, inter-union rivalry, lack of training for union members and cooperation from members, union leader conflicts, intervention into union activities, etc. Lack of financial resources, in particular, means that unions are reliant on either larger unions, federations, councils or outside organizations for assistance. Thus, unions cannot be independent in their functioning to provide services for their members. In spite of all these weaknesses, there are some factors that contribute to the strengths of the unions. These include the higher education of new generation union leaders, the oligopolistic nature of the enterprises (especially the public enterprises), interests of the management, and the political consciousness of the union members.

The activities of employers' organizations, on the other hand, have been undertaken by the council of employers which is the highest level organization. Most of the activities have been focused on providing assistance to alleviate social problems and member employers' organizations. These have included providing training and educational programs on labor relations, labor and management education, and various seminars both inside and outside of the country.

Table 7.7 Number of Grievances Received and Workers Involved in Thailand, 1980 - 2007

Year	Grievance Received (Number)	Workers Involved (Number)
1980	4,697	22,527
1981	3,933	15,579
1982	4,361	19,680
1983	3,858	20,512
1984	3,932	22,493
1985	3,749	23,773
1986	3,645	25,448
1987	3,121	16,817
1988	2,772	15,451
1989	2,458	14,361
1990	2,610	16,190
1991	3,697	25,472
1992	3,975	30,394
1993	5,002	40,678
1994	6,145	47,904
1995	6,054	53,225
1996	6,488	56,787
1997	8,252	75,815
1998	9,081	64,707
1999	7,708	40,555
2000	7,070	31,398
2001	6,976	28,622
2002	4,615	13,516
2003	6,421	19,891
2004	8,272	22,971
2005	9,228	27,083
2006	8,473	21,685
2007	8,785	33,201

Source: Yearbook of Labor Statistics, Various issues, Dept. of Labor Protection and Welfare, Ministry of Labor and Social Welfare

Table 7.8 Number of Grievances Received by Major Issues and Workers Involved in the Whole Kingdom, 1994-2007

Issues	Grievances Received													
	1994	1995	1996	1997	1998	1999	2000	2001	2002	2003	2004	2005	2006	2007
Total	6,145	6,054	6,488	8,252	9,081	7,708	7,070	6,976	4,615	6,421	8,272	9,228	8,473	8,785
Severance Pay	1,409	3,711	1,317	1,750	2,322	1,613	1,282	1,142	539	737	840	759	712	1,297
Wages	3,659	3,711	4,053	5,178	5,093	3,535	3,085	3,024	1,895	2,344	2,849	3,070	2,766	3,339
Overtime Pay	22	23	31	29	44	33	40	39	17	20	36	38	31	505
Damage Deposit	117	84	103	23	169	307	322	290	294	128	429	450	395	899
Payment for Work Done on Holidays	44	31	34	15	15	18	13	23	13	14	23	37	25	224
O.T. Pay on Holidays	-	-	-	-	-	-	-	-	5	2	5	7	4	76
Savings Fund	30	35	34	106	49	41	44	36	-	-	-	-	-	-
Minimum Wage	101	85	47	25	24	12	16	11	-	-	-	-	-	-
Two or More Issues Combined	763	770	853	1,075	1,345	1,944	2,057	2,188	1,627	2,633	3,637	4,328	4,083	863

Table 7.9 Number of Labor Disputes, Strikes and Lockouts by Industry in the Whole Kingdom, 1997-2007

Year	Labor Disputes (times)	Employee Involved	Strikes			Lockouts		
			(times)	Employee Involved	Mandays Lost	(times)	Employee Involved	Mandays Lost
1997	187	56,603	22	8,950	117,196	17	7,832	102,738
1998	121	35,897	4	1,209	161,856	4	935	84,688
1999	183	74,788	3	909	8,422	13	6,958	134,491
2000	140	50,768	3	2,165	192,845	10	3,804	57,403
2001	154	47,759	4	449	4,527	1	77	1,540
2002	110	41,717	4	1,369	18,691	2	511	5,211
2003	97	43,801	1	1,700	5,100	4	1,876	18,951
2004	123	76,210	1	93	372	1	100	100
2005	87	29,111	3	348	2,112	6	803	43,745
2006	80	32,807	2	900	24,000	0	0	0
2007	100	48,069	2	183	1,323	3	437	10,278

Source: Yearbook of Labor Protection and Welfare Statistics, 1997-2007, Department of Labor Protection and Welfare, Ministry of Labor.

Until now, in the Thai context, collective bargaining has not been as an ideal process of decision-making between employer and employees of the enterprise in question. Most of the conflicts are solved only when employees resort to the power structure (namely, political entities or military groups) which acts as a third party to intervene and thus make their demands to the employers materialize. Here again, the concept of patron-client is exhibited. Most of the workers' organizations have to demonstrate or publicize the conflict in order to gain support from the public and to put pressure on employers to concede to their demands. For most of the employees who are not members of the unions, when they are not satisfied with their jobs or are unfairly treated, often they choose to quit rather than bargain with the employers. This is more evident when the economy is experiencing an economic boom. In fact, it can be one reason explaining why there have not been many strikes in recent years. High quit rates have reduced the competitiveness of such firms. Therefore, it is proposed that bipartism be resorted to as a means to enhance productivity and well-being of the parties involved at the workplace level. In the Thai context in which confrontation is usually avoided, joint consultation can be another mechanism to produce the desired outcomes. Though some labor leaders seem to prefer employees' committees or workers councils to joint consultation committees (JCCs), in principle they have no objection to the establishment of JCCs. This is on the condition that the labor unions are first consulted before JCCs are established and that the employee members are either nominated by labor unions (where unions exist) or elected by the employees (where it is non-unionized). The bipartite nature of their composition has been attributed as one of the main reasons for the acceptance of JCCs by employers.

4. CONCLUSION

Starting in 2007, Thailand experienced a lot of political instability and social turmoil in the southern provinces. In addition to this, the U.S. which is Thailand's main export market experienced the financial crisis. As a consequence, Thailand's economic growth is expected to be significantly affected from this economic recession in the U.S. market. Many firms had to layoff workers and many labor protests were displayed and publicized. The government agencies had to intervene to resolve the conflicts and helped relieved the workers' plights.

In effect, the cycle of rapid economic growth for Thailand as a developing country has been rather short of about 10 years of import substitution and almost ten years of export and in the next decade, it is likely that the country should focus more on developing its domestic and neighboring countries' market development such as those in the Southeast Asian nations (known as ASEAN) and strengthen its own societal order to gain sustainable development while expanding to some extent to other potential markets. In addition, the country should develop more capability and better technological infrastructure to bid for outsourcing projects in certain manufacturing and services industries from more advanced economies. This should enhance the employment growth and strength of industrial relations system.

5.   CASE STUDIES

5.1   Toyota Motor Thailand Co. Ltd.

Toyota Motor Thailand Co. Ltd was established in Thailand in 1962 having Mr. Yoshiaki Muramatsu as its President in 1997. It had as its registered capital 4,250 million baht.

Workers' Organization

The Toyota Co. Union was established on November 12, 1981. The factors leading to the establishment of the union include the dissatisfaction with the management policies. There was the need to change the then terms and conditions of employment and to stimulate for the management system to improve wages and salary, welfare, etc. At that time, the Toyota Co. Ltd. was not the leading company in terms of wages and salaries compared to other firms in the same neighborhood, such as N.S. Steel, Signetics, etc., which are located in Samutprakarn Province. There were then also more Japanese expatriates. Many of them were at the middle-level management. Therefore, there was some misunderstanding between the Thai workers and the Japanese expatriates. Part of it was due to the inability to communicate with each other and the cultural differences which reflected in the work value orientations. However, later most of the Japanese expatriates were reduced as the Thai counterparts became competent to take up the responsibilities in the view of the Toyota Co. headquarter in Japan.

The organization of the union was not well-received by management. Yet, management recognized this legal entity. In the early stage of organizing, there were not so many members. After the registration of the union organization, the membership campaign was made among the workers. In 1999, right after the financial crisis and when the case study was prepared, the union members are about 70 per cent of the company's total work force of 4,000 persons.

Since its establishment, there have been some labor disputes. During 1983-1984, a strike was held. However, the duration was short. Employees gathered in front of the office in Bangkok by taking the bus from Samutprakarn Province where the plant was located. It was a peaceful strike, no case of violence occurred during the strike period.

The demands submitted by the union had mostly been dealt with wages and salaries, as well as bonuses.

Labor-Management Relations after the Financial Crisis

In 1996, before the financial crisis took place and due to the management's proactive strategy, a declaration between management and the union was made. In the Declaration, an agreement for non-strike period was made. This was witnessed by many people, including those representatives from the then Ministry of Labor Protection and Social Welfare. In return the management agreed to provide flexibility to the union's rank-and-file to work full-time for the union. For example, the president and the secretary of the union could work full-time for the organization and were provided with office space in the company compound. The company offered the union's office car at the lowest price. In addition to this, the company also had been organizing an overseas visit to other company branches, such as in Japan, the U.S. and other countries. This allowed the union representatives (its rank and file members) to learn and share their ideas of union administration with other unions in the company's branches. In the same tours, the management representatives, such as the human resources managers also joined the group. Thus, in a way, a better rapport and relationship between the management and union was built. In general, information sharing has been done more frequent than it had been before the union was organized. This was hoped to create a better understanding of the company's and the workers' situations. Union has been consulted and informed in case that there is a new car models to be produced, as it would affect the work organization in the workplace.

When the financial crisis started, the company asked for agreement from the union not to pay for some welfare items, and other trip provisions, etc. There was a discussion on bonuses which the company had negotiated to pay for two months. In general, the company had undertaken many measures to reduce costs with cooperation from workers and the union as the main channel of communication. There was no layoff as the company advocated its life-time employment policy. Job rotation had been used. In addition, the company contacted the Association of Overseas Technical Scholarship to send some employees to training programs in Japan. This was hoped to build the company's competencies during the recession to cope with the economic recovery in the future.

In addition to the company union, the company also has a workers' council of which its members are the same as that of the union. This is because the majority of the company's workers (over 70 %) are union members. However, there are certain issues that cannot be discussed in the workers' council except through collective bargaining represented by the union as indicated by law.

The relationship between management and labor was satisfactory in the 1990s. One of the reasons was due to the fact that both sides had good knowledge of labor laws and observed the rules and regulations set up in the workplace together very well. The strengths of the union-management relationship at the Toyota (Thailand) Co. Ltd. is that the union has more experience and has somewhat become mature. However, there was still some weaknesses in the labor relations process as some of the union' s rank-and-file who were elected by focusing more on self-interest issues rather the majority's interest. One observation is that the employees at the Toyota (Thailand) Co. Ltd. are also well educated and thus tend to be rational. In the negotiation, reasoning is used more than emotion. So, it contributes to the understanding and peaceful relationship. In addition, the employees are skilled which make them highly valued to the firm. Their bargaining power is therefore comparatively higher than for other types of workers.

5.2   The ATP Industry Co. Ltd.

Company Profile

The ATP Industry Co. Ltd. is a subsidiary firm of Yontrakij Co., which is a family business. In 1999, the Company had over 5,000 employees in all its subsidiaries. There was no accounting department in all subsidiaries of Yontrakij Co. Everything was reported to the headquarter in the city. The ATP Industry Co. Ltd. (hereafter ATP) produced auto parts, such as exhaust pipes, jigs, electric wires, wheel caps and car windows for European cars. Yontrakij Co. Ltd. had received the contracts to produce these parts and components as well as assemble cars for Peugeot 505, Citroen, BMW and other makes such as Lancia. The ATP as a subsidiary gets their job orders from the

Yontrakij Co. From 1992, ATP started to accept subcontracting jobs but eventually stopped in 1998.

Company's Employee Profile

ATP had 377 employees on its payroll in 1999. Most of the employees hired were skilled although the minimum requirement was four years of formal schooling. This is simply the ability to read and write that is required of operational employees. This group of four to ten years of education (Grade 4 – *'Maw Saam'*) composed the largest group of employees of the company at the time. Most of the employees were from rural areas. There were some who had obtained their bachelor's degree. In addition, there were over ten engineers in the plant. The personnel manager himself was an architect. In the engineering division, some vocational and technical trained people were hired. In the assembly line, the level of education of workers was generally lower. In the engineering division, the wages were better than the production division. This company did not have a mandatory retirement age. As long as employees could work, they could continue their jobs. Everyone was treated more like family members.

Workers' Organization

The union was organized in 1983 by Mr. Jamras Chailangkar. At the time of organizing, there were only 10 members as required, by the Labor Relations Act, 1975. When the union was registered, the campaign for membership started. The union's structure has its rank and file members as required by the law.

The reasons leading to the organization of the union was that during that time, there were problems about terms and conditions of employment. The company often changed its employment policies. In the 1983, the company hired more employees but it reduced the fringe benefits earlier provided to workers. For example, workers used to have Saturdays and Sundays off, then, it changed its policy to have only Sundays off. The workers were not satisfied, so the company union was organized. There were about 400 employees at the time and over 200 of them joined in the submission of workers' demand. However, many workers were somehow forced to withdraw their names. Therefore, there were only over 100 employees in the movement for collective bargaining. At that time, the group was supported by the International Metalworking

Federation (IMF) union. Since then, collective bargaining has been held between union and management annually. In 1991, the company was split into two companies and thus the workforce was redistributed among the two entities. This union was then renamed the Auto Assembler Union of Thailand. The union membership was reduced to about 280 persons in 1999. The union membership fee was 200 baht per year. Members got the following services from the union: training and educational activities, information relevant to the employment conditions, in the early stage of union operation, training was provided once a year, as well as the report of the annual union meeting; welfare for members, e.g. visits to sick members at the hospitals, wreaths for the funerals of members or members' parents and relatives; the setting up of a credit union within ATP.

Collective Bargaining Processes

During the first stage of development, there were legal advisors for the company involved in collective bargaining. The involvement of the legal advisors was regarded by the union to have created problems in negotiation. According to the union leader, most of these legal advisors had an anti-union attitude. They also focused on the minimum requirements indicated in the labor law. In addition, whatever the union demanded and got from the employer would be somehow offset by the management's demand for something in return. The demands submitted usually included issues about holidays, annual wage increase, diligence allowance for those employees who had never taken any leave of absence throughout the year, and working conditions such as lighting, safety, drinking water, etc.

Generally, collective bargaining took months to get every issue settled. The negotiation was conducted every week. Most of the time, the negotiation went well. There had never been any strike. Until 1999, there had been only three times that mediators were needed in the process. What the two social partners in this company did was to discuss issues of concern in the workers' council first. Then, the issues of concern defined by labor law were covered in collective bargaining. This procedure had been positive to the work process as it is realized that time needed in the collective bargaining was reduced compared to the earlier practices when workers' council was not in existence. Earlier, when collective bargaining was initiated by workers, most of the workers automatically stopped working and waited for the results of the negotiation. This slowed down the operation. The union did not hold a meeting every three months as required by labor law. On the contrary, it called for a meeting whenever needed.

The workers' council of this company was composed of nine members all of whom came from the union committee members; while the latter was composed of fifteen members. With the company being divided into two new companies, there were over 200 union members for the new entity. Their membership fee was 150 baht/month, or annual fee of 1,800 baht. Prior to 1999, there were more job orders and the employees were working overtime more often. In fact, their overtime pay was a bigger proportion of their total earnings from work. In early 2000's, many supervisory unions were also set up.

Company's Employment Measures during the Financial Crisis
During November to December of 1998 and January 1999, company workers had to stop working. Actually, there had been no work since May 1997. But the company just asked their workers to stop coming to work in late 1998 and early 1999. Yet, the company did not lay off any workers. It just cut down about 10% of the salary of those who receive more than 5,000 baht per month. At YMC, which is another subsidiary of the same holding company, there were some repair jobs that were brought in for employees. However, at ATP, such activities could be generated as it is mainly the car parts production.

During this financial crisis period and starting from 1996, the company did not hire any new employees. The situation had led to more frequent communication between labor and management. There seemed to be an understanding among both parties. For example, workers agreed not to receive bonuses during the time of the financial crisis, no increase in wages and salaries. However, the company still paid 700 baht/month for those who earned less than 10,000 baht and some cash for their work diligence (for example, never absent from work) every month.

Because of the changes in the external environment, the company expected more automation in its system. In 1999, the company had also been able to secure contracts from Audi Volkswagen and Siet. This had helped alleviate the employment situation within the company.

5.3 Far East Knitwear Co. Ltd.

In 1999, Far East Knitwear Co. Ltd. (hereafter, FEK) had over 1,200 employees. Most of them are female industrial sewing machines operators. There were only about 10% male employees. Most of the male employees worked on general tasks and some also operated the sewing machines.

The employment practices were of three types: (1) contract work (i.e., by dozens of pieces sewed; (2) daily; and (3) monthly. The company's layout of work organization was arranged in such a way that the machine operators would be working on two floors and the rest of the six-storey building was for work activities such as cutting, ironing and packing. There was no shift work at this company. At the time, the company subcontracted some job orders. Generally, the company hired people who could read and write as a minimum employment requirement. The employees' age ranged from 18 – 40 years old. Then, it would train these new employees how to do their jobs. Usually, in about 2 months, these new hires would be able to do the jobs well. For those who were contract workers, they earned about 30 baht per dozen of pieces sewed. Therefore, they would be able to earn around 6,000 – 10,000 baht per month depending on their skill and experience on the job. Earlier on, all workers were daily workers. The employment changed to the three categories as mentioned above in the late 1990s. There was however a high turnover rate of workers, even though there was a good working relationship between workers and supervisors. Generally, workers would quit after they were older than 40 years old. This is partly due to the fact that at that age, their dexterity would slow down and they would not be able to make enough compared to when they were younger.

The FEK Company union was established in about 1984. It was also registered as the workers' council, as most of the employees were union members (i.e., over 500 persons out of about 1,000 employees). The union has its officers as follows: president, vice president, secretary, treasurer, labor protection officer, education, public relations, logistics. The total number of the officials was fourteen. Usually, collective bargaining was not held every year. Sometimes, the union took initiatives to suggest quality improvement of the products. An annual meeting was regularly held. The membership fee was ten baht/month. This rate was the same for both contract workers and daily workers. The fees would be collected by the rank and file officers who are members of the particular work groups. The union election is held every two years.

The union communicated its activities and other employment-related issues to members through the leaders of the work groups. It usually organized some recreation activities outside of the workplace. The union itself as an organization participated in the public activities organized by the Congress of Labor of Thailand such as Women's Day, Labor Day, and the training activities of the ILO. Until 1999, there had been no cases of layoffs since the financial crisis. The workers felt that their work load was still the same, according to the union leader. In fact, the company started to send job orders to outside subcontractors. So, the company was actually not so much affected by the crisis. The company's main market was Europe. In case that any member of the union was punished for tardiness or absenteeism or not being given jobs to do and it was regarded to be unfair by the member, then the union stepped in by discussing the case with the supervisors.

5.4 Asia Garment Co. Ltd.

Company's Profile

Asia Garment Co. Ltd. (hereafter, AGC) was established in 1971 with the registered capital of 70 mil. baht and under the BOI promotion program. Its plant was located in Samutprakarn Province. In 1999, its total workforce was about 700 employees, of which 650 were production workers and the rest consisted of office staff, personnel managers, accountants, financial managers, marketing managers, etc. There were altogether over 500 machines. Its production line was well known for its finest quality apparel and its flexibility to adapt quickly to serve its customers.

The company produced and gained its expertise in ready-made casual apparel and sport wear garments such as track suits, woven suits, jogging suits, sweatshirts, jackets, running suits, track pants, polo shirts, uniforms. Its production capacity was 150,000 pieces per month. About 95% of the production were made-to-order contract from foreign customers under their patents and design specifications. The remaining 5% was made with the company's own brand name. AGC was committed to increase production efficiency and improve product quality.

Employment Practices

In 1999, AGC had about 700 employees of which about 500 were contract workers, 100 daily workers, and 100 monthly employees. There were altogether about ten managerial personnel. The length of service of these employees was about 5-7 years. The turnover rate was about 3-5% per month which was considered high. This however was experienced among the contract workers who changed jobs often. The company provide training and development for its employees. It emphasizes productivity improvement, ISO 9000 and Safety and Health issues, 5S [2]. All these were provided as in-house training and some are off-the-job training. Generally, lower level employees will have to go through training program before start working. The personnel department has its training and development plan. This company was a Thai family business. Welfare was provided to employees according to what is regulated by the Labor Law. Other types of welfare provided included: diligence award of 150 baht/month; 3 uniforms/ year; and free food.

Labor Relations Situation in the Company

Working together in the company, there existed a labor-management cooperation. This was a non-union company. The atmosphere was that of a family. Everybody helped each other out. Up until 1999, the company had been established for 28 years, there had never been any labor disputes or submission of demands from workers. The communication was both formal and informal. For formal communication, this included the company's announcements, circulars and other memos, etc. For informal communication, the supervisors oversaw their own subordinates and helped solve whatever problems they encountered.

Activities Promoting Good Labor-Management Relations

1.   Effective communication system – there are frequent meetings between supervisors and subordinates as well as meetings between management and employees;

2.   Suggestion box at various places in the plant to encourage employees to express their opinions and ideas. Most of the suggestions are more on day-to-day type on production system, work environment which can be handled easily;

3.   Management-employee joint- safety inspection committee to improve the working conditions and reduce hazards in the plant. The company emphasizes safety and there are 3 safety personnel in the plant.

4.   Sports events and annual get-together

5.   Promotion and support training and development activities particularly computer and e-mail usage to employees;

After the Financial Crisis

Since 1997, general economic conditions had worsened. However, the company was not much affected as over 90% of the company's products was exported. The company's performance during 1992-1997 had not decreased, which was countercyclical to that of other industries. The company's customers were mainly from Europe and there had been an increase in orders. Therefore, the company's profits had not decreased and hence, there had been no need to layoff workers.

Company's Measures during the Financial Crisis

The company slowed down its recruitment activities since 1997 by not hiring more employees in response to natural attrition. There was an organizational restructuring. But there was no layoff/discharge policy. FEK encouraged all units to reduce costs and improve work efficiency.

Strengths and Weaknesses in FEK's Labor Relations Processes

Strengths included the fact that employees worked with management within a family-like atmosphere. Everyone was treated like relatives. There were discussions, but no submission of demands or strikes. Weaknesses were however that most of the employees generally did not express their ideas. Most of them were not highly educated.

Hence, the company needed to provide a more participative management style as well as non-formal education opportunities to employees to enhance their quality of life even after they retire.

6. DISCUSSION ON CASE STUDIES

In our case studies, we found that all the companies did not have any layoff policy. In the worst case, layoff was used as the last resort of the firms. However, the companies tried to either find more markets for their products, such as in the garment industry, or use natural attrition and early retirement packages as their strategies in downsizing. This practice fit well with the flexible organization model proposed by Salaman (1992). This model proposes an organizational structure with core and peripheral groups of employees, with the rest in subcontracting activities and through contact with employment agencies. In our case studies, we find the evidence of such practices in the garment industry. Although, the companies did not layoff workers, they did subcontract their job orders. However, the problems they faced was high turnover rate among the contract workers. This is because these employees, once they had acquired the skills needed, they would move to other enterprises. The main reason was because they did not get fringe benefits or welfare from the company as did the daily or monthly workers who worked on a full-time basis. It was also very hard for these workers to organize, as they were not a stable workforce for the company. Therefore, an industrial union may be needed in order to provide them with some employment protection. However, a close look at these workers also suggested that these workers earned by their skills and experiences. Thus after about 2 months on a probation period learning how to sew on the industrial sewing machines, most of them can actually earn more than the minimum wage rates per month. Some can earn from 6,000 – 10,000 baht per month (the average of the minimum wage rates during 1997 -1999 was about 6,900 baht/month) depending on their skills. However, most of them will have to quit the job after they are over 40 years old, as most of them by that age are not be able to work fast and effectively on the machines. So, they will not be able to earn as much as they used to earn when they were younger, although the company practice paying minimum wages. The garment workers may however be luckier than their counterparts who work in the other stages of the textile industry, like fiber plants or spinning processes. Those who work in these stages do not actually learn any skills that they can use to become an entrepreneur. For those who work in the garment or clothing industry, most of them will be able to become a dress-maker easily with some further training. This is a policy implication which has been taken up by Labor Skills Development Department.

Another observation about the garment industry is that it is very much labor intensive as suggested by the share of total employment in the textile industry as a whole. In addition, these workers are generally of low educated, as what is required by the employer is only the ability to read and write. The employers are willing to train them to operate on industrial machines. In fact, it takes only a week to know how. But to be very good for some workers, it may well take at least two months. However, as the incentive pay is used, most workers will have the motivation to learn and do better as fast as they can so that they can earn more.

The implications for the worker's organization activities is that it would be difficult to organize and develop over time as these workers are not stable. They move in and out of the organization very often. So, workforce stability as well as employment stability has an impact on the union's organization and growth. But would we expect a fundamental change in the current industrial relations system wherein the Buddhist cultural values tend to be influential? Probably not, the same question has been asked of the Japanese industrial relations system by Benson (1998). He examined the labor management during recessions in the Japanese manufacturing enterprise in 1990s with respect to the changes in labor management and strategy. He concluded that despite some significant modifications, the basic configuration of Japanese labor management has remained intact.

In our case studies, we found that the dialogue between management and labor took place on a continual basis in the workers' council in the case of companies which have a union. For the non-unionized company, supervisor tends to play a significant role of communication mediation between management and labor. The dialogue in the workers' council is found to be useful for both parties as it functions to an extent as a forum for the concerned parties to voice their interests and ideas on various activities that affect employees. Also, once the issues concerning wages and benefits are brought to the collective bargaining table, less time is spent in reaching the agreement. This is because during the workers' council meetings, information sharing and exchange of ideas have already taken place. Some attitudinal restructuring processes of the two parties have been developed. So, it is not surprising that during the economic boom period of the country, there were fewer strikes. In short, it is hypothesized that the workers' council functioned very well in that period and that management well accepted and encouraged the functioning of the council. For Thai cultural values, the workers' council imply a consultation approach rather than the confrontational approach of the collective bargaining. Hence, in most non-unionized companies, workers' council seems to work very well.

7.   QUESTIONS FOR DISCUSSION

1.   From the discussion above, what do you think are the impact of globalization on Thailand labor markets?

2.   What can be the Government and private sector firms' strategies to cope with changes in the labor markets? Would the Government and the business firms act differently in view of the anticipated recessionary economic period in the next decade?

3.   What should be the role of labor unions? How can they increase their membership? What can be the unions' strategies to protect and enhance at the same time their members and organization's need for job security, survival and growth?

4.   With respect to the case studies, what factors do you think contribute to the effective labor-management relations at the firm level? Can these practices be transferred to other firms? Why and How?

ENDNOTES

This paper is based on the earlier version of the report prepared for the ILO during 1999 - 2000 on Industrial Relations and Recession in Thailand. I am grateful to the ILO for the financial support and especially Dr. Duncan Campbell of the EASTMAT Team, ESCAP, Bangkok in 2000 for having invited me to investigate on the financial crisis impact on industrial relations at the firm's level. I thank many colleagues, various informants in the relevant industries, union leaders and rank-and-file union members of the cases presented herein for their kind cooperation and information, insights. Any remaining errors are however solely my responsibilities.

[1] The IMF-supported programs for Thailand focused on the objectives to reduce poverty by maintaining macroeconomic stability and implementation of firm's key structural reforms. The strategy to address the crisis had three main components: financing, macroeconomic policies, and structural reforms (See IMF,2000).

[2] Five *Ss (5 S)* are work practices in Japanese management system that is believed to help improve productivity at the workplace. The 5S concept includes *Seiri, Seiton, Seiso, Seiketsu,* and *Shitsuke. Seiri* is to sort out what is necessary or needed and what is not, then, to get rid or dispose of what is not necessary or needed. Make sure that only necessary things are kept at the workplace. *Seiton* is to make sure that there is a place for everything and everything is in its place. *Seiso* is to make sure that the workplace and equipments are clean. Cleaning is inspection. *Seiketsu* is to maintain present standards and keeps improvement. *Shitsuke* is to develop positive work attitude.

Chapter 8

GLOBALIZATION AND INDUSTRIAL RELATIONS
IN THE PHILIPPINES

Maragtas V. Amante

1. INTRODUCTION

Philippine enterprises operate in an environment of a country and people who continue to face the most difficult challenges. Every kind of possible disaster, whether man-made or natural, happens in the Philippines. A wide variety of political and economic problems, ranging from the mundane to the complex looms in the horizon, both with opportunities and threats for enterprise survival and growth. In this difficult environment, Philippine businesses fall and rise in competition. Some rise up, persevere, and survive to move on as success stories – as long as they know how.

Various factors are influencing changes in the Philippine industrial relations system. These include pressures from the globalization process, international norms, labor market changes and conventions on corporate social responsibility, development of management practices, cultural values at both corporate and national levels. Case studies of selected enterprises show that to achieve desired results, human resource development and management strategies should go hand in hand, and not in isolation of industrial relations. It is important that human resource development (HRD) and human resource management (HRM) strategies support and accommodate policies to promote decent work, notably freedom of association and collective bargaining, workers rights including health and safety, and other basic labor standards, to ensure skills formation, and motivate productivity of the workforce.

2. THE PHILIPPINE LABOR MARKET CONTEXT

Basic facts about the Philippine labor force from 1990 to 2006 are shown in Table 8.1. Per capita Gross National Income (GNI) is estimated by the World Bank at US$ 1,300, in 2005. While the Philippine population grows at an average annual rate of 2.0 percent, unemployment is at 10.9 percent, more apparent among women (10.3 percent to 11.7 percent) and the youth (19.7 percent to 21.7 percent). Youth accounted for almost half (49.7 percent) of the total unemployed. From 24.5 million workers in 1990, the labor force (total of employed and unemployed workers) is now estimated at 35.6 million. An additional 2.8 percent women and men joined the labor force in 1990; and 1.4 percent in 2006.

Table 8.1 Basic Characteristics of the Philippine Labor Market

	1990	2000	2006
Population (millions)	61.0	76.3	88.7
Population growth rate (%)	2.3	2.1	2.0
Labor force (millions)	24.5	30.9	35.2
Annual change in labor force (%)	2.8	0.7	1.4
Labor force participation rate (LFPR) (%)	64.5	64.3	66.5
Male LFPR (%)	81.8	80.3	82.9
Female LFPR (%)	47.5	48.4	50.2
Employed persons (millions)	22.5	27.8	32.9
Share of employed persons (%) in:			
Agriculture, forestry, fishery	45.2	37.4	37.1
Industry (manufacturing, mining ...)	15.0	16.0	15.4
Services	39.8	46.6	47.5
Unemployment rate (%)	8.1	10.1	10.9
Underemployment rate (%)	20.5	22.3	22.7
Overseas Filipino Workers (OFWs)	446,095	841,628	980,000

Sources of statistics: Philippine Statistical Yearbook (1990, 2000); Bureau of Labor Statistics <www.bles.dole.gov.ph>, National Statistics Office <www.census.gov.ph>; Philippine Overseas Employment Administration <www.poea.gov.ph>

According to the October 2006 labor force survey by the National Statistics Office, there were 55.3 million Filipinos of working age. Of this number, 35.2 million were either employed or looking for jobs, among whom 2.8 million could not find any. The unemployment rate has steadily increased from 5.4 percent in 1975 to 11.30 percent (7.3 percent using ILO definition) in 2005. This number of unemployed would have increased had not some 980,000 workers went abroad as Overseas Filipino Workers (OFWs) to work for foreign employers. It is estimated that 7.8 million Filipinos are permanent, temporary or undocumented migrants worldwide. These OFWs and migrants provided the Philippines a crucial lifeline in managing the balance of payments deficit, with remittances amounting to US$ 12.8 billion in 2006, an increase of 19.4 percent over the previous year.

Underemployment averaged 12.7% from 1975 to 1980. It ballooned to 20% in the next two decades, tapering to 22.7% in 2006. The underemployed are those who either wanted to work full-time, get second jobs or move to other jobs that would pay better. This means that as a result of jobless growth, the jobs generated in the past were short not only in quantity but also in quality. The labor supply of workers has been increasing faster than jobs are being created. While more than a million new workers joined the labor force in 2006, only 750,000 new jobs were created from January 2005 and January 2006.

The dilemma of jobless growth underlines the impact of globalization in the Philippine labor market, in addition to the persistent underemployment, mismatch in skills and jobs demanded, growth in short term contractual employment, and expansion of the informal sector. The informal sector includes wage and salary workers in family-based or unregistered economic units, industrial home workers, the self-employed, and the unpaid family workers.

As the pressure for global competition intensifies, enterprises have introduced changes in the organization, new work methods and technology, together with the implementation of productivity based employment conditions. Employers emphasize the need to "compete, survive and succeed in global competition". Companies resort to relentless organizational changes to achieve the best results, i.e., high quality products and services. Continuous reorganizations, reengineering and rightsizing are linked to more contractual employment, to lower payroll costs. Very common strategies in human resource management include job evaluation, greater emphasis on performance appraisal, HR systems for productivity, the use of a variety of incentives and flexible pay, and investments in human resource development through short term training.

At the national level, reforms in the Philippine labor market policy attempt to fill the gaps by providing, among others, public employment service centers, regulation of job contracting, a voluntary labor standards enforcement framework, and favorable rules to business process outsourcing (i.e., exemptions from prohibition to night work of women in business process outsourcing, such as call centers, etc.). Dependence on overseas employment of Filipino workers (OFWs) estimated at 1.3 million in 2005, who bring in remittances of US$ 12 billion every year, greater than the top industry export, remain to be a key feature of the Philippine labor market.

3. PHILIPPINE INDUSTRIAL RELATIONS

To survive and compete, Philippine employers resort to functional flexibility and more cooperative employment relations, with an anti-union thrust. The logic of competition induced firms to adopt practices that promote numerical flexibility such that a core-periphery workforce is created. Philippine unions however are unable to effectively counter employer strategies, due to low numbers in membership, fragmentation and an unfavorable public-policy environment. Philippine organized labor however, made some recent gains in organizing and inter-union coordination, and in parliamentary and extra parliamentary struggles to highlight policy issues. While the basic framework of industrial relations remains firm, government policies, strategies and resources were inadequate to counteract the negative effects of global market integration on workers, and to launch the Philippines economy into a sustainable high road of industrialization.

Philippine labor is actually composed of a diverse workforce of Indo-Malayan ethno-linguistic groups who live in 7,000+ islands. Local work values are a product of the historical blending of ideas, beliefs and customs of these ethno-linguistic groups, along with more than 330 years of Spanish colonial dominance and 45 years of American rule, together with about 5 years of Japanese military administration in World War II.

Colonial American patterns of work and pay, Spanish habits, patronage and land owning elites, and Chinese merchant traders shaped the idiosyncrasies of Filipino culture - also described as a Latino nation in Asia. More than 6 million Muslim Filipinos in Mindanao and numerous tribal groups contribute to the diversity of the work culture and employment practices in the Philippines.

Most Filipino workers came from rural backgrounds. It is inevitable that rural patterns of behavior persist even in urban-based employment. It is important to have a basic understanding of "Filipino values" underlining workplace behaviour, particularly between subordinates and superiors, and between co-workers. Jocano (1988) argued that understanding Filipino culture is important in understanding corporate behavior.

Box 1: "The Philippines should be growing ....

" ... [The Philippines] is a country of vast natural resources that can be responsibly developed in a way that brings jobs and investments, ... and that need to be preserved to promote tourism. ... This country also has a very great resource in its people. This is a country with a very entrepreneurial population. I have known Filipinos as friends and colleagues throughout the world, and when you come here and see the population, you know that these are people who are kind, caring, creative and technology-friendly. ... ...

This is also a place of incredible diversity and I mean that in the very best way, because I think it is quite unique. ... I have never had the privilege of living somewhere where that is so cherished and valued. Filipinos are proud of the fact that when you travel to another part of the country – another island – they speak a different dialect or will serve you a different food. This is also a very literate population. Most people here read and write, many of them more than one language. English is well spoken here, as well as other languages. That is a real asset in today's world. ...

The growth rate here looks extremely good given the part of the world I have just been in. But compared to some of the dynamic, fast-moving economies in Asia, the Philippines is not where it ought to be. ... "

-- *U.S. Ambassador **Kristie Kenney**, excerpts of speech before the American Chamber of Commerce in the Philippines, 19 April 2006, Shangrila Hotel, Makati City*

Philippine industrial relations is an amalgam of Spanish and American colonial patterns of assets ownership and commercial business practices, laws and institutions. Philippine labor laws were copied from American legislation which emphasized collective bargaining and disputes settlement, without regard to adversarial consequences. As a result, Philippine industrial relations became an almost exclusive world for lawyers, arguing and negotiating cases, from the 1950s onwards. As a response, union militancy could be traced to revolutionary movements against Spanish and American colonial rule (Villegas, 1988). Labor laws, social legislation and bureaucracies were created by the colonial state both to suppress and appease widespread and spontaneous workers protests and peasant unrests, while maintaining the status quo on land ownership, access to national resources, and asset distribution.

The Philippines ratified the fundamental conventions of the International Labor Organization (ILO) on industrial relations as early as 1953, particularly ILO Convention 27 on Freedom of Association (1948), and ILO Convention 98, on the Right to Organize and Collective Bargaining (1949). Commitment to the United Nations Declaration on Human Rights (1948) is also an important part of the country's fundamental framework. These commitments to international norms are reflected in part or in whole through the Philippine Constitution, and various labor laws and social legislation enacted through the years. The fundamental framework of global standards and the constitution-guided policy and practice in the field of industrial relations, including collective bargaining and disputes settlement.

The Philippine Constitution provides the fundamental framework for industrial relations, when it declares:

> **"The State** shall afford full protection to labor .... It shall guarantee the rights of all workers to self organization, collective bargaining and negotiations, and peaceful concerted activities including the right to strike in accordance with law. They shall be entitled to security of tenure, humane conditions of work, and a living wage. They shall participate in policy and decision-making processes affecting their rights and benefits as maybe provided by law." [4]

In addition, the Philippine Bill of Rights guarantees "the right of the people, including those employed in the public and private sectors, to form unions, associations or societies for purposes not contrary to law ... " [5]. These guarantees are likewise extended to the public sector: "The right to self-organization shall not be denied to government employees" [6].

3.1 Government

The fundamental framework guarantees the right to organize unions for purposes of collective bargaining for workers both in the private and public sector. National laws enacted by the Philippine Congress, and policy directives by the executive branch of

---

Box 2. Basic features of collective bargaining in the Philippines

- Collective bargaining is enterprise-based. There is no tradition of industry bargaining in the Philippines.
- Collective bargaining may cover one enterprise unit, or separate bargaining units within the same enterprise.
- There may be two more unions in an employer or bargaining unit, but only one union may represent the entire unit for collective bargaining. The union representative is called the "exclusive bargaining agent".

What conditions must be satisfied before collective bargaining starts?

- Union must be legitimate, and registered with the Department of LaborLabor and Employment (DOLE).
- Union must be the exclusive bargaining agent, either through certification election or voluntary recognition.
- Union must make a demand to bargain.
- There must be no registered collective bargaining covering the same bargaining unit; if there is, bargaining must be done during the freedom period.

How many years is a CBA contract?

- An exclusive collective bargaining agent has five years to represent the members of the bargaining unit
- A collective bargaining agreement has a term of five years, but may be renegotiated prior to the end of third year.

Source: Director Hans Cacdac, National Conciliation & Mediation Board, Department of LaborLabor and Employment (NCMB-DOLE).

government repeat the basic guarantees, and provide for their implementation. Another source of regulation and guidance are the decisions issued by the Philippine courts, on various labor cases and disputes. These judicial and quasi-judicial bodies include the Secretary of Labor, the labor arbiters, voluntary arbitrators, the National Labor Relations Commission, the Court of Appeals, and the Supreme Court.

The Philippine Labor Code of 1974 is the key legislation on industrial relations, as well as collective bargaining, disputes settlement and social dialogue. Among others, the law provides for recognition of labor organizations, as well as procedures for collective bargaining, disputes settlement, and strikes.

A key provision in the Labor Code is the mandate of the Philippine State to: " ... promote and emphasize the primacy of free collective bargaining and negotiations ..." (*Article 211(a), Philippine Labor Code*).

The Labor Code also declares as state policy the promotion of " ... free trade unionism as an instrument for the enhancement of democracy and the promotion of social justice and development"; (*Article 211(b)*); " ...to ensure a stable, dynamic and just industrial peace"; and " ... to ensure the participation of workers in decision and policy making processes affecting their rights, duties and welfare *(Article 211(g)*". Furthermore, "... to encourage a truly democratic method of regulating the relations between the employers and employees by means of agreements freely entered into through collective bargaining, no court or administrative agency or official shall have the power to set or fix wages, rates of pay, hours of work or terms and conditions of employment", except as otherwise provided in the Labor Code *(Article 211(g)*. It is also the state policy "to ensure the the participation of workers in decision and policy-making processes affecting their rights, duties and welfare... (and) to encourage a truly democratic method of regulating the relations between the employers and employees by means of agreements freely entered into through collective bargaining..." *(Article 212 (B)*.

In keeping its commitments arising from the ratification of various ILO conventions to promote decent work, the Philippines legislated and put in place social and labor standards in the following areas:

- Employment standards and non-discrimination
- Workers rights: freedom of association, unions
- Collective bargaining
- Hours and conditions of work
- Wages and benefits
- Social security
- Occupational safety and health

3.2 Employers

The Employers' Confederation of the Philippines (ECOP) safeguards the interests of business in all areas related to labor-management relations, including social and economic policy matters affecting such relationship, and the promotion of industrial harmony, social and national growth. The ECOP is the umbrella organization for 451 foreign and local chambers of commerce, industry and professional associations, in both large and small enterprises. It has also 513 corporate members. The ECOP serves as the employers' voice concerning employment, industrial relations, labor and social policies.

There are about 826,769 business establishments in the Philippines, of which 91 percent are micro-enterprises which employ less than 9 workers. In 2003, there were 66,734 enterprises with 10 or more employees. The Employers' Confederation of the Philippines (ECOP) is the umbrella organization for 45 chambers of commerce, industry and professional associations representing SMEs and large enterprises. It has also 513 corporate members. The ECOP serves as the employers' voice concerning employment, industrial relations, labor and social policies.

ECOP safeguards the interests of business in all areas related to labor-management relations, including social and economic policy matters affecting such relationship, and to the promotion of industrial harmony, social and national growth. The ECOP represents employer interests in the formulation and recommendation of policy proposals on issues affecting labor-management relations, as well as other social and economic policy questions before regional or international government agencies and organizations. ECOP accepts the need to encourage and ensure the success of the tripartite consultation machinery in order for workers, employers and government agencies to work harmoniously and effectively towards greater productivity and national progress.

Small and medium enterprises (SMEs) generate employment. SMEs must be allowed to seek their competitive niches and establish business linkages through franchising and subcontracting under a deregulated and flexible labor market. As an employers' organization, ECOP seeks to expand its programs and services to SMEs by responding to their specific needs by developing new, or enhancing existing services. In achieving the goals of employment, ECOP places a significant importance to an effective labor market, and with an enabling legal environment to ensure adequate flexibility. A priority of the ECOP's objectives is to lobby for labor law reforms, which enhance the country's ability to achieve the national economic agenda.

ECOP promotes socially responsible behavior of the enterprises at the workplace and has developed a Corporate Social Responsibility (CSR) program, including the promotion of Equal Employment Opportunity (EEO) among managers, promotion of self-assessment and social accountability tools as well as child-friendly and family-friendly workplace initiatives (Leogardo 2004, 2005).

3.3 Worker Organizations

There is a diversity of union organizations -- plant level unions could affiliate and be represented by federations, or could be independent. Labor laws provide that at least 10 percent of the workforce belonging to a bargaining unit could apply for registration, and stand for "certification election", if there are other unions within the enterprise, to represent the workforce in collective bargaining negotiations. Thus, how to extend the benefits of unionism to the non-organized, informal sector is a major challenge. Labor management cooperation (LMC) mechanisms recognize as pro-active mechanisms towards non-adversarial industrial relations.

Only about five percent of the employed workforce is unionized, which raises the question on the welfare and protection of those who are not organized. There is a diversity of unions, federations and national labor centers of which eight are officially recognized. Only about half a million workers are covered by collective bargaining agreements, against a claim of 3.47 million members by the unions. There are problems of double counting in union membership, which is 24% of the 14.6 million wage and salary workers, but only five per cent of the total employed workforce of 30.252 million.

There are 21,022 Philippine trade unions representing 1,483,382 workers [7]. Unionized workers represent five per cent of the employed workforce of 31.6 million, and nine per cent of 16.7 million workers who are paid wages and salaries. There are ten labor centers, and 171 federations. There are 254,369 workers (17% of claimed union membership) covered by 1,296 collective bargaining agreements. A 2004 survey by the Bureau of Labor and Employment Statistics reported that unions cover 15% of non-agricultural (industry and services) establishments with 20 or more workers. There are 14.2 percent of establishments with collective bargaining agreements. In the public sector, there are 1,358 unions representing 264,000 government employees (18 percent of the total). An overwhelming 95 percent of Philippine workers remain unorganized, which is a significant gap in industrial relations. Non-union members have no rights to exercise collective bargaining and negotiations, and concerted action to improve working conditions, health & safety, and wages, among others, for workers who do not belong to unions.

Through militancy and political work, the Philippine trade unions started to appreciate non-traditional, sometimes non-collective bargaining activities, including investments in labor enterprises, worker cooperatives, and renewed political unionism and organizing workers in the informal sector of the economy. The Philippines has the advantage of a rainbow labor movement with diverse ideologies. Ideological competition however is also an obstacle to strong solidarity. Diverse ideological approaches to solve the worker problem were offered by the major trade union groups, including the Trade Union Congress of the Philippines (TUCP), the Federation of Free Workers (FFW), and the Alliance of Progressive Labor (APL) [8] Many militant trade unions organized party-list groups to participate in parliamentary elections and represent workers in legislation. These include the Kilusang Mayo Uno (May First Movement) which organized the

Anakpawis (literally means 'Toiling Masses') and the *Bayan Muna* (Nation First); and the *Partido ng Manggagawa* (Workers Party), the women's party *Gabriela*, and the *Akbayan*. Militant party list representatives were elected as lawmakers in the Philippine Congress, but as a minority, they influence debates but not significantly alter the balance of parliamentary votes with respect to the majority interests of traditional economic and political elites. The ECOP has vigorously opposed many of the populist labor law proposals from the militant party list lawmakers, such as a legislated P125 across the board wage increase.

There are also independent labor groups with no direct stake in union organizing in the auto industry, such as; the National Confederation of Labor (NCL), the Trade Unions of the Philippines and Allied Services (TUPAS), the National Labor Union (NLU), the Philippine Transport and General Workers Organization (PTGWO), the National Alliance of Trade Unions (NATU), and the Associated Marine Officers and Seafarers Union of the Philippines (AMOSUP) including several public sector unions.

4. CONCLUSION

The need for struggle and survival skills highlight the experience of Philippine industrial relations, as employers and employees wind through the labyrinth of processes and mechanisms for human resource development and management (HRD/HRM) to improve performance and raise productivity at the enterprise, and national policy level.

With the increasing pace of globalization, countries open up their borders to flows of trade and investments, through less regulations, more incentives, and infrastructure support. Both foreign and local firms adopt management practices that have proved successful. For multinational corporations, there is a greater need to identify the means to effectively manage employees located in different social and political environments. In their HRM decisions, companies with operations in different locations face the "global or local question" – whether they should adopt globally uniform corporate employment relations policy or tailor them to suit local environments.

Personnel strategies employed by both foreign and local firms may be tailored-fitted, and "custom designed" to their production strategy and manufacturing practices. In this context, competencies and skills are important, on what works, with respect to personnel functions like recruitment, training, compensation, performance appraisal and rewards, including issues concerning non-regular workers and the role played by the unions and workers' committee.

The effective utilization of human capital for economic development requires productive and harmonious relations between the workforce and the employers through a stable, responsive web of rules which promote decent work and livelihood. While the East Asian region works towards greater economic integration as a free trade area, there is greater attention to human resource development, as well as effective management strategies to improve employee performance and enterprise raise productivity.

Issues concerning industrial relations may appear to be marginalized in globalization, and in the context of the shift from industry to services, knowledge-based and ICT − intensive "new economy". The experience in the Philippines clearly shows the need to for supportive HRD and HRM to achieve sound and harmonious industrial relations. Employers are more preoccupied with product quality, and the shift from mass production to flexible specialization. New technology however results in a shift from production based industry to knowledge-based organizations, such as teleworking, flexible work hours, and work done at home. The Philippine case studies given below clearly show that a neglect of decent work and sound industrial relations would eventually defeat and undermine HRD and HRM strategies.

The increasing globalization of work affect national labor markets, with inevitable impact upon employment, education and training, industrial relations, compensation and work rules. It is important to ensure that industrial relations reinforce HRD & HRM strategies, and vice versa, to achieve fair globalization and decent work. It is important for both employers, leaders of workers organizations, and officials of relevant government agencies to acquire the competencies and skills needed to translate broad macro economic objectives, into relevant micro level practices and link industrial relations with supportive HRD/HRM practices at the enterprise or workplace to achieve successful results, as well as to continuously struggle and survive in a difficult competitive environment *(Box 6)*.

5.   CASE STUDIES

The interface between local and foreign management in the Philippines is reflected in many practices at the workplace. Both Western and Japanese style work practices are popular in the management training circles, disseminated by various consulting companies. Popular management training concerns quality improvement, flexibility in the job and pay structure, performance, productivity through good housekeeping, and development of positive work values in the workforce. In interviews and field work, the author has identified some of the key points of tension.

5.1   The Struggle of Nestle Workers in the Philippines [9]

One of the well-known cases of the Philippine adversarial industrial relations is the struggle of the Union of Filipino Employees (UFE) against the management of Nestle, Philippines. UFE is an affiliate of the Drug, Food and Allied Workers' Federation (DFA), which is a member of the most militant labor center Kilusang Mayo Uno (KMU) or the May First Movement. The union supports the militant party list groups *Anakpawis* (Toiling Masses) and *Bayan Muna* (Nation First) which have elected representatives in the Philippine Congress who have championed the cause of the union in various public venues, including rallies and demonstrations.

Nestle Philippines is a Swiss based multinational which is on top of the milk and dairy industry in the Philippines. It has its central office in Makati, Metro Manila, with factories in Alabang and Cabuyao, both in south Luzon, and in Cagayan de Oro, in Mindanao. Nestle was twelfth among the top 1,000 corporations in the Philippines in 1989 with net sales of P7.5 billion (US$278 million) and a net profit of P491 million (US$18.2 million).

According to the union account, the organizing effort started in 1982. Even with no one union representing the Nestle workers, the UFE-DFA-KMU launched a sympathy strike for non-payment of a Christmas bonus and other unfair labor practices. A few days earlier workers under the union, NPAFW (Nutritional Products Association of Food Workers), at the Alabang and Cabuyao factories also went on strike due to a deadlock in the collective bargaining negotiations. The 75-day strike of the two unions, the UFE and NPAFW, successfully ended on March 19, 1982, which made their members realize the value of coordinated mass action. The two unions merged under the UFE in 1984 after a certification election. Thus, UFE was recognized legally as the sole and exclusive bargaining agent of the Alabang and Cabuyao workers.

After more than two months at the bargaining table, UFE and Nestle entered into a collective bargaining agreement (CBA), effective July 1, 1984. Union members were workers from the Alabang and Cabuyao factories. The CBA had provisions for wage increases and new benefits considered to be one of the best agreements in the industry at that time. Nestle later agreed to extend the same benefits granted to the Alabang and Cabuyao workers to its employees in Makati, Cebu, Davao and Cagayan de Oro. All existing CBAs in the different worksites of Nestle were synchronized to expire on June 30, 1987.

After some time, the union alleged that Nestle started to renege on some provisions of the CBA. Benefits were unilaterally withheld and gradually withdrawn by the company. A big number of casual workers were hired to perform the functions of regular workers at Nestle's Alabang and Cabuyao plants. Company rules and policies were enforced strictly. The company also did not grant the one-month productivity bonus, and the profit sharing plan, which were agreed in the CBA. Union leaders were harassed. The UFE was thus forced to again declare a strike on Jan. 22, 1986, on numerous grounds of unfair labor practices, union busting, non-payment of legally mandated holiday pay and productivity bonus.

The union views the strike which lasted for almost two months as a contribution of Nestle workers in the movement to oust the Marcos dictatorship. The period from 1982 to 1986 also saw a political upheaval, in the protest campaigns against the Marcos regime. Workers on strike were always present in mobilizations for protest rallies and demonstrations. The UFE union was one among the numerous unions most actively involved in the campaign.

Marcos was ousted and left the Philippines in February 1986. The UFE strike ended in March 15, 1986, through the mediation of the new minister of labor, Secretary Augusto Sanchez, to reinstate the striking workers. Sanchez was later sacked by the newly installed Aquino government because of the pressure from the employers, mostly the TNCs in the Philippines.

In 1987, all the unions at Nestle, including all sales personnel in the Luzon provinces, those at the Cebu and Davao sales offices as well as at the factory at Cagayan de Oro, were consolidated under the banner of UFE-DFA-KMU. This move boosted the bargaining posture of the union vis-a-vis Nestle's management. Nestle workers also participated actively in the campaign to promote workers rights, including other national issues such as the non ratification of the US bases treaty.

With the new round of CBA negotiations, Nestle management stood steadfast on its "first and final offer". The workers considered this management posture unreasonable and unjust. The UFE was forced to declare a deadlock in collective bargaining negotiations after more than three months at the bargaining table. On Sept. 11, 1987, UFE declared a strike. At this point, Nestle management dismissed almost all of the 70 officers of the UFE, barely four days after the strike.

At the same time, Nestle, using its vast resources, went on a propaganda blitz in the mass media, branding the UFE strike as communist-inspired, meant to subvert the economy and the new Aquino government. On Oct. 20, 1987, President Corazon Aquino declared a "total war policy" against labor in a speech before employers of mostly multinational enterprises in the Philippines. She authorized the police and military to immediately dismantle illegal barricades set up by workers in front of strike-bound establishments.

A few days later, the picket lines established by UFE at Nestle's factories at Alabang, Cabuyao and Cagayan de Oro were dispersed by heavily armed military personnel, resulting in injuries to several strikers. Some workers were detained with no charges. In one of the dispersal operations at Cabuyao, one of Nestle's trucks forced its way through the picket lines and killed three innocent bystanders. However, the company filed murder charges against the striking workers. The strike-bound Nestle factories were virtually transformed into military camps. Meanwhile, a new secretary of labor, Mr Franklin Drilon, replaced Sanchez, who was considered pro-labor. Mr Drilon was formerly the vice president of the Employers Confederation of the Philippines. He later became executive secretary, secretary of justice, and president of the Philippine Senate.

Nestle management was able to secure a ruling from the labor arbitration of the National Labor Regional Commission (NLRC) that the 1986 strike was illegal and thus, the strike leaders could be dismissed from employment.

The UFE union leaders decided a temporary stop to the strike on December 16, 1987. In a spirit of reconciliation, the union leaders called for the resumption of negotiations. Sensing a victory, Nestle turned down all these reconciliatory moves of the union leadership. Meanwhile, a new company-friendly union was organized, drawn from ex-pelled UFE members and other pro-management employees. The company also refused to release union funds of around Pesos 3 million (US$111,000).

Despite setbacks, the UFE continued to consolidate their ranks. On January 20, 1989, the union president, Mr. Meliton Roxas was assassinated by an unknown assailant in front of the Nestle Cabuyao factory. The union publicly accused both the Nestle management and the Philippine military for complicity in the murder of Roxas.

In 2005, the Nestle Philippine union president who succeeded Roxas was also murdered. After attending a union leader meeting, on September 22, 2005, Mr. Diosdado Fortuna passed by the picket line of striking workers at the Nestlé factory in Cabuyao, Laguna, for an on-site study forum with some students who were visiting in solidarity, and share the union's experience in three years of struggle. Later, as he went home and entered his subdivision, unidentified men on board a motorbike shot him. He died instantly.

The union has resolved to continue with the struggle against Nestle management, and has rallied the rank-and-file workers, and their shop stewards for this purpose. The union has pledged that "every arbitrary action of management must be immediately answered by a concerted workers' action". The saga continues, avidly monitored by nervous employers in the south Luzon industrial area.

5.2   The Philippine Auto Industry and Toyota Motor Philippines

The Philippine automotive and vehicle parts supply industry consists of fourteen passenger car assembly companies, twenty passenger vehicle assembly companies, seven motorcycle assemblers and a conservative estimate of 256 auto parts suppliers. There are about 240 dealer outlets. Investment consists of Pesos 40 billion (US$ 800 million) from car companies, and 28 billion pesos ($560 million) from auto parts suppliers. The industry employs about 74,700 workers. There are 15,000 workers in the car assemblers and distributors, 44,000 in the auto parts suppliers, and 15,700 in the dealers.

The industry exported US$ 1.95 billion worth of vehicles in 2005. There were $ 150 million in vehicle exports, and $ 1.8 billion in auto parts and components. The government earned Philippine Pesos 11.5 billion ($230 million) in taxes and duties from the industry in 2003. Employees also contribute to the government through their income taxes. Retrenchment of employees means less government tax from this sector. In 1997-99, due to the Asian financial crisis, there were 6,914 retrenched employees from the industry. There were 1,248 retrenched employees from Mitsubishi Philippines, 500 from Toyota, 292 from Nissan, 380 from Isuzu Philippines, 494 from Honda Cars, and 4,000 estimated from various car parts suppliers.

Reports from the Chamber of Automotive Manufacturers of the Philippines (CAMPI) and the Truck Manufacturers Association (TMA) show that sales in 2005 grew by 20 percent in January 2006. The main explanation is the rush by people who are buying vehicles to avoid higher prices due to the value added tax (VAT). The 2005 sales reports by company are presented in Table 8.2.

Table 8.2 Philippine Vehicle Sales for 2005

Company	Vehicle units sold	Market share (%)
Toyota	35,513	36.59%
Honda	9,797	10.09%
Mitsubishi	12,984	13.38%
Nissan	4,860	5.01%
Columbian Autocar	2,711	2.79%
Asian Carmakers (BMW)	802	0.83%
Scandinavian Motors	345	0.97%
Commercial Motors	72	0.07%
Universal Motors	3,006	3.10%
Philippines Hino	1,212	1.25%
Ford Motor Co. Phil.	8,336	8.59%
Isuzu Philippines	9,644	15.70%
General Motors	2,410	2.48%
Columbian Motors Corp.	272	0.28%
Fil-Daewoo	32	0.03%
Hyundai	4,924	5.07%
PGA Cars	139	0.05%
Total vehicle sales	**97,063**	**100.0%**
Compare to 2004	88,075	10% increase

Source: Chamber of Automotive Manufacturers of the Philippines, Inc.

Local assemblers sold 7,739 units in January 2006, compared to 6,456 units in the same month in 2005. Turnover of commercial vehicles mirrored the overall market performance with an increase of 22.1 percent. Industry leaders expected that sales of utility vehicles, light commercial vehicles, trucks, and buses would increase in 2006. Toyota Motor Philippines Corp (TMPC) stayed in the lead with 35.4 percent of the market, and Mitsubishi Motors Philippines Corp. (MMPC) had 13.8 percent of the market. Honda Cars Philippines was third, with 12.4 percent and Ford Philippines exported 646 completely built units. Some experts have pointed out that if the country is able to put in place the correct policies, the Philippines could become a significant player in the auto industry in the region.

The problem of second hand vehicle imports is also significant. The transition in the life cycle of cars, from production of new, used and overused status is fast, even in countries such as Taiwan and China. Surplus cars need to be dumped. Some second hand units arrive as separate parts, called "chop chop" cars then re-assembled. The risks to traffic and safety are enormous with these unregulated second hand vehicle imports whose quality has no guarantee. There is no fair level playing field in competition with these second hand vehicle imports, since taxes are not properly paid.

Industrial Relations in the Toyota Motors Philippines Corporation

Court and other records show the various possibilities of confrontational and legal strategies to realize worker exercise of the rights to organize a union and to engage in collective bargaining and negotiations. On the other hand, the company exerted all out efforts to fight and frustrate the union in every step they took through legal means. Eventually, in at least two cases, the Supreme Court decided in favor of the union, but only after a long, expensive and dreadful legal process which is still ongoing. This case is a good study on *how not to use too much legal strategy* in achieving results in industrial relations [10].

The Toyota Motors Philippines Corporation (TMPC) started operations in 1988. There were 1,242 employees in 2005. Toyota Japan owns 34 percent of the company, and 30 percent is owned by the Metrobank Group of George Ty, a Filipino Chinese taipan. Another local investor group, Titan Resources Corporation owns 21 percent. The rest is owned by others.

On November 26, 1992 the Toyota Motor Philippines Corporation Labor Union (TMPCLU) filed a petition for a certification election before the Department of Labor and Employment-National Capital Region (DOLE-NCR) office. TMPCLU's petition was dismissed on the grounds that the labor organization's membership was composed of supervisory and rank-and-file employees in violation of Art. 245 of the Labor Code, and that at the time of the filing of its petition, TMCPLU had not even acquired a legal personality yet. The TMPCLU appealed, and the Secretary of Labor directed the holding of a certification election among the regular rank-and-file employees of TMPC. But the Toyota management (TMPC) blocked the election by employees to choose a union, in a case before the Supreme Court which ruled that since TMPCLU's membership list contained the names of at least twenty-seven supervisory employees in

---

Box 3. Toyota Japan Policy on Relations with Employees:
To What Extent Does it Influence Toyota Philippines?

"Foster a corporate culture that enhances individual creativity and teamwork value, while honoring mutual trust and respect between labor and management."

Toyota has adopted the Basic Principles of Human Resources Management:

1. Creating a workplace environment where employees can work with their trust in the company.
   - Stable employment where lay offs and dismissals are not readily made
   - Steadily maintain and improve working conditions from a medium to long term perspective
   - Ensure fairness and consistency
   - Ensure high employee morale.

2. Creating a mechanism for promoting constant and voluntary initiatives in continuous improvements
   - Share management mindset and sense of critical urgency through communication.
   - Promote employee participation in corporate activities.
   - Reflect business results in working conditions.

3. Fully committed and thorough human resources development.

4. Promoting teamwork aimed at pursuit of individual roles and optimization of the entire team.
   - Through consensus building and achievement in single thrust
   - Team results and creating a sense of unity.

Source: Toyota website. Responsibility.Relations with employees.
http://www.toyota.co.jp/en/relationship/index.html [Accessed 5 January 2007]

Level Five positions, "the union could not, prior to purging itself of its supervisory employee members, attain the status of a legitimate labor organization. Not being one, it cannot possess the requisite personality to file a petition for certification election."

On February 19, 1997, the Supreme Court ruled that the employees of the respondent Toyota Motor Philippines Corporation (TMPC) belonging to the Level 5 positions under its Single Salary Structure set up were supervisory employees.. The decision became final, and the company implemented its Three-Function Salary Structure for employees.

On April 24, 1997, the Toyota Motors Philippines Corporation Employees and Workers Union (TMPCEWU) filed a Petition for Certification Election before the Med-Arbitration Unit of the DOLE-National Capital Region (DOLE-NCR) seeking to represent the rank-and-file employees of the manufacturing division from Levels 1 to 4 of Toyota Motor Philippines Corp. (TMPC).

On May 13, 1997, while the case was pending hearing, the Toyota Motors Philippines Corporation Labor Union (TMPCLU) claimed to be the legitimate labor organization, filed a Motion to Intervene with Opposition to the Certification Election. It claimed that the TMPCEWU petition was premature due to an earlier resolution by the Secretary of Labor ordering the conduct of a certification election among the rank-and-file employees of TMPC represented by petitioner which was the subject of certiorari proceedings before the Supreme Court and still awaiting final resolution at the time; and, that the collective bargaining unit which respondent TMPCEWU sought to represent violated the "single or employer" unit policy since it excluded the rank-and-file employees in the other divisions and departments in respondent TMPC.

On February 4, 1999, Toyota Motors Philippines Corporation Workers' Association (TMPCWA) filed a petition for certification election seeking to be recognized as the sole and exclusive bargaining agent of all rank-and-file employees at the Bicutan and Sta. Rosa plants of the Toyota Motors Philippines Corporation (TMPC). But this move was vigorously opposed by the Toyota Motors management on the grounds that a case was pending before the Supreme Court between it and another union, the Toyota Motor

Philippines Corporation Labor Union (TMPCLU) whose registration certificate has been cancelled. The company argued that the TMPCWA membership is the same as that of the TMPCLU, which sought to represent the same bargaining unit. The company further asserted that this petition repeated a previous petition dismissed on June 18, 1998.

On March 29, 1999, the regional office of the DOLE dismissed the petition. The union appealed, and Undersecretary Rosalinda Dimapilis-Baldoz of the DOLE reversed the decision on June 25, 1999, and ordered the conduct of a certification election.

The TMPC filed a petition with the Court of Appeals, alleging grave abuse of discretion on the part of the Secretary of Labor and Employment (SOLE), which was denied. The certification election was set on March 8, 2000. During the inclusion and exclusion proceedings on whom among the employees has the right to vote, the company submitted a list of 1,110 employees at its Bicutan and Sta. Rosa Plants in the payroll list. The TMPCWA however, questioned the eligibility of 120 employees in the list, contending that they were not rank-and-file employees but supervisory employees of the respondent, on the basis of a previous Supreme Court decision.

The company asserted that the establishment of its Three-Function Salary Structure had already superseded the Supreme Court decision. The real supervisors or managers were distinguished from the rank-and-file employees in terms of the duties and functions of the employees. Nonetheless, the certification election proceeded as scheduled. During the certification election, 105 out of the 120 employees whose eligibilities had been questioned by the petitioner were able to cast their votes, but these votes were not opened and considered. With 503 affirmative votes and the exclusion of the 105 challenged votes, the TMPCWA asserted that it garnered the majority votes of the 943 votes cast (less the challenged votes); hence, it sought to be declared as the certified bargaining agent of the respondent at its Sta. Rosa and Bicutan Plants.

On May 4, 1999, the arbiter at the Department of Labor and Employment-National Capital Region (DOLE-NCR) conditionally dismissed the petition. TMPCWA immediately filed an appeal before the Secretary of the Department of Labor and

Employment. Pursuant to a decision dated June 25, 1999 granting the appeal, the Department of Labor and Employment, through Undersecretary Rosalinda D. Baldoz ordered the conduct of a certification election. The results of the election held on March 8, 2000, turned out in favor of TMPCWA. Out of the 1,110 employees, 1,063 cast their votes, with 105 votes being challenged for allegedly being cast by supervisory employees.

A total of 503 votes were in favor of the worker's union while 440 votes were against it. The union then filed a motion to be certified as the sole and exclusive bargaining agent of all the rank-and-file employees of Toyota Motor Philippines Corporation. But Toyota Motor Philippines Corporation did not accept the results of the election and insisted that the 105 questioned votes be opened for purposes of determining the majority of the valid votes cast. This was notwithstanding the fact that these 105 challenged and segregated ballots were cast by employees occupying position levels 5 and upwards and considered as supervisory employees in accordance with a previous Supreme Court ruling. Management insisted that a new three-function salary scheme had superseded the previous ruling. Nonetheless, on May 12, 2000, the Med-Arbiter declared the challenged votes as ineligible and subsequently TMPCWA was certified as the bargaining agent of the rank and file employees of the company. The TMPC appealed the decision, but the Secretary of Labor denied the appeal. But when TMPCWA submitted its CBA, the TMPC management refused to negotiate.

TMPC filed a Motion for Reconsideration of the DOLE secretary's decision and to the union's surprise an order requiring both parties to a hearing was issued. Obviously alarmed, the union decided to hold an assembly after the scheduled hearing to express their dismay at the decision. The TMPCWA filed a formal request to the Toyota management on behalf of the workers to join the assembly while expressing willingness to work without overtime pay on rest days to make up for lost time.

On March 16, 2001, the 227 union officers and members were shocked to receive a decision from Toyota Corporation terminating 227 union officers and members and suspending 64 union members for 30 days for participating in the assembly from 21 to 23 February 2001. The union filed a notice of strike. While the union was preparing for a strike vote, protest actions were organized in front of Toyota's two plants to persuade management to retract its decision. A full-blown strike subsequently took place when management paid no attention to the protests.

On April 4, 2001, the National Labor Relations Commission issued a Temporary Restraining Order which practically allowed management to disperse the striking members. On April 9, 2001, while most of the striking union members went home to visit their families, around 100 policemen and security guards dispersed the picket line and forcibly took all the strike paraphernalia. At the same time, busloads of scabs and managerial employees were escorted inside the plants.

A day after the violent dispersal of the striking union members, the Secretary of Labor assumed jurisdiction over the labor dispute and ordered the strikers to return to work. Though unconvinced with the decision of the Secretary of Labor, the union members complied with the return to work order. The union then questioned the assumption of jurisdiction by the Secretary of Labor before the Supreme Court, but the high court sustained the DOLE Secretary's decision

After the Secretary of Labor certified the labor dispute to the National Labor Relations Commission, the union requested to defer hearing on the certified cases. The National Labor Relations Commission declared the protest rallies illegal and decided that the termination of 227 members who participated in those assemblies was justified. It also declared that the union officers and directors have forfeited their employment status for having led the protest assemblies.

Toyota management implemented the NLRC decision, and more than half of the membership of the union was dismissed, including the entire union leadership. Toyota also filed criminal complaints against several union members and officers for grave coercion.

Meanwhile, on March 19, 2001, the union proposed to the company that a conference be held between them on March 21, 2002, to settle all issues amicably, including their current labor dispute and CBA regulations. On March 21, 2001, the company filed a petition before the Court of Appeals to nullify the decision of the Secretary of Labor to recognize the TMPCWA as exclusive bargaining agent for the rank and file employees. The company argued that the union failed to obtain a majority vote of the workers. The company opposed the TMPCWA in representing the workers in collective bargaining, and argued that:

- The TMPCWA was coercing and urging its members to force the company to start negotiations for collective bargaining, despite the serious question on the status of the union as the exclusive bargaining agent of the rank-and-file employees;
- 300 employees refused to render overtime service on February 21, 2001 and deliberately did not report for work February 22 and 23, 2001;
- Operations in the production plant was paralyzed and lost potential sales for the amount of P40,000,000;
- The government would suffer considerable losses in taxes from lost potential sales;
- If the challenged voters were not finally resolved, it would result in their mass promotion not on the basis of their work performance, but simply on the opinion of the Secretary of Labor;
- If operations of the company were paralyzed due to the dispute on the status of the challenged voters, its 1,600 employees would be adversely affected, and the company would resort to cost-reduction or even the closure of its business, thus contributing to the already worsening unemployment condition of the country.

The Secretary of Labor and Employment however assumed jurisdiction over the Toyota labor dispute, and ordered all union members and officers who staged the strike to return to work. The DOLE Secretary determined that the auto industry is indispensable to the national interest. The union gave assurances that its members and officers would no longer stage a strike because of the certification election.

On September 24, 2003, the Supreme Court issued a decision favorable to the TMPCWA, and denied the injunction requested by the company, against the union representing Toyota workers in collective bargaining.

Before the Supreme Court issued its favorable decision, on February 2003, the TMPCWA filed a complaint to the ILO Freedom of Association Committee against the government of the Philippines and the Toyota Motor Philippines Corporation for infringement of ILO conventions 87 and 98 at ILO/CFA. In November 2003, the ILO/CFA recognized the complaint and ruled that the Philippine government did infringe on these ILO conventions (Freedom of Association and Protection of the Right to Organize Convention, and Right to Organize And Collective Bargaining Convention) and made several recommendations, including: 1) the reinstatement of all the 233 dismissed union members, 2) the immediate resumption of CBA in order to establish healthy labor relations, 3) the withdrawal of criminal charges against union members, 4) acceptance of ILO delegation, and 5) the amendment of relevant legislative provisions in the country's Labor Code.

- In 2003, the ILO Committee on Freedom of Association completed its report to the ILO Governing Body concerning the complaint. The ILO urged the Philippine government not only to review its labor legislation, but to introduce fair, independent and speedy procedures in the certification process, to recognize a union to represent workers in collective bargaining negotiations. Likewise the ILO Committee requested the government to amend the Labor Code, as it has allowed the Secretary of Labor and Employment to submit the Toyota dispute (and any dispute likely to cause a strike) to compulsory arbitration with the argument that the Toyota Motor Company represents "an industry indispensable to the national interest" – which totally contradicts the provisions of ILO Conventions 87 and 98 ratified by the Philippines. In addition, it observed that the administrative labor court decisions in the Toyota case contained disproportionate sanctions for participating in an illegal strike. It urged the government to facilitate the reinstatement of the 227 dismissed workers and 15 trade union officers who lost their employment status, and to provide for their compensation if reinstatement is not possible."

The ILO observed that Philippine labor laws which provided for the penalty of dismissal from employment are disproportionate to the act of participation in a peaceful strike. A "back to work order" in strikes which do not threaten the life, health, and safety of the population is also not in conformity with ILO Conventions 87 and 98 on freedom of association. The ILO recommended that the government amend its labor laws to be in conformity with these conventions. The ILO noted that it took more than one year to organize a certification election to recognize the union, and another year to have the union confirmed as the exclusive bargaining agent with the Toyota Motor Corporation. The ILO Committee noted that these delays resulted from the various petitions, appeals and motions filed by the Toyota Motor Corporation with the labor authorities, particularly with the Secretary of the Department of Labor and Employment [11].

On July 11, 2005, the Department of Labor and Employment (DOLE) granted the petition for certification election filed by another union, the Toyota Motor Philippines Corporation Labor Organization (TMPCLO). The TMPCWA opposed this action, and argued that there is already a certified bargaining agent, and accused the latter as a yellow union supported by the company.

The Philippine DOLE went ahead and approved the rules and the official list of voters for a Certification Election which was held on February 16, 2006. The TMPCWA organized a picket protest to what they referred to as unjust rules by the labor department, but the union also took part in the election. The TMPCWA lost (237 votes) against TMPCLO (424 votes), out of a total of 894 employees who voted. Under the law, there is failure of election if the winner does not get a majority vote (at least one half plus one of the total votes). There were 121 challenged voters, and an additional 89 dismissed workers. The TMPCWA argued to consider the challenged votes in the result, and filed a protest to question the results, with alleged violations and harassments. It is expected that whatever is the outcome of the case at the lower level, appeals would be filed by either party up to the Supreme Court. As in previous cases in Toyota, this dispute may take many years to resolve.

Meanwhile, on June 6, 2006 the International Metalworkers Federation (IMF), which includes auto industry workers unions all over the world, launched a global campaign to win the reinstatement of the TMCP workers fired, and to encourage the Toyota Motor Philippines Corporations to bargain in good faith with the TMPCWA [12].

Interface in IR, HRD & HRM in the Philippine Auto Industry

Diverse interests motivate the actions and strategies of stakeholders in human resources and industrial relations in the Philippine auto and vehicle supply parts industry. These interests involve the top Japanese auto companies and their local partners, worker unions, and government agencies with a mandate to promote decent work, create jobs, and labor justice. Global players include the International Metalworkers Federation (IMF), and the multinational auto companies in the Philippines: Toyota, Mitsubishi, Nissan, Isuzu, and Honda. Each local stakeholder competes to expand influence and achieve its distinct goals in the sphere of political action, union organizing, and solidarity (in the case of the workers organization), and increase in market share and stability in labor management relations (in the case of the employers). The

---

Box 4. Bone of Contention: Toyota MPC's 3 Function Salary Level with Blurred Distinctions between Supervisors and Rank and File, Japanese Style

SUPERVISORY employees are those who belong to:

The General Staff

Salary Levels 9-10 (Supervisors)

Salary Levels 7-8 (Group Heads, if they function as such, i.e., they are staff with subordinates for whom they are responsible in terms of daily work supervision)

Line Employees – refers to factory workers assigned at the manufacturing plants.

Salary Levels 9-10 (Foremen)

Salary Levels 7-8 (Senior Group Chiefs)

Salary Levels 5-6 (Junior Group Chiefs: Group Leaders & Team Leaders)

Note: Levels 5-10 are considered supervisors only when their actual functions dictate such categorization.

RANK-AND-FILE employees are not included in the managerial or supervisory classes:

The General Staff

Salary Levels 8 and below – function as ordinary staff; no subordinates.

Line Employees – refers to the factory workers, those who are assigned at the manufacturing plants: Salary Levels 1-4.

Office Staff: Salary Levels 1-6.

Source: Toyota Motors Phils. Corporation Worker's Association (TMPCWA) v. Court of Appeals, GR 148924, Supreme Court of the Philippines, 24 September 2003
GR 148924. Supreme Court of the Philippines. 24 September 2003

---

government's goal is to achieve industrial peace, settlement of disputes, and the balance of the protection of interests of both workers and employers *(Box 4)*.

Industrial relations is given more prominence due to increased union organizing among workers in the industry, with some support from the International Metalworkers Federation (IMF), and legal and non-legal conflict among the rival militant unions. Philippine workers organizations however emphasize independence or autonomy from the IMF. The Philippine Metalworkers Alliance (PMA) suspended its relations with the IMF, due to rivalry with the militant Kilusang Mayo Uno (May First Movement) affiliate in Toyota Motors. The KMU affiliate successfully filed a case of violation of freedom of association in Toyota Motors Philippines Corporation with the ILO. Government intervention in labor disputes is possible through conciliation, mediation, voluntary and compulsory arbitration through the courts. Policy changes through new rules and laws in labor relations are not expected to change significantly in the Philippines.

Auto and vehicle employers need to understand and realize the importance of respecting freedom of association, and being neutral in intra-union rivalry and conflicts caused by ideological differences among the union leaders. The goal must be to provide an environment of freedom to facilitate collective bargaining negotiations, and the use of labor-management committees (LMCs), grievance committees, and other bilateral mechanisms to reach agreement with the unions. It is urgent that both employers and the workers be provided with the necessary skills and competencies for negotiations, bargaining, and voluntary modes of disputes settlement. Top management and industry leaders need to appreciate that in the absence of competencies and skills in industrial relations, risk of jeopardizing costly investments will be greater.

It is expected that Philippine industrial relations in the auto and vehicle supply parts industry will increase in significance, as the stakes are high for all parties involved. It is important to strengthen mechanisms that will promote respect of the competing and overlapping interests of both employers and workers, and find venues and opportunities for negotiations and dialogue towards a win-win achievement of mutual goals *(Box 5)*.

Box 5. Extent of Influence of Toyota Japan HRM Policies in Toyota Motor Philippines Corp.: Relations with Employees

Toyota Japan	Toyota Motor Philippines
"Foster a corporate culture that enhances individual creativity and teamwork value"	5S: "seiri, seiso, seiketsu, seiton, shitsuke" Gemba shugi. "Muda, mura, muri,
"Honoring mutual trust and respect between labor and management."	Industrial relations is subject to Supreme Court rulings and ILO opinion asking the company to reinstate dismissed workers. TMPC actively opposed union formation.
"Stable employment where lay offs and dismissals not readily made."	Dismissal of workers who formed a union and organized protests against company not recognizing the union.
"Mechanism for voluntary initiatives in continuous improvements."	Kaizen activities. Suggestion schemes.
"Committed and thorough HRD"	Toyota Philippines has an active HR group, and a skills training center.

Note: Toyota Japan owns 34 percent of Toyota Motor Philippines. The majority ownership is by the local Filipino Chinese taipan, Metrobank Group of George Ty.

The employers, whose views and opinions were diligently sought for this study, agree that customers or buyers of auto vehicle products are not much concerned about union activity. The industry has not experienced organized customer boycotts which succeeded in the past. But it may be deduced that with industry unions on the rise through the Philippine Metalworkers Alliance – AIWA, the standardization and narrowing of differentials of wage rates and other economic allowances or incentives may become a possibility.

The AIWA has 15 union affiliates from the following Japanese auto companies: Mitsubishi, Toyota, Nissan, Isuzu and Honda. There are also affiliate unions from among auto parts makers and car dealerships. There are at least 20,000 workers who are members of 15 union affiliates of the AIWA. This makes up about 27 percent of the total estimated workforce of the 75,000 workers in the auto industry. The PMA has a total worker base of 40,000 from 27 union affiliates.

While union militancy may affect employee motivation and productivity, there are various means which could be harnessed to channel the impact of militancy into positive results, particularly through venues such as labor-management meetings, informal dialogues, and in the mobilization of employee welfare programs to send a strong message that the "company cares" for each member of the production team from the rank and file up to the top tiers of the organization.

Employers themselves do not deny that there are benefits to compliance with labor standards. Most employers acknowledge that adherence to humane labor practices and standards empower people and increase employee motivation, which in turn, leads to better performance and productivity. The need to comply with laws and regulations which are often quite strict, even in developing countries, indeed, is a major consideration. But pressure from customers and civil society has also added as a factor in some sectors, especially where assets such as corporate brand and reputation are important and need to be protected. For in the end, employers have realized, good sales go hand in hand with a positive business image.

5.3 Non-Union HRM Strategies at Work: Labor Management Council in the *Enchanted Kingdom* Theme Park [12]

The *Enchanted Kingdom* is a popular theme park in south Luzon. Over a million people would head south of Laguna each year to spend a day or a week of fun-filled excitement at Enchanted Kingdom. But more than the exhilarating rides they have, the main attraction this time, focuses with the park's workforce that had, since it started operations in 1995, committed themselves to bring magic and smile to their customers. The owner, Mr. Cesar Mario Mamon is a known Filipino civic and religious leader and a self made entrepreneur. The company is owned fully by the Mamon family.

The Enchanted Kingdom employees are members of the Labor Management Council (EK-LMC). According to the company HR manager, the EK-LMC "focused on giving equal footing and opportunity to both the management and the workers of the company." The company attributes its growth into a world class theme park from this new and improved employee-employer relationship, through the LMC mechanism.

Company officials say that through the LMC, rank and file employees are given the chance to be valued on the same level as the company's shareholders, instilling transparency, unity and a sense of ownership. The result enabled the Enchanted Kingdom to gain momentum in sales and revenues, and establish itself as a "world class" amusement park incomparable to any other in the country.

The creation of EK-LMC not only improved management relationship but also paved way for Enchanted's once unstable revenue to expand and rise optimistically. Melissa Monicayo, Assistant Vice President for Finance said Enchanted' financial condition has greatly improved since the company started reorganizing its personnel.

"Before, Enchanted's revenue was on a roller-coaster ride. Park attendance was poor and labor management relationship was strained. But when we started the LMC in 2000, our focus changed. Our revenues slowly but surely inched its way up despite the economic backdrop and our relationship not only improved but made us closer with each other", Monicayo said.

Enchanted has at least 220 regular employees. During lean and peak season, its cast members reach to play for the success of the company. They are assigned at the park's 16-hectare playground in Sta. Rosa, Laguna, where over one million people visit annually to relish the exhilarating rides and features of the park.

Executives of the company touched base with government officials and the academe like the Department of Labor and Employment (DOLE), University of the Philippines School of Labor and Industrial Relations (UPSOLAIR), and the Department of Trade and Industry (DTI) Center for Competitiveness for their company reorganization. Company officials said there were efforts to organize a union, but these did not prosper due to company initiatives to promote employee welfare and performance.

The EK-LMC is divided into six committees, namely Personnel and Policies, Communications and Concerns, Productivity and Quality, Recreation and Socials, Livelihood and Benefits and Safety and Health. Each committee is headed by four labor representatives and two from the management.

Remarkably, its attempt to prioritize its labor force has paid off. "We always want to make sure that the labor representatives outnumber the management representatives in each committee because we want to give importance to our employees", Lolita C. Torres, Enchanted's Assistant Vice President for Human Resources said.

The change in the management approach has also paved way for the company's remuneration package and incentives in the region. Regular employees' families are also taken care of by the company even after their employees have reached retirement. "This is our way of showing that we also care for their families. We also want them to feel they are still part of the group even if they are no longer working with us," Torres said. Aside from the medical benefits, LMC has also paved way for revenue generating projects for its employees. LMC has matured us. There is shared planning and shared decisions. It has formed unity and trust within the labor management and has instilled in us a sense of transparency and ownership," Torres said.

6. QUESTIONS FOR DISCUSSION

1. With more severe competition due to globalization, what should the three actors in the Philippines industrial relations system do to enhance the competitiveness of the country's economy?

2. Based on the case studies given in this chapter, which approach you would follow if you were a union leader? Which industrial relations approach would you take if you were on the management team?

3. How could labor-management relations at the workplace level be improved and strengthened? How can collective bargaining in good faith be developed? If you were the manager in charge of industrial relations issues, what would be your strategies to develop a sound industrial relations system at your workplace?

4. In your view, how could unions serve their members better in the globalization era while contributing to the competitiveness of the firm?

Box 6 Summary of Goals and Strategies for Stakeholders of Industrial Relations in the Philippine Auto & Vehicle Parts Supply Industry

Stakeholders	Goals	Strategy
Worker organization:		
Philippine Metalworkers Alliance + Alliance of Progressive Labor (AIWA - APL)	Promote industry wide bargaining through responsible unionism.	Union organizing, petition for certification elections. Court cases.
Rival unions: Kilusang Mayo Uno (KMU), Bukluran ng Manggagawang Pilipino (BMP)	Expand membership. Solicit support from ILO, IMF and the public.	Picket, strikes.
Employers:		
Subsidiaries of car companies: Toyota, Mitsubishi, Honda, Isuzu, Nissan	Expand, increase or stabilize market share. Minimize disruption in production.	Increase negotiations skills, pro active competencies in IR & HR.
Government: Dept of Labor & Employment (DOLE):		
DOLE in relation to employers	Compliance with labor standards & policies, create jobs, stabilize employment and promote foreign investment.	Conciliation, mediation, voluntary and compulsory arbitration through labor court.
DOLE in relation to unions	Protection of workers rights.	Information sharing.
DOLE in relation to IMF	Respect for freedom of association.	Monitoring.
Arbiters, National Labor Relations Commission, Court of Appeals, Supreme Court	Settlement of labor disputes through compulsory arbitration, based on Philippine labor laws.	Temporary restraining orders, injunctions, execution of decisions.
International Metalworkers Federation (IMF)	Achieve international worker solidarity, industry bargaining & coordination. International framework agreements.	Solidarity, support with PWA, KMU, IMF Philippine Council. Pressure multinational auto employers.
International Labor Organization (ILO)	Promote decent work, monitor compliance with international labor standards	Investigation, pressure to DOLE & government

**Box 7. How to Link Sound Industrial Relations with HRD/HRM:
A Guide to Competencies**

Macro economic dimensions & national industry policies	Competencies required to link with micro level (enterprise) practices
Development of critical professional competencies & skills development.	Career track development & supportive HRM strategies; firm's human capital formation.
National income & value added; minimum wages; living standards	High performance & productivity improvement schemes. Performance based compensation.
Respect for workers' rights. Tripartite disputes settlement & stable IR	Bipartite labor management relations at the workplace, with minimum government intervention
Maintenance of purchasing power & low inflation	Allowances & income supplements.
Work & life balance. Gender sensitivity.	Flexible work hours. Family support. Support for solo parents. Employee housing program.
Health & safety at the workplace.	Health clinics. Programs to address psycho-social problems at the workplace (harassment, alcoholism, unwanted pregnancies, drugs ...)
Social security.	Pension plans. Early (voluntary) retirement plans.
Labor laws & policies.	Compliance with labor standards; Corporate Social Responsibility (CSR). Respect for diversity.

ENDNOTES

1. *Manila Bulletin*, "RP overseas remittances hit US$ 12.8 billion", 15 February 2007.

2. "Survive, compete, succeed in global competition" is the theme of the National Conference of the Employers Confederation of the Philippines (ECOP) in May 2006 (see: www.ecop.org.ph).

3. National Statistics Office, "2005 Survey of Overseas Filipinos" www.census.gov.ph [Accessed 30 November 2006].

4. Article XIII, Section 3 on "Social Justice and Human Rights" of the 1987 Philippine Constitution.

5. Section 8, Article III on the Bill of Rights of the 1987 Philippine Constitution.

6. Section 2(5), Article IX-B of the 1987 Philippine Constitution.

7. Bureau of Labor Relations, Department of Labor and Employment, www.blr.dole.gov.ph. Special release on industrial relations. Manila: DOLE-BLES [Accessed 25 April 2006].

8. Statements and activities of the major trade union organizations could be accessed in the following websites: TUCP, www.tucp.org.ph; Federation of Free Workers (FFW), www.ffw.org.ph; Alliance of Progressive Labor (APL), www.apl.org.ph

9. This case study is from various news reports and a paper on the "Analysis on the Present Struggle of the Nestle Workers in the Philippines," a report of the Union of Filipro Employees (UFE) 1991, and the author's observations during fieldwork with both union and management officials.

10. This section is based on public court records and interviews with industry leaders.

11. The full text of the ILO Committee on Freedom of Association report on the Toyota Motor Philippine

12. The IMF global campaign webpage could be accessed at www.imfmetal.org/toyotaphiilppines [Accessed 15 January 2007].

13. Condensed from a news article by Hannah L Tarragoza, *Manila Bulletin*, 19 September 2005, page C1. Supplemented by interviews of the author with Enchanted Kingdom management.

APPENDIX 1. IMPORTANT LABOR LAWS IN THE PHILIPPINES

1. Freedom of Association and Union Rights

Item	Provision	Main features
Workers rights	Art. 3, Section 8, Philippine Constitution	State shall assure the rights of workers to self-organization, collective bargaining, security of tenure, and just & humane conditions of work.
Union rights & registration	Art. 234 to 240, PLC	Association or unions entitled to rights and privileges granted by law.
Rights against unfair labor practices	Art. 247 to 249, PLC	Defines unfair labor practices of both employers & labor organizations, with criminal sanctions.
Right to strike	Art. 263 & 264, PLC	Workers have right to engage in concerted action for purposes of collective bargaining.
Right to collective bargaining	Art. 250 to 259, PLC	Procedures for CBA, to be enforced for 5 years.
Grievance procedure	Art. 260 to 262, PLC	Grievance machinery & procedure, including voluntary arbitration.
Arbitration	Art. 261, PLC	Parties shall name a voluntary arbitrator for disputes settlement.
Public sector unions	Executive Order 180 (1987)	Right to form unions and engage in collective negotiations among government employees.

2.   Employment Standards

Item	Source of legislation	Main features
Minimum age	Art. 139, PLC	No child below 15 years shall be employed. Those between 15-17 years of age maybe employed in non-hazardous jobs.
Non discrimination	Art. 135, PLC	Unlawful to discriminate against women employees with respect to terms and conditions of employment.
	Art. 3, PLC	State shall ... ensure equal work opportunities regardless of sex, race or creed.
Regularization	Art. 280 & 281, PLC	Probationary employment not to exceed 6 months. Employee shall be considered regular if allowed to work after 6 months. Employees could be regularized if duties are necessary or desirable in the usual business or trade of the employer.
Subcontracting	Art. 106, PLC	DOLE may restrict, prohibit the contracting out of labor. Prohibits "labor only contracting" -- where the person supplying workers to an employer does not have substantial capital or investment in the form of tools, equipment, machineries, work premises, among others.
Security of tenure	Art. 279, PLC	Regular employee could only be dismissed for just or authorized business causes.
Night work, women	Art. 130, PLC	Women prohibited from working between 10 pm to 6 am.
Forced labor	Art. 114 & Art. 116, PLC	While there is no direct mention against forced labor, these articles prohibit actions that result in indebtedness or bond.

3. Wages

Item	Source of legislation	Main features
Minimum wages	Art. 99; Art. 120 to 127, PLC	Provides for minimum wages, based on regional rate as determined by tripartite wage boards.
Overtime pay	Art. 87, PLC	Provides for overtime work: at least 25% of regular pay.
Premium pay on holidays & rest days	Art. 93 & 94, PLC	Provides for compensation for rest days, Sundays or holiday, special holiday work-- at least 30% of the regular pay.
Night shift pay	Art. 86, PLC	Provides for a 10% night shift differential.
13th month pay	PD 851	All employers required to pay 13th month pay.
Non diminution in pay	Art. 100, PLC	Prohibition against elimination or diminution of benefits.

* 'PLC': Philippine Labor Code (1974), as amended.

4. Hours of Work

Item	Source of Legislation	Main Features
8 hours of work	Art. 83, PLC	Defines the normal hours of work, not to exceed 8 hours/day
Meal periods	Art. 85, PLC	Provides for meal periods, not less than 60 minutes time-off for regular meals.
Weekly rest period	Art. 91 to 92, PLC	Provides for weekly rest periods after 6 consecutive working days, not less than 24 hours.
Paternity leave	RA8187	Seven days paternity leave.
Solo parent leave	RA8972 (2000)	Enterprises must set up a system to recognize and help solo parents, including solo parents leave.

* 'PLC': Philippine Labor Code (1974), as amended.

5. Health & Safety

Item	Source of Legislation	Main Features
Paid maternity leave	Art. 133, PLC	Maternity leave at least 2 weeks before delivery and 4 weeks after delivery
Medical and dental services	Art. 156 to 161	First aid, medical and dental services, health program, 1 full time nurse for at least 200 employees.
Health & safety	Art. 162 to 165	Safety and health standards, and administration
Sexual harassment	RA 7877	Enterprises must provide for a Code of Discipline to prevent and deal with sexual harassment.

6. Social Security

Item	Source of Legislation	Main Features
Employees Compensation	Art. 166, PLC	Social security and employee's compensation
Social security	RA 1161	Social security law of 1997 compulsory coverage.
GSIS law	RA8291	Government employees social security law (1997)
HDMF law	(Pag-ibig Law)	Membership in the Home Development Mutual Fund
Philhealth	RA7575	National health insurance (enhanced Medicare)

Sources: Philippine Labor Code (PLC) (1974) and Implementing Rules, as amended, unless otherwise indicated; Azucena (2005); ILS-DOLE (2000)

Chapter 9

MAKING INDUSTRIAL RELATIONS WORK IN THE GLOBALIZATION ERA: CHALLENGES AHEAD FOR KNOWLEDGE-BASED ECONOMIES

Sununta Siengthai, John J. Lawler, Chris Rowley and Hiromasa Suzuki

1.   SUMMARY AND CONCLUSION

This book has analyzed how globalization has affected industrial relations relations at the enterprise level in general and the effect of the Asian financial crisis and its aftermath on industrial relations in the Asian knowledge-based economies in particular. Siengthai and Pitayanon (Ch.1) describe and discuss the economic environment and employment growth of Japan, Korea, Taiwan, Singapore, the Philippines and Thailand in the past decade and their current economic situations. Based on the available statistics, they discuss the changing trends in industrial relations in these countries. They find industrial action (strike days, etc.) has decreased in spite of the fact that the number of union organizations has increased in recent years in Korea, Taiwan, and Thailand. As there has been no specific empirical studies undertaken to explain such phenomena, this finding gives some support to the system model proposed by Siengthai (Ch.2) which asserts that effective human resource management (HRM) and industrial relations will lead to organizational learning, firm innovation and productivity improvement. The illustrative case studies on industrial relations processes at the enterprise level for these selected economies are given by HRM/IR scholars in each country chapter.

In Japan, the research by Suzuki and Kubo (Ch.3) focuses on the transformation of Japanese firms and their HRM system. Indeed, the traditional function of HRM was central to organizational building and control of Japanese firms. It is observed that top management relied on a personal network of managers to control the different departments and activities, in contrast to the US firms, which tend to stress financial controls. With increasing overseas production, Japanese firms try to set up new ways of communication and controls with or without the central HRM department. Suzuki and Kubo first look at the long-term changes in the Japanese economic and social context. They also examine structural elements such as demographic trends. Their investigation suggests that Japan is currently experiencing a rapidly aging population. In addition, the level of female labor force participation is rising as is the growth of atypical employment. Then, the authors describe changes concerning the actors in the industrial relations and HRM systems and offer a case study which illustrates the HRM practices in a Japanese multinational firm with special reference to the recent changes in pay policies (i.e., pay for performance system) which is also evidenced in other countries in this book.

In Korea, Park (Ch.4) observes that since 1987, in terms of industrial relations system development, the country has seen the promotion of labor rights, reduced state intervention into union activities and the establishment of a system of collective bargaining to determine wages and working conditions in Korean workplaces. However, the price of this transformation has been substantial. Consecutive wage rises, often surpassing productivity gains, have become a heavy burden on the competitiveness of Korea's companies. The Korean economy has also had to pay a high price due to the frequent strikes and work stoppages that occurred during this period. In 1997, a new set of the labor laws was passed. However, even before the most controversial provision of the 1997 labor law amendment became effective, Korea was hit by the Asian financial crisis.

Park illustrates the development of trade unionism in the country from late 1980 to the early 2000s. The analysis of trade union development suggests the strong intervention of the government before 1987 and its recognition of the role of the union in industries in the late 1990s after the financial crisis. White-collar unions, mostly those in the banking sector, were formed in the late 1980s. The growth of the unions experienced a decline in the late 1990s.

Lee (Ch.5) notes that Taiwan has enjoyed enormous success in its ongoing economic development for over fifty years, and as a result, the island has gained international recognition for this 'economic miracle'. Furthermore, due largely to the extraordinary transformation of Taiwan over a period of less than two decades, from an authoritarian state to an open and democratic society, this 'economic miracle' has subsequently been developed into a 'political miracle'.

Lee began with a brief description of the industrial relations system during the former industrial era in Taiwan, before going on to examine the new development. The banking industry was then used as a case to illustrate the changing face of industrial relations within a KBE. The banking industry was selected as the case because this industry has been traditionally accounted for a substantial share of white collar workers enjoying high employment stability and good levels of pay and benefits in Taiwan. The rapid emergence of Taiwan as a global hub of the electronics and medium-heavy industrial sectors has mirrored the rapid industrial development of its Asian neighbors, Japan and South Korea. Concomitant with Taiwan's economic emergence has been a placid industrial climate, policed by a strong national government with pervasive influence over organized labor and governmental agencies of labor administration.

Political changes have also led to new dynamics in Taiwan's industrial relations. New labor representative organizations that emerged only defined themselves in terms of their independence from, and indeed a level of antipathy towards, many of the elements of central authority. Even though its manufacturing sector is still strong, the rapid economic growth and the emergence of the mainland manufacturing sector will likely require that Taiwan change its economic role from a primary manufacturer to a facilitator of manufacturing within the region. These challenges associated with this new role, and the developing trading and investment ties between Taiwan and mainland China, have driven the development of a less centralized, more market-driven industrial relations system in Taiwan.

On the other hand, changes in various aspects of employment have been experienced in Taiwan in recent years. These include increasing employment insecurity, changes in pay systems, changes in employment standards, erosion of life-long employment for senior managers, increases in employment flexibility, moves towards demarcation (categorization), and deskilling of the workforce. The responses of workers, particularly in the banking *industry case,* have been in terms of collective bargaining agreements, and the appointment of bank employees to boards of directors.

Employers are much more aware of the important contribution of human resources. Many employers, particularly those in the high-tech industries are paying greater attention to HRM principles and trying hard to develop human capital within their enterprises. Thus, we have seen an emphasis on individualism by employers on one side, while the government and unions strive for collectivism on the other. Clearly, however, employers, unions and the government in Taiwan must search for an optimum combination of individualism and collectivism suitable for Taiwan's special social and cultural background.

Wan (Ch.6) provides a brief introduction to industrial relations in Singapore in general and a case study of the various industrial relations issues between Singapore International Airlines (SIA) and its five unions. The case study traces the intense union-management relationship occurring during the period from the September 11 tragedy to crisis management immediately after the SARS outbreak. The SIA group was chosen as the point of focus because it is in this particular industry (the global airline industry) and this enormous *organization,* that the climate of industrial relations attracts the most attention from the government, the labor movement, employers in general and the mass media. Given the significance of Singapore as an indisputable international air hub and SIA as a showcase of the country's (business) success story, good industrial relations, mutual acceptance, teamwork and the avoidance of industrial conflict are not only indispensable, but also must be maintained at all cost. The case provides a vivid example of the so-called 'non-adversarial problem-solving approach' which was applied to an industry which has been negatively affected by economic slowdown, high oil prices, constant threat of terrorism, emergence of regional budget airlines and the occasional health disaster like SARS.

Siengthai (Ch.7) describes the changes Thailand had experienced immediately after the 1997 Asian financial crisis and its economic adjustment processes. The development of the industrial relations system in the country is discussed. Selected case studies of the industrial relations in the auto-related and textiles industries are given to illustrate how cooperative industrial relations has been able to foster company's survival and growth.

Previous to 1975 workers associations were formed. However, trade unions in Thailand have only been legal since 1975, and strikes legal since 1981. The trade union movement has been weak, both in coverage and in workplace industrial relations. The low level of union density in the private sector reflects difficulties faced by unions in their organizing efforts. Companies have used various tactics to undermine strikes which were regarded by the organized workers as the only powerful industrial action to bargain with their employers for better terms and conditions of employment. These include tactics which are illegal or exploit "legal loopholes" to maintain non-union status, temporary company shutdown, mass terminations, sacking of union leaders and use of temporary workers.

Until recently, in the Thai context, collective bargaining is not effectively resorted to as an ideal process of decision-making between employer and employees of the enterprise in question on issues that would affect the latter. Most of the conflicts will be solved only when employees resort to the power structure (namely, political entities or military groups) which acted as a third party to intervene and thus make their demands to the employers materialized. Here again, the concept of *the 'patron-client'* is exhibited. Most of the workers' organizations have to demonstrate or publicize the conflict in order to gain support from the public and to put pressure on employers to concede to their demands. For most of the employees who are not members of the unions, when they are not satisfied with their jobs or are unfairly treated, often they choose to quit rather than bargain with the employers. This is more evident when the economy is experiencing an economic boom. In fact, it can be one reason explaining why there have not been many strikes in recent years. High quit rates have reduced the competitiveness of such firms. In the Thai context in which confrontation is usually avoided, joint consultation therefore can be another mechanism to produce the desired outcomes which include industrial peace.

In short, Thailand is still far from achieving an effective industrial relations system whereby the two sides are considered equal partners. The reasons include the lack of effective conflict resolution mechanisms which provide satisfaction to both employers and employees, lack of understanding and training about the industrial relations system as a useful concept for rule-making and conflict-resolution among both employers and employees and lack of a country-wide training and education on existing labor laws.

Amante (Ch.8) notes that in the Philippines various factors are influencing changes in the industrial relations system. These include pressures from globalization process, international norms and conventions on corporate social responsibility, cultural values at both corporate and national levels. To survive and compete, Philippine employers resort to functional flexibility and more cooperative industrial relations, with an anti-union thrust. The logic of competition induced firms to adopt practices that promote numerical flexibility such that a core-periphery workforce is created. Philippine unions however are unable to effectively counter employer strategies, due to low number in membership, fragmentation and an unfavorable public-policy environment. While the basic framework of industrial relations remain firm, the Philippine government policies, strategies and resources were inadequate to counteract the negative effects of global market integration on workers, and to launch the economy into a sustainable high road of industrialization.

Of all the selected countries in this study where union memberships statistics available, it is found that the union membership is declining in the Philippines. Whether the decline of trade unions mean that they have lost their economic and social roles in the society, it is interesting to observe in the next decade. For example, in Japan's case, it is asserted that Japanese labor unions are faced with many challenges to their raison d'etre. Similar to some other countries represented in this book, few employees actually participate in union activities.

In conclusion, the case studies provided in all chapters suggest that each country still experiences a different stage of industrial relations system development due to various factors in both the internal and external environments faced by the country. However, due to the intensive pressure from the globalization process, there seems to be an emergent pattern among these countries that HRM is taking a significant role in enabling private sector growth. With the population in each country being more educated and skilled, higher levels of job mobility may be possible for workers and hence there is less need for traditional labor unions which are adversarial in nature. In combination with Asian values regarding harmony, awareness of external pressures may lead to more cooperative labor-management relations. Evidently, flexibility is one of the 'core' concept to be achieved by firms to sustain their organizational competitiveness in global markets. To achieve this, they must have effective HRM practices which advocate proactive HRD and labor-management relations. Both HRM and industrial relations must be aligned to the business strategies of the firms. The effective utilization of human capital for economic development requires productive and harmonious relations between the workforce and the employers through a stable, responsive web of rules which promote decent work and livelihoods.

2.   MAKING INDUSTRIAL RELATIONS WORK FOR COMPETITIVE ADVANTAGE

As demonstrated in many cases in this book, industrial relations in the economically environments of the knowledge economies has suggested many areas of improvement for the industrial relations mechanisms at the enterprise level. We would like to make the following recommendations with respect to the enterprise level industrial relations:

1. Enterprises should improve their communication approaches and channels. This has proved to be effective and positive to the relationship of both parties who are direct stakeholders of the business. In the ICTs environment, not only suggestion boxes or meetings but also email communications or web-based grievance procedures can be designed for employees to be able to have their voice heard. This also implies that companies that introduce the ICTs environment should provide training and retraining on computer literacy and skills so that they can work and use the ICTs effectively.

2. Management teams, especially, middle-level management and supervisors, should be educated about the industrial relations concepts and become more proactive in this area. There should be an attitudinal restructuring with regard to the role of workers organizations. Recognition given to worker organizations and cooperation in terms of information-sharing. The joint decision-making in some aspects that affect terms and conditions of employment in the workplace generally lead to job satisfaction, meaningfulness and sense of belonging for workers.

3. The concept of partnership should be cultivated among the two parties. While management may have capital, they need labor as another source of input in the production and service processes. Therefore, both are equally important to make business survive and grow. Thus, a 'win-win approach' should always be taken in handling industrial relations issues.

4. The concept of workers councils has proved to work well in some Asian countries, such as Japan and Thailand. However, as wages and salary issues are not allowed by law to be discussed legally in workers' councils, both management and workers must be educated about labor law and the mechanisms how to handle those issues effectively such as in the collective bargaining exercises. In many cases, particularly when workers are not well-educated, they are found to be ignorant about their rights and duties in law, and hence have a low level of interest in participating in union activities. In other words, union organizations exist with low levels of activities, as evidenced in Japan and Thailand.

5. On the employees' side, workers organizations should be more educated regarding how to run their organizations using management or union administration concepts. Many unions do not keep good records of their own organization. Therefore, it is very difficult for the learning process to take place in the organizations and hence there is a lack of union organization development.

6. In order to help maintain employment security of members and other economic and social objectives, unions must become an educational institution for union members, whose clear aim is the education of employees. Unions should advocate

that their members' long-term personal success is intertwined with their employer's prosperity. This simply implies that unions will transform traditional adversarial relationship with employers to ones which are more of an instrumental role while still maintaining the bargaining power to improve terms and conditions of employment for the benefits of members at large. Unions should also cooperate with the other two main partners in the industrial relations system, namely the employers and the government, to make education, training and retraining an integral part of every employee' s life.

7. As evidenced in the country cases, HRM practices in companies firms are changing towards more performance-oriented cultures rather than membership-oriented cultures. Thus, unions must try to ensure that employees are well-supported, are equipped with the skills and abilities to perform and are fairly treated with respect to employment and promotional opportunities. Unions should support and encourage member involvement and participation in decision-making processes at all levels of the organization that would affect terms and conditions of employment.

8. It has become more necessary that unions develop more services to cater to the needs of their members to increase membership and participation and involvement in union activities. With the emphasis on the superordinate goal of the firms, union organizations should be more constructive as change agents and able to align their long-term goal of survival and their beneficial role to their members, particularly the more disadvantaged members by background of training and education, for example, members of older generation with less education.

9. On the government's part, there should be an active role of the concerned ministry to provide education *about labor law* to both employers and employees, as well as the skill development programs to workers in various sectors. Incentives should be given to the firms that provide skill development programs to their workers on a continuous basis. The skill development fund concept should be implemented more effectively.

10. A bipartite relationship should be encouraged. The government should play down its role so that the two parties will resolve conflicts on their own. The government can develop certain schemes, such as social protection and social safety nets. It can encourage social dialogue among concerned parties at the enterprise level as well as at the national level on labor market issues and employment security as well as quality of working life. It can act more as an informant of the changes in the external socio-economic conditions for the two parties. In other words, the government will need to do more research and study on labor markets and send signals to the parties for their proactive planning. Hence, government's role will be on the rule and regulations set for the two players, not as the third party to intervene because of their interaction.

3. CHALLENGES AHEAD

It is clear that with the globalization process and the advent of information and communication technologies, economies cannot expect stable environments in the future. Those who are already players in the global market will be faced with the following challenges:

1. The role of the government as the largest employer in the economy: the government has often been the largest employer in *an economy*. Currently, countries represented in this study are going through public sector reform, privatization of public enterprises and downsizing. It is likely that this will be through changing employment systems, and outsourcing activities. How can the government be a good employer in applying the new employment practices?

2. The issue of regulating decent works: This can be through amendment of existing labor laws and encouraging the formation of vested interest groups, especially for workers at all levels by encouraging and training them to be able to manage their organizations and provide benefits to their members. But again, regulating decent work is not an easy task.

3.   Deskilling jobs due to technology – general skills needed by all industries rather than specific skills in especially in the service sectors. For example, the banking industry used to be the source of large number of jobs. Now, many of the traditional transactions are being automatically done by machines. Other examples include tourism and even in the educational service sector, where new internet or online services and programmes are available. All of these developments are made possible by the advancement of technology in general and information and communication technology in particular. These changes are taking place in all societal sectors which facilitate and enhance the transformation of the traditional to modern and knowledge-based societies. Hence, the efficiency and effectiveness of the market mechanism will only be achieved if market participants are knowledgeable and skilled and able to afford the access to such technology and become active participants in the market. The question raised from the findings from the cases in this study is then: what should be the role of the state to facilitate and cope with the globalization process and the technology environments which demand flexibility of firms to survive and grow in the highly competitive and borderless environment.

In Europe and the U.S. the central question concerns the new forms of social protection – labor market policies, in particular – that accompany a fast-evolving labor market as it can no longer deliver employment and social protection (Auer and Cazes, 2003). Labor market policies are an important element of employment and social protection, and their adaptation to the new, more flexible employment practices. (Auer and Cazes, 2003)

Thus, the state or government cannot leave market mechanisms alone. In fact, it seems to be even more important that state or government will need to make every effort to create and participate in the international dialogue and solve these market-related problems with respect to employment and well-being of its citizens in regional and global fora. The state needs to equip and provide access to its citizens who are labor market participants with good education and knowledge resources so that they themselves can be multi-skilled and become more flexible in term of their job roles. The state should provide incentives to companies to further invest in training and retraining the existing workforce so that they will be skilled and knowledgeable to cope with changes firms face. Hence, this is also where the role of HRM lies: HRD and performance management of the firm.

REFERENCES

Abegglen, J.C. (1958) *The Japanese Factory: Aspects of Its Social Organization,* Glencoe, IL: Free Press

Alic, John A. (1997) "Knowledge, Skill and Education in the New GlobalEconomy," *Futures*, Vol.29, No.1, pp.5-16.

Amante, Maragtas S.V. (1993) "Tensions in Industrial Democracy and Human Resource Management: A Case Study of Japanese Enterprises in the Philippines", *The International Journal of Human Resource Management.* February: 129-158.

Amante, Maragtas S.V. (1995) "Employment and Wage Practices of Japanese Firms in the Philippines: Convergence with Filipino-Chinese and Western-Owned Firms", *The International Journal of Human Resource Management.* September: 642-655

Amante, Maragtas S.V. (1996) "The 'Best Practice Model' and the Japanese Human Resource Approach in the Philippines" *Keio Business Review*, Keio University Press, Tokyo. Reprinted by The Japan Institute of Labour in *Frontiers of Human Resources* (a collection of essays in honor of Prof. Yoko Sano)

Amante, Maragtas S. V. (1997) "Converging and diverging trends in human resources management in the Philippines", *Asia Pacific Business Review,* Vol. 3 No. 3 & 4, (U.K.)

Amante, Maragtas (2005) "Social Accountability in Philippine Enterprises: Moving Ahead in Advocacy", *Multipartite Policy Dialogue in Social Accountability,* Dusit Hotel, Makati City, 15 March 2005, sponsored by the German Development Cooperation (GTZ) and the Employers' Confederation of the Philippines (ECOP).

Amante, Maragtas (2006) *Industrial Relations in the Philippine Auto Parts Supply & Vehicle Industry.* Quezon City: University of the Philippines School of Labour and Industrial Relations (UP SOLAIR) and Center for Labour Education & Research Development (CLEARED) Foundation. Unpublished report.

Andrea, D.; O' Brien, C. and Buono, A.F. (1996) " Building Effective Learning Teams: Lessons from the Field," *SAM Advanced Management Journal*, 61, 3:4-9, Summer.

Aoki, M. & Dore, R. (ed) (1994), *The Japanese Firm; Sources of Competitive Strength,* Clarendon Press Oxford

Argyris, C. (1993) Teaching Smart People How to Learn, in Robert Howard (ed.) (1993) *The Learning Imperative: Managing People for Continuous Innovation*, A Harvard Business Review Book, pp. 177-194.

Arom Pongpangan Foundation (1990) *The History of Labour Movement in Thailand: From the Early Stage to 1989*, December.

Auer, Peter and Cazes, Sandrine (eds.) (2003) *Employment Stability in an Age of Flexibility:Evidence from Industrialized Countries*, Interna- tional Labour Office, Geneva, 272 pp.

Azucena, Cesario A. (2005) *The Labour Code with Comments & Cases*. Manila: Rex Book Store.

Bacungan, Froilan M. (1999) "Philippine Labour Code for the 21st Century". *Philippine Industrial Relations for the 21st Century: Emerging Issues, Challenges and Strategies. Proceedings of the 1999 National Conference on Industrial Relations.* Gatchalian, J. C., Amante, M.S.V. & Gust, G. (editors) Quezon City: U.P. School of Labour and Industrial Relations, and Philippine Industrial Relations Society, pp. 93 – 114.

Bacungan, Froilan and Ofreneo, Rene (2002) "The Development of Labour Law and Labour Market Policy in the Philippines." In Sean Cooney, Tim Lindsey, Richard Mitchell and Ying Zhu (eds.) (2002) *Law and Labour Market Regulation in East Asia*. London: Routledge, pp. 91-121.

Brion, Arturo D. (1997) *Public Sector Unionism: A Proposed Re-configuration,* Manila: Civil Service Commission. Unpublished Manuscript.

Bamber, Greg J. and Lansbury, Russell D. (1998) *International & Comparative Employment Relations: A Study of Industrialized Market Economies*, Third edition, Sage Publication, London.

Bahrami, Bahman (1988) "Productivity Improvement Through Cooperation of Employees and Employers", Labour Law Journal, March, pp. 167 – 178.

Barney, J. (1991) "Firm Resources and Sustained Competitive Advantage", *Journal of Management*, Vol. 17, pp.99-120.

Bank of Thailand Monthly Bulletin. Various issues.

Bangkok Bank Annual Report (1999).

Batstone, Eric and Gourlay, Stephen (1986) *Unions, Unemployment and Innovation*, Basil Blackwell Ltd.

Becker, B. E. & Huselid, M. A. (1998) High Performance Work Systems and Work Systems and Firm Performance: A Synthesis of Research and Managerial Implications, *Research in Personnel and Human Resources Journal*, 16, (1), 53-101.

Beer, M.; Spector, B; Lawrence, P.R.; Mills, D.Q. and Walton, R.E. (1985) *Human Resource Management: A General Manager's Perspective*. New York: The Free Press.

Behrman, Jere R.; Deolalika, Anil B.; Tinakorn, Pranee with Chandoevwit, Worawan (2000) *The Effects of the Thai Economic Crisis and of Thai Labour Market Policies on Labour Market Outcomes*, Report prepared for the World Bank by Thailand Development Research Institute, November, 111 pp

Behrman, Jere and Tinakorn, Pranee (2000) *The Surprisingly Limited Impact of the Thai Crisis on Labour Including on Many Allegedly "More Vulnerable" Workers*, Thailand Development Research Institute Foundation.

Benson, John (1998) "Labour Management During Recessions: Japanese Manufacturing Enterprises in the 1990s," *Industrial Relations Journal*, Vol.29, No.3, pp.207-221.

Bergmann, Thomas and Roger J. Volkema (1989) "Understanding and Managing Interpersonal Conflict at Work: Its Issues, Interactive Processes, and Consequences," in *Managing Conflict: An Interdisciplinary Approach*, ed. By M. Afzalur Rahim, Praeger, N.Y., pp. 7-19.

Board of Investment (1998) *Thailand's textile industry in Thai Board of Investment*, April 10, 1998, Vol.7, No. 1.

Blau, P. M. (1964) *Exchange and Power in Social Life*, New York: John Wiley & Sons.

Breitenfellner, A. (1997) "Global unionism: A Potential Player" *International Labour Review*, Vol. 136, No.4, Winter, pp.531-555.

Boudreau, J.W. (1991) "Utility Analysis in Human Resource Management Decisions", in M.D. Dunnette & L.M. Hough (eds.) *Handbook of Industrial and Organizational Psychology*, Vol. 2, pp.621-745, Palo Alto, CA: Consulting Psychologists Press.

Burke, R. J. (1970) "Methods of Resolving Supervisor-Subordinate Conflict: The Constructive Use of Subordinate Differences and Disagreement", *Organizational Behavior and Human Performance*, 5, pp.393-411.

Cacdac, Hans J. & Audea, Teresita E. (2005) *The State of Philippine Voluntary Arbitration.* Paper presented in the Roundtable Research Conference sponsored by the Department of Labour and Employment Institute for Labour Studies (DOLE - ILS), 27 July 2005. Unpublished paper.

Cameron, Samuel. 1987. Trade Unions and Productivity: Theory and Evidence. *Industrial Relations Journal*, 18, 3:170-176, Autumn.

Cappelli, P. and Singh, H. (1992) "Integrating Strategic Human Resources and Strategic Management", in D. Lewin, O.S. Mitchell; and P. Sherer (eds.) *Research Frontiers in Industrial Relations and Human Resources*, pp.165- 192, Madison, WI: Industrial Relations Research Association.

Cappelli, P. (1999), *The New Deal at Work*, Harvard Business School Press.

Caspersz, Donella (2007) "The 'Talk' versus the 'Walk': High Performance Work System, Labour Market Flexibility and Lessons from Asian Workers," in Holland, Peter; Teicher, Julian and Gough, Richard (eds.) (2007) *Employment Relations in the Asia-Pacific Region: Reflections and New Directions,* Routledge, London and New York.

Chaitaweep, Saowaluck (1991) *The Role of Female Workers Leaders in the Textile Industry*: A Report prepared for the Arom Pongpangan Foundation with the support of the Friedrich Ebert Stiftung. (Text in Thai)

Chaichankul, Anchaleeporn (2007) *The Implementation of ILO Labour Rights Standard in Thailand.* A Master Research Submitted in Partial Fulfillment of the Requirements for the Degree of Master of Arts in International Relations, Faculty of Political Science, Thammasat University, 38 pp.

Chandran, R. (2005), *Employment Law in Singapore*, Pearson Prentice-Hall.

Chang, Pao-Long and Chen, Wei-Ling (2002) "The Effect of Human Resource Management Practices on Firm Performance: Empirical Evidence From High-Tech Firms in Taiwan", *International Journal of Management*, Vol.19, Iss.4, December, pp. 622 – 631.

Charoenloert, Voravit (1992) *Workers and Participatory Democracy, Labour and Participation*, Arom Pongpangan Foundation.

Chen, S.J.; Ko, J.H. and Lawler, J. (2003) "Changing Patterns of Industrial Relations in Taiwan," *Industrial Relations,* Vol.42, No.3, pp.315-340.

Cheng,T.J.(2001)"The Economic Significance of Taiwan's Democratization", in C.C. Mai and S.S. Shih (eds.) *Taiwan's Economic Success Since 1980*, Edward Elgar, pp.120-55.

Chew, S. B. and R. Chew (1995) *Employment-Driven Industrial Relations Regimes*, Avebury.

Daramas, Sukanya (1991) "The Development of Sound Labour Relations," in *The Development of Sound Labour Relations*, Report of the ILO/Japan ASEAN Sub-regional Tripartite Seminar, Kuala Lumpur, Malaysia, 5-8 March 1991

Debroux, P. (2003) *Human Resource Management in Japan: Changes and Uncertainties*, Ashgate.

Delaney, J.T. & Huselid, M.A (1996) "The Impact of Human Resource Management on Organizational Performance: Progress and Prospects", *Academy of Management Journal*, Vol. 39, pp.779-801.

Delaney, John T. and Godard, John (2001) "An Industrial Relations Perspective on the High-Performance Paragigm", *Human Resource Management Review*, vol.11, Issue 4, Winter, pp. 395-429.

Dessler, G. and C. H. Tan (2006), *Human Resource Management: An Asian perspective*, Pearson Prentice-Hall.

Development Analysis Network (2001) *Labour Markets in Transitional Economies in Southeast Asia and Thailand*, prepared by Cambodia Development Resource Institute; Cambodian Institute for Economic Management (Vietnam), Institute of Economics (Vietnam), National Economic Research Institute (Lao PDR), National Statistical Center (Lao PDR), Thailand Development Research Institute, supported by the International Development Research Center of Canada, Phnom Penh, March, 246 pp.

DGBAS (2005), *Monthly Bulletin of Manpower Statistics (November)*, Taipei: Directorate-General of Budget, Manpower and Statistics.

DGBAS (2006), *Yearbook of Manpower Survey Statistics*, Taipei: Directorate-General of Budget, Manpower and Statistics.

Donato, Demosthenes (2005) *Labour Juris 2005 Edition*, Manila: Central Books.

Dore, R. (1979) *Britisih Factory-Japanese Factory: The Origin of National Diversity in Industrial Relations*, London: George Allen & Unwin.

Dore, R. (2003) *Three lectures* (in Work in the Global Economy, ed. J.P. Laviec, M. Horiuchi and K. Sugeno), International Institute for Labour Studies, Geneva.

Doz, Y. (1990) "Managing Technological Innovation in Large Complex Firms: The Contribution of Human Resource Management", in Paul Evans; Yves Doz; and Andre Laurent (eds.) *Human Resource Management in International Firms: Change, Globalization, Innovation*, 200-215. N.Y.: St. Martin's Press.

Drucker, P. (1969) *The Age of Discontinuity: Guidelines to Our Changing Society.* New York: Harper and Row.

Drucker, P. (1993) *Post-Capitalist Society.* Oxford: Butterworth Heinemann.

Dunlop, John T. (1958) *Industrial Relations Systems.* New York: Holt, Rinehart, and Winston.

Edwards, Paul (2003) The Employment Relationship and the Field of Industrial Relations. In Edwards, Paul (ed.) *Industrial Relations: Theory and Practice*, Oxford: Blackwell Publishing Ltd. pp. 1 – 36.

Erickson, Christopher L.; Sarosh Kuruvilla; Rene E. Ofreneo; and Maria Asuncion Ortiz (2003) "From Core to Periphery? Recent Developments in Employment Relations in the Philippines", *Industrial Relations*, Vol. 42, July, pp. 368-395.

Ekalak Naew Na, 4 August 1995, pp.1,9. (Text in Thai).

Etzioni, A. (1964) *Modern Organizations.* Englewood Cliffs, NJ: Prentice-Hall, Inc .

Fashoyin, Tayo (2002) *Social Dialogue and Labour Market Performance in the Philippines, Working Paper,* Geneva: ILO In focus Programme on Social Dialogue.

Fells, Ray and Robert Skeffington (1998) "Moving Beyond Adversarialism: Industrial Relations and Change in the Australian Shearing Industry," *Industrial Relations Journal*, Vol. 29, No. 3, pp.234-246.

Flaherty, S. (1987) "Strike Activity & Productivity Change: The U.S. Auto Industry" *Industrial Relations*, 26, 2: 174-85, Spring.

Frederic C. Deyo (1981) *Dependent Development and Industrial Order: An Asian Case Study*, Praeger, Praeger Special Studies, 138 pp.

Folger, J. P. and Poole, M.S. (1984) *Working Through Conflict: A Communication Perspective,* Glenview, Illinois: Scott, Foresman.

Gough, R.; Holland, P. and Teicher, J. (2007) "Globalization, Labour Standards and Flexibility in the Asia-Pacific Region," in Holland, P.; Teicher, J. and Gough, R.

(eds.) (2007) *Industrial relations in the Asia-Pacific Region: Reflections and New Directions,* Routledge, London and New York.

Gough, Richard; Hollander, Peter and Teicher (2007) "Conclusion: Globalisation, Labour Standards and Flexibility in the Asia-Pacific Region", in Holland, Peter; Teicher, Julian and Gough, Richard (eds.) (2007) *Employment Relations in the Asia-Pacific Region: Reflections and New Directions,* Routledge, London and New York.

Ha, Bu-Young (2005) *What is the Problem in the Labour Relations at Hyundai Motor?* (Memeo in Korean)

Hansen, W. Lee (2002) "Developing new proficiencies for human resource and industrial relations professionals," *Human Resource Management Review,* pp.513-538.

Hendriks, P. H. (1999) "The organizational impacts of knowledge-based systems: a knowledge perspective," *Knowledge-Based Systems,* 12, pp. 159-169.

Hedberg, B. 1981. How Organization Learn and Unlearn. in P.C. Nystrom and W.H. Starbuck (ed.) *Handbook of Organizational Design,* New York: Oxford University Press.

Heracleous, L., J. Wirtz and N. Pangarkar (2006), *Flying High in a Competitive Industry: Cost-effective service excellence at Singapore Airlines,* McGraw-Hill.

Hirschhorn, L. and Gilmore, T. (1993) "The New Boundaries of the Boundaryless Company" in the *Learning Imperative: Managing People for_Continuous Innovation,* ed. by Robert Howard, A Harvard Business Review Book, pp.157-176.

Hirst, P. and Thompson, G. (1999) *Globalization in Question: the International Economy and the Possibilities of Governance,* Cambridge: Polity Press.

Hofstede, G. & Bond, M.H. (1984) "Hofstede's Culture Dimensions: An Independent Validation Using Rokeach's Value Survey", *Journal of Cross-Cultural Psychology,* 15: 417-433.

Holland, Peter; Teicher, Julian and Gough, Richard (eds.) (2007) *Industrial relations in the Asia-Pacific Region,* Routledge, London and New York, 145 pp.

Huselid, M.A (1995) The Impact of Human Resource Management Practices on Turnover, Productivity, and Corporate Financial Performance, *Academy of Management Journal,* Vol.38, Issue 3, 635-672.

Ichniowski, C. & Shaw, K. (1999) "The Effects of Human Resource Management Systems on Economic Performance: An International Comparison of U.S. and Japanese Plants", *Management Science*, Vol. 45, No.4, pp.704-21.

Ichniowsky, Casey; Kochan, Thomas A.; Levine, David; Olson, Craig; and Strauss, George (2008) "What Works at Work: Overview and Assessment", *Industrial Relations*, Vol. 35, Issue 3, published online in May, pp.299-333.

Ishida, H. (1985) *Nihon Kigyo no Kokusai Jinji Kanri (International HRM in Japanese Firms)*, Japan Association of Labour.

ILO (1991) *Report of the ILO/Japan East Asian Sub-Regional Tripartite Seminar on the Development of Sound Labour Relations*, Hong Kong, 25-28.

ILO (1994) *ILO National Tripartite Consultation Mechanism in Selected Asian Pacific Countries*, Asian Pacific Project on Tripartism.

ILO (1994) *Proceedings From A Regional Asian Pacific Symposium on Tripartism*, Asian Pacific Project on Tripartism, Vol.3, May.

ILO (2000) *Decent Work For All: Targeting Full Employment in Thailand.* Country Employment Policy Review, August, 124 pp.

ILO (2002) *Report VI: Decent Work and the Informal Economy.* International Labour Conference, 90th Session, 129 pp.

ILO (2003) *Case(s) No(s). 2252, Report No. 332 (Philippines): Complaint against the Government of Philippines presented by the Toyota Motor Philippines Corporation Workers' Association (TMPCWA)*, Vol. LXXXVI. Series B No. 3, Geneva: ILO.

ILO (2005) *National Philippine Action Plan for Decent Work*, Manila: Sub regional Office for Asia & the Pacific ILO SRO. Unpublished manuscript.

ILO (2008) *ILO Declaration on Social Justice for a Fair Globalization.* International Labour Conference, Ninety-Seventh Session, Geneva, 10th June.

IMF (2000) *Recovery from the Asian Crisis and the Role of the IMF -* http://www.imf.org/external/np/exr/ib/2000/062300.htm

Ivancevich, J. and S. H. Lee (2002), *HRM in Asia*, McGraw-Hill.

Jackson, S. E. and Schuler, R.S. (1995) "Understanding Human Resource Management in the Context of Organizations and their Environments", in J.T. Spence; J. M. Darley, and D.J. Foss (eds.) *Annual Review of Psychology*, Vol.46, pp.237-264. Palo Alto Annual Reviews, Inc.

Jacoby, S. (2005) *The Embedded Corporation*, Princeton University Press

Japan Labour Review (2004) *Changing Employment System and its Implications for Human Resource Management*, Number 3, Summer, JILPT.

Japan Labour Review (2007) special edition, *The Japan Institute for Labour Policy and Training*, vol. 4 No. 1.

Jimenez, Josephus (2003) *Philippine Country Paper on the Fundamental Framework of Industrial Relations and Legislation*. Japan Institute of Labour (JIL) Invitation Program for Senior Labour Officials, 6 to 13 July 2003, Tokyo. Unpublished.

Jocano, F. Landa (1988) *Towards Developing a Filipino Corporate Culture*. Metro Manila: Punlad Research House.

Jones, G.R. & Wright, P.M. (1992) "An Economic Approach to Conceptualizing the Utility of Human Resource Management Practices", in K. Rowland & G. Ferris (eds.) *Research in Personnel and Human Resources Management*, Vol.10, pp.271 – 299. Greenwich, CT, JAI Press.

Juniper, James (2002) "Universities and collaboration within complex, uncertain knowledge-based economies," *Critical Perspectives on Accounting*, 13, pp. 747 – 778.

Kakwani, N., and Pothong, J. (1998) "Impact of Economic Crisis on the Standard of Living in Thailand", *Indicators of Well-Being and Policy Analysis*, 2, No.4 (October): 1-20.

Karier, T. (1991) "Unions and the U.S. Comparative Advantage", *Industrial Relations*, 30, 1:1-19, Winter.

Katz, H.C.; Kochan, T.A., & Gobeille, K.R. (1983) "Industrial Relations Performance, Economic Performance, and QWL Programs: An Interplant Analysis", *Industrial and Labour Relations Review*, Vol.37, pp.3-17.

Katz, H.C.; Kochan, T.A., & Weber, M.R. (1985) "Assessing the Effects of Industrial Relations Systems and Efforts to improve the Quality of Working Life on Organizational Effectiveness", *Academy of Management Journal*, Vol.28, pp.509-526.

Kessels, Joseph W. M. (2001) "Learning in organizations: a corporate curriculum for the knowledge economy," *Futures*, 33, pp.497-506.

Kleiner, M.M. (1990) "The Role of Industrial Relations in Firm Performance", in J.A. Fossum & J. Mattson (eds.) *Employee and Labour Relations*, 4.23 – 4.43, Washington, DC: BNA Press.

Koike, K. & Inoki, T. (2003) *College Graduates in Japanese Industries,* The Japanese Institute of Labour, Japanese Economy & Labour series No. 8.

Kochan, Thomas A. (1999) Beyond Myopia: Human Resources and Changing Social Contract. *Research in Personnel and Human Resources Management.* Supplement 4.

Kochan, Thomas; Katz, Harry C.; and McKersie, Robert B. (1986) *The Transformation of American Industrial Relations.* New York: Basic Books.

Koike, K. & Inoki, T. (2003) *College Graduates in Japanese Industries*, The Japanese Institute of Labour, Japanese Economy & Labour series No. 8.

Korea Automotive Research Institute (KARI), 2004, *Korean Automobile Industry.* A report.

Korean Metal Workers Federation (KMWF), 2005a, *Changes of the Working Shift System.* A report (In Korean).

Korean Metal Workers Federation (KMWF), 2005b, *Modular Production of Hyundai Motor: the Case of Asan Assembly Plant.* A report (in Korean).

Kotha, S. (1996) "Mass-Customization: A Strategy for Knowledge Creation and Organizational Learning", *International Journal of Technology Management*, 11, 7,8: 846-858.

Kuruvilla, Sarosh and Erickson, Christopher L. (2002) "Change and Trans- formation in Asian Industrial Relations," *Industrial Relations*, Vol. 41, pp.171- 227.

Kuruvilla, Sarosh; Das, Subesh Kumar; Kwon, Hyonji and Kwon, Soonwon (2002) "Trade Union Growth and Decline in Asia," *British Journal of Industrial Relations*, Vol.40, pp.431 – 461.

Kuwahara, Y. (2004) *Employment Relations in Japan,* In G.J. Bamber, R.D. Lansbury and N. Wailes, *International and Comparative Employment Relations*, 4th edition, Sage publications

Lansbury, Russell D.; Kwon, Seung-Ho and Suh, Chung-Sok (2007) "Globalisation and Employment Relations in the Korean Auto Industry: The Case of the Hyundai Motor Company in Korea, Canada and India," in Holland, Peter; Teicher, Julian and Gough, Richard (eds.) (2007) *Employment Relations in the Asia-Pacific Region: Reflections and New Directions,* Routledge, London and New York.

Lauritzen, F. (1996), "Technology, Education and Employment", in *Employment and Growth in the Knowledge-based Economy,* Proceedings of the Conference on "Employment and Growth in the Knowledge-based Economy", Copenhagen, November 1994.

Lawler, John J. and Sununta Siengthai (1997) "Human Resource Management Strategy in Thailand: A Case Study of the Banking Industry," in *Research and Practices in Human Resource Management,* Vol.5, No.1, pp.73-88.

Lawler, John J.; Sununta Siengthai and Vinita Atmiyananda (1997) "Human Resource Management in Thailand: Eroding Traditions," in Human Resource Management in the Asia Pacific Region: Convergence Questioned, *Asia Pacific Business Review,* Vol.3, Summer, No.4, pp.170-196.

Lawler, J. J. and Atmiyananda, V. (2004) "HRM in Thailand: A Post-1997 Update", in Rowley, C. and Benson, J. (eds.) *The Management of Human Resources in the Asia Pacific Region: Convergence Reconsidered,* Frank Cass: London, U.K., pp.165-185.

Lee, J. S. (1995) "Economic Development and the Evolution of Industrial Relations in Taiwan, 1950-1993, in A.Verma et. al. (eds.) *Employment Relations in the Growing Asian Economies* (London: Routledge).

Lee, Byoung-Hoon and Steve Frenkel (2004) "Divided Workers: Social Relations between Contract and Regular Workers in a Korean Auto Company", *Work, Employment & Society,* Vol. 18, No. 3, pp. 507-530.

Lee, Byoung-Hoon (2003) 'Restructuring and Employment Relations in the Korean Auto Industry', *Bulletin of Comparative Labour Relations,* Vol. 45, pp. 59-94.

Lee, Byoung-Hoon and Young-bum Park (2006) *Globalization and employment relations in the Korean automotive industry* (mimeo).

Lee, J.S. (1988) "Labour Relations and Stages of Economic Development: The Case of the Republic of China", *Proceedings of the Conference on Labour and Economic Development,* held at the Chung Hua Institution for Economic Research, Taipei, Taiwan

Lee, J.S. (2000a) "Changing Approaches to Employment Relations in Taiwan", in G.J. Bamber, F. Park, C. Lee, P.K. Ross and K. Broadbent (eds.), *Employment Relations in Asia-Pacific: Changing Approaches*, London: Business Press, pp. 100-116

Lee, J.S. (2000b) "Employment Relations in Taiwan", in G. Bamber and R. Lansbury (eds.), *International and Comparative Employment Relations, 3rd edition,* (Chinese edition) Taipei: Commonwealth Publishing Company, pp.325-54

Lee, J.S. and C. Chen (2005) "The Internet, Trade Unions and Organizational Capital: The Case of Taiwan", *Journal of Asian Comparative Development*, 4, No. 1, (Spring): 135-59.

Leogardo Jr., Vicente (2004) "Addressing the Roots of Decent Work Deficits: Issues and Priorities," *2nd High-Level National Policy Dialogue on the Social Dimension of Globalization*, ILO Auditorium, ILO Manila, December 2, 2004.

Leogardo Jr., Vicente (2005) *Labour Standards and Self-Regulation in Business", Conference on Labour Code: 30 Years and Beyond.* OSHC, Quezon City, April 14-15, 2005.

Luca, L. de (ed.) (1998) *Labour and social dimensions of privatization and restructuring (Public utilities Water, gas, electricity)*: Part I: Africa/Asia-Pacific Region, ILO, Geneva. Part I: Africa/Asia-Pacific Region

Mabry, Bevars D. (1979) The Development of Labour Institutions in Thailand. Data Paper: No.112, Southeast Asia Program, Department of Asian Studies, Cornell University, Ithaca, New York, April, 144 pp.

Macaraya, Bach (2004) "The Labour Market and Industrial Relations Environment: Policy Issues and Option in a Global Economy", *Philippine Journal of Labour and Industrial Relations,* Quezon City: UP SOLAIR, pp. 1-32.

Macaraya, Bach and Ofreneo, Rene (1993) Structural Adjustments and Industrial Relations: The Philippine Experience", *Philippine Labour Review,* Manila: Department of Labour and Employment, pp. 26-86.

MacDuffie, J.P. (1995) "Human Resource Bundles and Manufacturing Performance: Organizational Logic and Flexible Production Systems in the World Auto Industry", *Industrial and Labour Relations Review*, 48, 2:197-221.

Mazzanti, Massimiliano; Paolo Pini; Ermanno Tortia (2007) " Organiza-tional innovations, human resources and firm performance: The Emilia-Romagna food sector" *The Journal of Socio-Economics,* 35 (2006) 123–141.

Miller, D. (1996) A Preliminary Typology of Organizational Learning: Synthesizing the Literature, *Journal of Management,* 22, 3:485-505.

Ministry of Interior (1990) *The Research Report on the Impact of Labour Relations Problems on the Private Business Organization Development.* Department of Labour, Ministry of Interior, Thailand

Naisbitt, J. (1987) "Re-inventing the Corporation", in Y.K. Shetty and Vernon M. Buehler (eds.) *Quality, Productivity and Innovation: Strategies for Gaining Competitive Advantage,* Elsevier.

Nakamura, K. and Nitta, M. (1995) in R. Locke, T. Kochan and M. Piore (ed) *Employment Relations in a Changing World Economy,* MIT Press.

National Statistical Office. Labour Force Survey. Various issues.

Naidu, D.P.A. and Navamukundan, A. (2003) *Decent Work in Agriculture in Asia.* Report of Asian Regional Workshop, 18th – 21st August 2003, International Labour Office, Regional Office for Asia and pacific, Bangkok, 737 pp.

Neumark, D. (ed.) (2000) *On the job: Is long-term employment a thing of the past?* (New York, Russell Sage Foundation).

Newmark, David and Deborah Reed (2004) "Employment relationships in the new economy," *Labour Economics,* Vol. 11, pp. 1 – 31.

NFBEU (2001-2008) *Yearbook of Taiwan Bank Employees,* Taipei: National Federation of Bank Employee Unions.

Nonaka, I. And J.K. Johanssen (1985) "Organizational Learning in Japanese Companies" in R.B.Lamb (ed.) *Advances in Strategic Management,* Greenwish, Conn.: JAI Press, 3:277-296.

Nonaka, Ikujiro (1993) "Ch.3: The Knowledge-Creating Co.", in *The Learning Imperative: Managing People for Continuous Innovation,* ed. by Robert Howard and Robert D. Haas, A Harvard Business Review Book, pp.41-56.

Nonaka, I. and Takeuchi, H. (1995) *The knowledge-creating company,* N.Y. Oxford Press

Ofreneo, Rene (2000) *Philippine Industrialization and Industrial Relations: State of the Nation.* Quezon City: Center for Integrative & Development Studies, University of the Philippines (UP CIDS).

Organisation for Economic Cooperation and Development (OECD) (1996) *Knowledge-based economy.* General Distribution, OECD/GD (96) 102, 46 pp.

OECD (1996*a*), *Employment and Growth in the Knowledge-based Economy*, Paris.

OECD (1996*b*), *Technology, Productivity and Job Creation*, Paris.

OECD (1996*c*), *Transitions to Learning Economies and Societies*, Paris.

Osterman, P. (1987) "Choice of Employment Systems in Internal Labour Markets", *Industrial Relations*, Vol. 26, pp. pp. 46-57.

Philippine Department of Labour and Employment. *Labour Code of the Philippines*. http://www.dole.gov.ph [Accessed 30 July 2006].

Piriyarangsan, Sungsidh and Kanchada Poonpanich (1994) "Labour Institutions in an Export-oriented Country: A Case Study of Thailand", in Gerry Rodgers (ed.), *Workers, Institutions and Economic Growth in Asia* (Geneva: International Labour Office, 1994), pp. 211-54.

Pissarides, C.A. (2001) "Employment protection", in *Labour Economics*, Vol.8, No.2, pp. 131-159.

Park, Tae-Joo (2006) *Evaluation of Labour Relations at Hyundai Motor*, the KLEI Working Report. (in Korean).

Park, Young-bum (2003) "Globalization and Employment Relations in Korea: Developments since 1997 Financial Crisis*", Bulletin of_Comparative Labour Relations*, Vol. 45, pp/ 17-32.

Park, Young-bum, Byoung-Hoon Lee and Seog-Hun Woo (1997) "Employment Relations in the Korean Automotive Industry: Issue and Policy Implications" *The Economic and Labour Relations Review*, Vol. 8 Number 2, pp. 248-268

Piriyarangsan, Sangsit (1995) "Labour Relations System for the Future: Suggested Recommendation," in *Labour and Thai Society: On the Path of Development* ed. by Bundit Thanachaisethavut, published by Arom Pongpangan Foundation; Faculty of Social Administration, Thammasat University; Thai Labour Museum; and Friedrich Ebert Stiftung.

Prasert, Suchinda (1997) "Participative Labour Relations at the Enterprise Level", in a *Collection of Essays on Labour Relations (Series I)* ed. By Chokechai Suttawet, October.

Psenicka, Clement and Rahim, M. Afzalur (1989) "Integrative and Distributive Dimensions of Styles of Handling Interpersonal Conflict and Bargaining Outcome", in M. Afzalur Rahim (ed.) *Managing Conflict: An Interdisciplinary Approach*, ed. By M. Afzalur Rahim, Praeger, N.Y., pp. 33-40.

Pucik, Vladimir; Noel M. Tichy; and Carole K. Barnett. 1992. *Globalizing Management: Creating and Leading the Competitive Organization*, John Wiley & Sons, Inc.

Rahim, M. A. (1986) *Managing Conflict in Organizations*, New York Praeger.

Rice, John (2007) "The Emergence of an Industrial Relations System in Taiwan: Historical and Contextual Challenges," in Holland, Peter; Teicher, Julian and Gough, Richard (eds.) (2007) *Industrial relations in the Asia-Pacific Region: Reflections and New Directions*, Routledge, London and New York.

Reich, R. (1991) *The Wealth of Nations: Preparing Ourselves for 21st Century Capitalism*. Simon & Schuster, London.

Rosenberg, Richard D. and Eliezer Rosenstein (1980) "Participation and Productivity: An Empirical Study", *Industrial and Labour Relations Review*, 33, 3: 355-378, April.

Robbins, S. P. (1978) "Conflict management and conflict resolutions are not synonymous terms", *California Management Review*, 21, 2:67-75.

Rooney, D.; G. Hearn; T. Mandeville and R. Joseph (2003) *Public Policy in Knowledge-Based Economies: Foundations and Frameworks*. Cheltenham: Edward Elgar.

Salamon, Michael (2000) *Industrial Relations: Theory and Practice (4th Edition)*, London: Prentice Hall-Financial Times.

Sano Yoko (1995) *Human Resource Management in Japan*. Tokyo: Keio University Press, Inc.

Schein, Edgar H. (1996) "Three Cultures of Management: The Key to Organizational Learning", *Sloan Management Review*, 38, 1:9-20, Fall.

Schuler, R.S. (1992) "Strategic Human Resource Management: Linking People with the Needs of the Business", *Organizational Dynamics*, Vol.20, pp.19-32.

Schuster, Michael (1983) "The Impact of Union-Management Cooperation on Productivity and Employment" *Industrial and Labor Relations Review*, 36, 3:415-430, April.

Senge, Peter (1996) "Leading Learning Organizations", *Training & Development*, 50, 12:36-37, December.

Shirai, T. ed. (1983) *Contemporary Industrial Relations in Japan*, University of Wisconsin Press.

Shirai, T. (2000) *Japanese Industrial Relations.* The Japan Institute of Labour (Japanese Economy and Labour Series No. 5).

Shiraki, M. (1995) *Nihon Kigyo no Kokusai Jinteki Shigen Kanri (International Human Resource Management of Japanese Firms),* Japan Institute of Labour.

Shiraki, M. (2006) *Kokusai Jinteki Shigen Kanri no Hikaku Bunseki (Comparative Analysis of International HRM),* Yukikaku.

Stewart, P. (ed.) (2005) *Employment, Trade Union Renewal and the Future of Work: The Experience of Work and Organisational Change,* Palgrave Macmillan, 290 pp.

Sugeno, K. (2002) *Shin Koyou Shakai no Ho (Law in a Society of Employees)* new edition, Yukikaku

Siengthai, Sununta (1994) Tripartism and Industrialization Process of Thailand in *National Tripartite Consultation Mechanism in Selected Asian Pacific Countries,* Asian Pacific Project on Tripartism, International Labour Organization, Vol.2, pp.358-407.

Siengthai, Sununta (1996) *The Impact of Globalization on Human Resource Management Practices: A Case Study of Textile Industry.* A paper prepared for the International Industrial Relations Association, 3rd Asian Regional Congress, Sept. 30-Oct. 4, Taipei, Taiwan.

Sibunruang, Atchaka and Peter Brimble (1992) *Export Oriented Industrial Collabouration: A Case Study of Thailand.* Report prepared for the United Nations Centre on Transnational Corporations, May.

Smith, K. (1995), "Interactions in Knowledge Systems: Foundations, Policy Implications and Empirical Methods", *STI Review,* No. 16, OECD, Paris.

Soontornpak, Natcha (1987) *The Study of the Bangkok Bank Union and Participation in the Bank's Operation.* A research report as a partial requirement for the Master's Degree Program in Social Work, Thammasat University.

Siengthai, Sununta and Bechter, Clemens (2001) "Strategic Human Resource Management for Firm Innovation and Competitive Advantage," *Research and Practice in Human Resource Management,* Vol. 9, No.1, July, pp. 35 – 57.

Snell, S.A. & Dean, J.W. Jr. (1992) "Integrated Manufacturing and Human Resource Management: A Human Capital Perspective", *Academy of Management Journal,* Vol. 35, pp.1036-1056.

Szulanski, Gabriel (1996) "Exploring Internal Stickness: Impediments to the transfer of best practice within the firm", *Strategic Management Journal*, 17, Winter, pp. 27-43.

Tan, C.H. (2004), *Employment Relations in Singapore*, Prentice-Hall.

Teicher, J.; Gramberg, B.V. & Holland, P. (2007) "Trade Union Responses to Outsourcing in a Neo-Liberal Environment: A Case Study Analysis of the Australian Public Sector," in Holland, P.; Teicher, J. and Gough, R.(eds.) (2007) *Industrial relations in the Asia-Pacific Region: Reflections and New Directions*, Routledge, London and New York.

The Textile Garment and Leather Workers'Federation of Thailand (1994) Annual Report, 20 August 1995. (Text in Thai)

Thanachaisethavut, Bundit (1995) "The Analysis of the Labour Relations Law, Unions and the Tripartite Systems in the Thai Society," in *Labour and Thai Society: On the Path of Development* ed. by Bundit Thanachaisethavut, published by Arom Pongpangan Foundation, Thai Labour Museum, Friedrich Ebert Stiftung, August.

Tjosvold, D. (1985) "Implications of Controversy Research for Management", *Journal of Management*, 11:19-35.

Tjosvold, D. (1989) "Interdependence and Power Between Managers and Employees: A Study of the Leader Relationship", *Journal of Management*, Vol. 15, No.1, pp.49-62.

Tsuru, Y., Abe, M. and Kubo, K. (2005) *Nihon Kigyo no Jinji Kaikaku (Reforms of HRM in Japanese Firms)*, Toyo Keizai Shinposha.

Tushman, Michael and David Nadler (1986) "Organizing for Innovation", *California Management Review*, 28, 3:74-92, Spring.

Unger, Danny (1998) *Building Social in Thailand: Fibers, Finance, and Infrastructure*, Cambridge University Press, 227 pp.

Van Mannen, John and Schein, Edgar (1979) "Toward a Theory of Organizational Socialization." In B.Staw (ed.) *Research in Organizational Behavior*, Vol.1, Greenwich, Connecticut, JAI Press, pp. 209-269.

Villegas, Edberto M. (1988) *The Political Economy of Philippine Labour Laws*. Quezon City: Foundation for Nationalist Studies.

Wang, J.C. (2004), 'Taiwan's Knowledge-based Service Industries', in T.J. Chen and J.S. Lee (eds.) *The New Knowledge Economy of Taiwan*, Cheltenham, UK: Edward Elgar, pp. 168-87.

Wichitrakorn, Sopon (1991) "Good Labour Relations: A Key to Industrial Peace and Economic Prosperity," in the *Development of Sound Labour Relations,* Report of the ILO/Japan ASEAN Sub-regional Tripartite Seminar, Kuala Lumpur, Malaysia, 5-8 March 1991.

Womack, James P.; James, Daniel T.; and Roos, Daniel (1990). *The Machine That Changed the World.* New York: Rawson Associate.

Weick, K. E., & Ashford, S. J. (2000) "Learning in organizations" In F. M. Jablin, & L. L. Putnam (Eds.), *The New Handbook of Organizational Communication*, pp. 704-731. Thousand Oaks, CA: Sage Publication.

Wong, E. (1987) "*Industrial Relations in Singapore*", paper presented at the First Asian Regional Congress of Industrial Relations, Singapore, 9-11 February 1987.

Woolsan Maeil Simun March 31, 2005 (A local newspaper)

Yearbook of Labour Protection and Welfare Statistics 1997-2007, Department of Labour Protection And Welfare, Ministry of Labour, Thailand.

Yuchtman, E. and Seashore, S.E. (1967) "A System Approach to Organizational Effectiveness", *American Sociological Review*, Vol.32, pp.981-1003.

Printed in the United States
By Bookmasters